A CENTURY OF BRITISH NAVAL AVIATION, 1909–2009

A CENTURY OF BRITISH NAVAL AVIATION, 1909–2009

David Wragg

Pen & Sword
MARITIME

First published in Great Britain in 2009 by
PEN & SWORD MARITIME
An imprint of
Pen & Sword Books Ltd
47 Church Street
Barnsley
South Yorkshire
S70 2AS

ISBN 978-1-84884-036-2

A CIP catalogue record for this book is available from the British Library

Typeset by Concept, Huddersfield, West Yorkshire
Printed and bound in England by the MPG Books Group, Bodmin, Cornwall

Pen & Sword Books Ltd incorporates the Imprints of Pen & Sword Aviation, Pen & Sword Maritime, Pen & Sword Military, Wharncliffe Local History, Pen & Sword Select, Pen & Sword Military Classics, Leo Cooper, Remember When, Seaforth Publishing and Frontline Publishing

For a complete list of Pen & Sword titles please contact
PEN & SWORD BOOKS LIMITED
47 Church Street, Barnsley, South Yorkshire, S70 2AS, England
E-mail: enquiries@pen-and-sword.co.uk
Website: www.pen-and-sword.co.uk

Contents

List of Maps

Acknowledgements

In researching and compiling a book such as this, an author is heavily dependent on the help and assistance of many others. In particular, I am indebted for the provision of photographs and other material to the late Lord Kilbracken, who, as John Godley, flew as an RNVR pilot, eventually reaching the rank of lieutenant commander, during the war; to the late Mrs Marjorie Schupke; to my father, the late Lieutenant S.H. 'Harry' Wragg, RN, for his collection of wartime photographs and other material.

Inevitably, official and semi-official sources have also been invaluable. Like many other researchers, I am grateful to both the Fleet Air Arm Museum and the Imperial War Museum.

No work on something as vast as our long history of naval aviation can cover every inch of ground, and for those whose appetite is whetted by this book, I would draw their attention to the bibliography at the back. There are accounts of the air war at sea from every perspective, including the all-important personal accounts, as well as volumes of sheer factual matter, essential for the serious student and the modeller alike.

Glossary

(A) – Air Branch of the RN or RNVR.
AA – Anti-aircraft.
AB – Able seaman.
ADDL – Aerodrome dummy deck landing.
Aeronautics – Embraces both lighter-than-air flight, or aerostation, and heavier-than-air flight, or aviation.
Aerostation – Lighter-than-air flight or ballooning.
AFC – Air Force Cross.
Airship – A balloon that is streamlined and with a torpedo-like shape which can be powered and steered.
AM – Albert Medal, predecessor of the George Cross (GC).
ASH – Air-to-surface vessel radar (US-built).
ASV – Air-to-surface vessel radar (British-built).
Aviation – Heavier-than-air flight, including gliding as well as powered aircraft.
Balloon – A lighter-than-air vehicle with an envelope that can be inflated either by hot air or by gas, originally usually hydrogen. It has no means of control other than ascent and descent, and is at the mercy of the prevailing wind.
BPF – British Pacific Fleet.
CAG – Carrier Air Group.
CAM-ship – Catapult-armed merchant vessel.
CAP – Combat Air Patrol.
Capt – Captain.
CB – Commander of the Order of the Bath.
CBE – Commander of the Order of the British Empire.
CCA – Carrier controlled approach.
Cdr – Commander.
Charliere – A hydrogen balloon, named after the inventor in 1783, Professor Jacques Charles. During the nineteenth century, the high cost of producing hydrogen sometimes meant that coal gas was used instead.
C-in-C – Commander-in-Chief.
CMG – Companion of the Order of St Michael and St George.

CO – Commanding Officer.
CPO – Chief Petty Officer.
CVE – Escort carrier, more usually known in the RN as auxiliary carriers.
CVO – Commander of the Royal Victorian Order.
DFC – Distinguished Flying Cross.
DLCO – Deck Landing Control Officer, more usually known as the 'batsman'.
DLP – Deck landing practice.
DLT – Deck landing training.
DSC – Distinguished Service Cross.
DSO – Distinguished Service Order.
Dt – Detachment.
E-boat – German MTBs or MGBs.
Empire – Prefix for name of merchantmen owned by the British government but managed by shipping lines.
FAA – Fleet Air Arm.
Fixed-wing – Aircraft other than a helicopter, and including naval aircraft with folding wings as well as variable-geometry aircraft.
Floatplane – The correct term for a seaplane, a name supposedly invented by Winston Churchill when First Lord of the Admiralty.
Flt – Flight.
Flying boat – A hydroaeroplane that has its hull sitting in the water.
FRU – Fleet Requirements Unit. A squadron based ashore that provided anti-aircraft training for ships of the fleet and also, on occasion, other miscellaneous duties.
GC – George Cross.
HMS – His/Her Majesty's Ship.
HMAS – His/Her Majesty's Australian Ship.
HMCS – His/Her Majesty's Canadian Ship.
Hydroaeroplane – Any aircraft that can land on water, whether it is a seaplane, floatplane or flying boat.
KCB – Knight Commander of the Order of the Bath.
Lt – Lieutenant.
Lt Cdr – Lieutenant Commander.
MAC-ship – Merchant aircraft carrier (a merchant vessel with a flight deck).
MBE – Member of the Order of the British Empire.
MGB – Motor Gunboat.
MONAB – Mobile Naval Air Base.
Montgolfiere – A hot-air balloon, named after the inventors, the Mongolfier brothers, who discovered this means of making a balloon rise in 1783.
Monitor – A warship designed specifically for coastal bombardment, usually with a single turret with two heavy calibre guns, which can be 11-in or more.

MTB – Motor Torpedo Boat.
MV – Motor Vessel.
NAS – Naval Air Squadron.
OBE – Officer of the Order of the British Empire.
OS – Ordinary Seaman.
PO – Petty Officer.
PR – Photo Reconnaissance.
RAAF – Royal Australian Air Force.
RAF – Royal Air Force.
RAN – Royal Australian Navy.
RCAF – Royal Canadian Air Force.
RCAN – Royal Canadian Navy.
RFC – Royal Flying Corps.
RM – Royal Marines.
RMLI – Royal Marine Light Infantry.
RN – Royal Navy.
RNethN – Royal Netherlands Navy.
RANVR – Royal Australian Naval Volunteer Reserve.
RCNVR – Royal Canadian Naval Volunteer Reserve.
RNR – Royal Naval Reserve.
RNVR – Royal Naval Volunteer Reserve.
RNZNVR – Royal New Zealand Naval Volunteer Reserve.
RP – Rocket projectile.
SAAF – South African Air Force.
SANF(V) – South African Naval Force (Volunteer), equivalent of RNVR.
Seaplane – A hydroaeroplane that has floats and the fuselage clear of the water.
TAG – Telegraphist Air Gunner.
TBR – Torpedo Bomber Reconnaissance.
TF – Task Force.
TSR – Torpedo Spotter Reconnaissance.
U-boat – German submarine.
USN – United States Navy.
USS – United States Ship.
VC – Victoria Cross.

Introduction

No one could have realized the impact of air power on warfare at sea when they signed the tender documents for the Royal Navy's first airship on 7 May 1909. That the Royal Navy's first airship was a complete failure would only have made practical air power seem even less likely, but the aeroplane had already arrived, and the achievements of the Wright brothers had been recognized on both sides of the Atlantic, and beyond. In the years that remained before the outbreak of the First World War, the early naval flyers divided their time between showmanship and experiment. The former was undoubtedly necessary to raise the profile of naval aviation, and the latter, which included the first dropping of a torpedo from an aircraft, was equally necessary to prove that the new arrival was a practical addition to the Royal Navy's capabilities.

The years before the start of the First World War have often been presented as an age of innocence for the aeroplane, but it was also an age of experiment, and during the war years, rapid strides were made in aviation in particular. Desperate measures were sometimes resorted to: the need to get landplanes to sea led to experiments in flying aircraft off lighters towed behind destroyers steaming at high speed. The aircraft carrier steadily evolved as the embarrassing 'light battlecruiser' HMS *Furious* was converted in stages to become the world's first aircraft carrier, and in due course between the wars her two sisters, *Courageous* and *Glorious*, followed her. By this time, the first carrier-borne strike had been flown off *Furious* in August 1918, and the design of the aircraft carrier had finally been settled, with the first ship designed as such, the small HMS *Hermes*.

Yet this progress was not without its problems. The Royal Navy had lost control of its own aviation with the creation of the Royal Air Force on 1 April 1918, so the inter-war years were also ones of inter-service rivalry as the Admiralty fought the political battle to regain control of its own air element. A small number of naval airmen were allowed in the RAF squadrons that comprised the inter-war Fleet Air Arm, itself an RAF creation within Coastal Area, but for most of them, naval aviation meant flying the seaplanes and amphibians that were operated from battleships and cruisers for reconnaissance and spotting the fall of shot. Two problems resulted from the loss of naval aviation to the RAF. The first was that a generation of senior naval officers was produced that was largely ignorant of the potential and the threat of air power at sea. The second was that, starved of funds between the wars, the RAF neglected the provision of modern aircraft for the fleet.

Both services suffered from conservatism. The RAF selected the Fairey Swordfish and, in particular, Gloster Sea Gladiator biplanes because they resisted the appeal of monoplanes, but the Royal Navy thought that high-performance aircraft could not be flown off ships!

Nevertheless, elsewhere the aircraft carrier was showing what it could do, as the Imperial Japanese Navy provided support for the advance by Japanese forces into China. Substantial carrier fleets were already part of not just the Royal Navy, but also the United States Navy and the Imperial Japanese Navy. The French had just one obsolete aircraft carrier, but as war loomed, both Germany and Italy started work on carriers of their own.

Even before war broke out, the Admiralty realized that they did not have enough aircraft carriers, and at one stage conversion of even the two largest ships in the world, the Cunard transatlantic liners RMS *Queen Mary* and RMS *Queen Elizabeth*, the pride of the British Merchant Navy, was considered and wisely rejected as these two ships would be needed as troopships in wartime. The problem was that the British carrier fleet by this time was aging, with only three ships, the new HMS *Ark Royal*, only the second purpose-built British carrier, and *Courageous* and *Glorious*, both of a reasonable age, being conversions with flight decks that were less than their full length. The four older carriers were due to be replaced by four new, fast, armoured ships, and fortunately, an additional two ships were then ordered, as well as a maintenance carrier, *Unicorn*, which also saw action. Yet, in a time of need, even the four elderly ships were to find themselves in the front line at sea.

Meanwhile, the Admiralty had finally regained control of the Fleet Air Arm. The transfer was not complete, as the Fleet Air Arm still depended on the RAF for training aircrew and ground crew. It was fortunate indeed that some 1,500 RAF personnel elected to transfer to the RN, and after the outbreak of war, even before the United States entered the conflict, the USN started to provide aircrew training in the United States under the 'Towers Scheme'.

The first year of war saw the loss of two British aircraft carriers, the sisters *Courageous* and *Glorious*, but not before the Fleet Air Arm had managed to sink the first major operational warship to be lost to air attack, the German light cruiser *Konigsberg*. Aerial reconnaissance had also contributed to the loss of the German *Panzerschiff*, or 'pocket battleship', *Graf Spee*. Before 1940 was over, the Fleet Air Arm scored a remarkable victory over the Italian Navy at Taranto, where three of Italy's six battleships were put out of action, although this achievement was never accorded the recognition it deserved. Most of the major naval battles of the Second World War, and all but one of the Allied assaults on enemy territory, that at Anzio, relied heavily on naval aviation. The Fleet Air Arm contributed to the sinking of the German battleship *Bismarck*, and to the victory at Matapan.

One of the major contributions to the war at sea, and to the survival of the United Kingdom and eventual victory, was the success in the convoy war against German U-boats. This was aided by the advent of the auxiliary aircraft carrier, converted merchantmen, known more generally as escort carriers, the numbers of which were steadily growing, and by the stop-gap measure of putting wooden flight decks on grain carriers and tankers to create merchant aircraft carriers or MAC-ships. The latter also introduced the Dutch to naval aviation with one naval air squadron manned by Royal Netherlands Navy personnel.

If the Battle of the Atlantic was essential to the survival of the United Kingdom and for the building up of forces for the invasion of first North Africa and then Europe, the Arctic convoys were essential for the supply of war materiel to the Soviet Union. These were amongst the hardest-fought convoy battles of the war, with the weather being as great an enemy as the Germans, who were able to use U-boats, surface raiders and shore-based aircraft to mount attacks that, in the long Arctic summer days, could be continuous. The Fleet Air Arm was there as soon as escort carriers became available, starting with convoy PQ17. Yet, escort carriers were never enough for a Malta convoy, as the beleaguered islands needed fleet carriers to ferry aircraft for the defences and for the great convoy, Operation Pedestal, of August 1942 that lifted the siege of the islands, and on which one of the four fleet carriers was sunk.

With war drawing to a close in Europe and the Battle of the Atlantic won, the Royal Navy returned to the East, with the creation of the British Pacific Fleet, the largest and most balanced fleet the United Kingdom has ever deployed. The Fleet Air Arm learnt about massed air attack from the United States Navy, and encountered fierce Japanese opposition as it attacked the oilfields and refineries in Sumatra, so much so that some naval aviators of the period believe that the achievement on these raids was even greater than that at Taranto. These operations saw widespread fighter cover. The USN didn't want the Fleet Air Arm in the way, but no doubt appreciated its actions off the Sakishima Gunto, where it stopped the Japanese flying in reinforcement aircraft to replace their losses. At the bitter end, the Fleet Air Arm was flying strikes against Japanese shipping in the Home Islands.

The return of peace saw the Fleet Air Arm foster naval aviation in Australia, Canada and the Netherlands, and, much later, India, as well as helping the French Navy, the *Marine Nationale*, re-establish its air arm, *L'Aeronavale*. Peace was all too short, however, as the Fleet Air Arm provided the British air contribution to the Korean War, something brought about not just by the RAF's other post-war commitments, but also by the shortage of good bases ashore as North Korea nearly overran the South. The Korean War was the last conflict dependent upon piston-engined aircraft, but even so the Fleet Air Arm managed to use a Hawker Sea Fury to shoot down a North Korean Mig-15, while others were damaged.

The Suez Campaign of 1956 has become one of those conflicts that politicians like to forget, but not only did the Royal Navy, operating alongside the French Navy, do all that was asked of it, striking at Egyptian airfields and military installations, it also marked the first airborne assault from the sea using helicopters from two aircraft carriers. In this way, the concept of the commando carrier was born, proving a useful addition to Britain's defence capabilities during the brush fire wars of the Cold War era. The Royal Navy played a vital role in the Indonesian confrontation with Malaysia in the 1960s, helped quell a mutiny in East Africa and also prevented a threatened Iraqi invasion of Kuwait, all in the same decade! Naval aviation was vital to all of these and in Kuwait, HMS *Victorious*, the much modernized Second World War veteran, provided fighter control for the RAF fighter squadrons when they eventually arrived. Less appealing roles for the Fleet Air Arm included using the Royal Navy's carriers to enforce sanctions against Rhodesia after that country declared its unilateral declaration of independence, with ships mounting a blockade off Mozambique, the so-called 'Beira patrol'.

Yet controversy and a settled existence, still less an assured future, still seemed to evade the Fleet Air Arm even when at the peak of its powers, at last flying carrier-borne aircraft that were a match for those based ashore in the form of the Buccaneer bomber and the Phantom jet fighter. With the two largest aircraft carriers ever operated by the Royal Navy, HMS *Ark Royal* and *Eagle*, worthy successors to the wartime *Illustrious* and her sisters, two even larger ships were promised – CVA.01 and CVA.02 – and although they would have been commissioned no doubt with inspiring names, they were cancelled. The whole future of fixed-wing aviation in the Royal Navy was once again doomed. Fortunately, this coincided with the appearance of the vertical take-off Harrier, and someone thought of the idea of building a new generation of light fleet carriers, although this time they were known as 'through-deck cruisers', which some cynics have suggested was an idea to fool the RAF into not objecting!

A cynical ploy or not, the first of these ships, HMS *Invincible*, played an important role in the liberation of the Falklands after the Argentine invasion in 1982. Yet the limitations of the ship were clear alongside the last of the old carriers, HMS *Hermes*, which had been converted from an aircraft carrier into a commando carrier, and then converted again to carry the BAe Sea Harrier, and which had a far larger aircraft capacity. While no one can lament the Invincible-class ships, they were badly designed with lifts that obstructed the flight-deck runway, and an overlarge superstructure.

Today, the Fleet Air Arm has lost its air-defence capability with the retirement of the Sea Harrier and the substitution of the Harrier GR9, an effective aircraft but basically a bomb truck designed to support ground forces rather than defend the fleet or attack enemy warships. This will change once the Lockheed Martin F-35 V/STOL fighter enters service after 2014, by which time the Royal Navy should have two large new aircraft carriers from which to operate these aircraft – but haven't we been here before?

Chapter 1

In the Beginning

The British Army was the first of the British armed services to take to the air with the Royal Engineers forming a balloon section at Woolwich as early as 1878. The advantage of being able to rise above the surface had been appreciated almost from the earliest days of the balloon age, which began in 1783 with the invention of both the hot-air balloon, or *Mongolfiere*, and the hydrogen balloon, or *Charliere*. By 1794, the French Army was using a balloon at the Battle of Maubeuge, with the balloons, or aerostat, giving the user the advantage previously only conferred by holding the high ground. It took some time for the true value of the balloon, or aerostat, to be fully appreciated, and the early commanders had to drop notes to the ground so that their forces could make use of this intelligence.

One can discount the use of a coal barge, the *G.W. Parke-Curtiss*, as a transport to carry and tow observation balloons for the Unionist Army during the American Civil War, as an early maritime use of the balloon. In the same way, the use of small balloons, unmanned, to carry messages from HMS *Assistance* in 1856, while searching in the Canadian Arctic for the ill-fated expedition led by Sir John Franklin, was imaginative, but not a true naval use of the technology, such as it was.

The fact was that navies were far slower to make use of the balloon. The reasons for this were practical rather than any lack of imagination or an excess of conservatism. Not only was there less need for a balloon on a warship at sea, with lookouts posted in its masts and later gunnery direction platforms high above the rest of the superstructure, there were problems with the balloon itself. The simple balloon, regardless of whether it was hot air or hydrogen, could only be used at sea, even when tethered, in flat calm conditions with the ship not under way, and therefore a sitting duck. It was not until the arrival of the airship, or dirigible, pioneered in Germany by Zeppelin and in France by the Lebaudy brothers, that a practical means of using aeronautics at sea could be realized with aerostats that could be powered and steered.

The first senior officer to appreciate the opportunities and threats that the air posed was Admiral of the Fleet Sir John 'Jacky' Fisher, who was First Sea Lord from 1904 to 1910. It was Fisher who famously predicted that the future of naval warfare lay under the waves and above them. By this, Fisher meant the airship. While the Wright brothers had made their first flights in December 1903, it was not until 1908, when they demonstrated their invention first to the United States Army and Navy at Fort Myers, Virginia, and then brought it to Europe, that their achievement was widely recognized, even though a United States Coast Guard sufman had been present at their first flight, and had even taken a photograph of it for the brothers. The airship was showing its potential during the first decade of the twentieth century, while the aeroplane was frail and at first more of a novelty or plaything.

The USN was slow off the mark. Meanwhile the estimates for the Royal Navy in 1909 included £35,000 for the purchase of an airship, and the Admiralty tender for HMA.1 (His Majesty's Airship No. 1) was signed on 7 May. This marked the start of the race amongst navies to get into the air, with France, the United States, Imperial Russia, Sweden, Japan, Germany, Norway and then Denmark, all buying or, in the case of Sweden and Norway, being presented with, aircraft during the next few years. By 1913, even Brazil had aircraft for naval use and, the following year, Greece was doing the same, with British assistance.

It shouldn't be thought that the British were content with an airship. During the early days of aviation, it was the Royal Aero Club that issued pilots' licences, not the government, and in 1910, the Royal Aero Club put two Short biplanes, based at Eastchurch on the Isle of Sheppey, at the disposal of the Royal Navy for any naval officers who wished to learn to fly. When young officers seemed backward in taking advantage of this opportunity, that December the Commander-in-Chief at the Nore, Admiral Sir C.C. Drury, drew the attention of his officers to the availability of the aircraft, describing them as 'biplanes of the most modern type, fitted with Gnome motors', adding that they were available 'at all times and without charge'. The only conditions were that any damage be repaired at the cost of the pilot concerned, and that those using them become members of the Royal Aero Club.

It is easy to overlook Drury's intervention. Naval aviation histories so often point out the way in which senior officers, even as late as the 1930s, thought it a kindness to discourage bright young officers from becoming involved in aviation, and not just in the Royal Navy but in others as well, including the Imperial Japanese Navy. Drury was the exception.

As a further incentive, before the year was out, King George V approved an Order in Council giving a daily allowance to naval airmen of six shillings for officers and half-a-crown for chief petty officers, petty officers and leading seamen, while able seamen received two shillings. It is perhaps reassuring that flying pay was available from the beginning!

Nevertheless, aviation medicine was clearly in its infancy, as *The Lancet*, then as now a leading British medical journal, ran an article on the blood pressure of airmen, suggesting that they keep to a low and steady altitude. Others also had concerns, with a correspondent for the new magazine, *Flight*, warning against shooting at aeroplanes as they flew over in case the crew decided to drop a bomb – clearly someone who had got cause and effect badly muddled.

Nevertheless, amidst this interest in aeronautics, there was a big disappointment for the Royal Navy. Its first airship, HMA.01 was finally completed at Barrow-in-Furness, but appeared to be too heavy to be successful. Workers quickly set about lightening the structure of the craft, which had been named *Mayfly*, but the lightened structure collapsed, breaking almost in two halfway along the airship, as she was moved outside her shed on 24 September 1911. It was not until 27 November 1916 that the RNAS had its first successful rigid airship, *R9*.

Some Royal Navy officers must have been attracted to flying, or at least tempted by the King's six shillings, for on 25 April 1911, the service received the first four pilots from Eastchurch. These were Lieutenants Arthur Longmore, R. Gregory and Charles Rumney Samson, all RN, and Lieutenant E.L. Gerrard of the Royal Marine Light Infantry.* Some idea of the spirit which these young men possessed was that at the time the Royal Aero Club had issued just fifty-five pilots' certificates, suggesting that almost 8 per cent of British aviators were members of the Royal Navy and Royal Marines! These were the first, but others soon followed. One of these was Sub Lieutenant F.E.T. Hewlett, who had been taught to fly by his mother, who seems to have been a woman of considerable character since she flew in bad weather wearing sabots, a type of wooden clog.

Naturally, the Royal Navy was not the only service interested in aviation, as we have already seen. In mid-November 1910, Lieutenant Eugene Ely of the United States Navy had taken off from a wooden platform built over the forecastle of the light cruiser USS *Birmingham* as she lay at anchor, while in January 1911, he landed on the cruiser USS *Pennsylvania* as she too lay at anchor, and took off later to fly back to his base at Selfridge Field. His landing had been helped by a primitive arrester wire system, with wires strung across the landing platform and kept in place by 100-lb sandbags at each end. Meanwhile in Italy, before the end of 1911, Captain Claudio Piomatti produced a paper on the role of the aeroplane in naval warfare.

The pace of development was indeed accelerating. In 1908, the aeroplane was a spectacle, an amusement and something of awe, but by 1911 it was beginning to grow up and show that it could have a practical benefit. In France, there were experiments with float-gliders, but it was in the United

* The Royal Marine Light Infantry (known as the 'red' marines because of their uniform jacket colour) were disbanded in 1923, when all marines adopted the blue of the Royal Marine Artillery.

States in 1911 that Glenn Curtiss built the first practical floatplane, which he flew for the first time on 26 January 1911 at San Diego, California. The following year, he used this aircraft as the basis for the first flying boat, but he had a rival, Denhout, in France, who that same year also built and flew the successful Donnet-Leveque flying boat. Curtiss continued his work on flying boats up to the outbreak of the First World War in Europe. He was assisted by a retired Royal Navy officer, Lieutenant Commander J.C. Porte, and together they designed the large twin-engined biplane flying boat *America*, which was sold to the Royal Naval Air Service in 1914.

Meanwhile, in a display of private initiative, Lieutenant (later Commander) Oliver Schwann RN bought an aeroplane privately, and fitted it with floats and gas bags to make a water take-off in November 1911. This was no light venture as, given the knowledge of the day, he could so easily have lost his aeroplane, or even his life. One of the original four Eastchurch graduates, Lieutenant Arthur Longmore, flew a Short S27 biplane fitted with airbags onto the River Medway on 1 December, and was able to take off again.

Longmore was the most successful of the original Eastchurch graduates, transferring to the Royal Air Force on its formation and eventually attaining the rank of air chief marshal. On 28 July 1914, at Calshot near the mouth of Southampton Water, already a squadron commander, he made the first drop of a standard naval torpedo while flying a Short Folder seaplane. The torpedo was carried on an improvised rack between the seaplane's floats.

Another of Longmore's group at Eastchurch, Lieutenant Charles Romney Samson, had the distinction of making the first take-off from a British warship. Wednesday, 10 January 1912 dawned grey and misty, but the mist began to clear in the late morning, making flying possible. At noon, Samson climbed into the same Short S27 used by Longmore the previous December and flew from the airfield at Eastchurch to land at Cockleshell Hard. On landing, the plane was manhandled onto a lighter, to which it was secured, and then towed by a pinnace to the battleship HMS *Africa*, moored in Sheerness Harbour, whose derrick lifted the aircraft onto the launching platform, which consisted of planks running from the top of 'A' turret down to the bows. At 14.20, with the ship still moored, the S27's 50-hp Gnome rotary engine was started and the aircraft started its run forward down the platform, before starting to climb away from it. Once in the air, Samson flew over the destroyer HMS *Cherwell* before turning back to fly over *Africa*, and then along the River Medway to the village of West Minster at an altitude of some 800 feet on his way back to Eastchurch. Samson's S27 was fitted with airbags in case an emergency landing in the Medway was necessary, and one senior officer present, Admiral E.H. Seymour maintained that he was 'heartened' by the ability of the frail aircraft to land on the water without sinking.

During the early years of the twentieth century, the Royal Navy held regular naval reviews, in marked contrast to more recent years. The 1912 Annual Naval Review was held off Portland in early May and the Royal Navy took no less than four aircraft to the review: two Short biplanes, a Deperdussin monoplane and a Nieuport. One of the Short biplanes had been converted by Samson into a hydroaeroplane by the simple expedient of fitting it with three torpedo-shaped floats, and naming it HMS *Amphibian*. Being Samson, there can be little doubt that this was done without reference to the Admiralty Ships' Names Committee! Official support was not lacking, however, as the battleship HMS *Hibernia* had a ramp constructed forward for the launching of landplanes, and was also formally referred to as a hydroaeroplane mother vessel. As for the airmen, they showed a flare for showmanship as well as airmanship that must have done much to raise the profile of naval aviation.

Needless to say, the flying was started by none other than Samson. He took off from Portland in his 'HMS' *Amphibian* and flew over the fleet which was lying at anchor. What really delighted the onlookers, however, was when the newly promoted Captain Gerrard RMLI took off with a young lady as passenger. They might have been even more delighted, or even impressed, had they known that the young lady was none other than the daughter of the C-in-C, Admiral Callaghan. Compared to this piece of showmanship, and courage on the part of the admiral's daughter, flights by Lieutenant Grey in both the Nieuport and Deperdussin, and that by Longmore in his trusty S27, were dull routine.

Towards the end of the review, Samson used *Amphibian* to carry a messenger with a letter for King George V, landing alongside the Royal Yacht *Victoria and Albert*, with the messenger transferring from the aircraft in a dinghy. As a further demonstration of the capabilities of the aeroplane, while Samson was delivering his messenger, Lieutenant Grey flew past the *Victoria and Albert* at 500 feet and dropped a 300-lb dummy bomb at a safe distance. He then flew past the battleship HMS *Neptune*, but suddenly dived, causing considerable alarm amongst those watching, pulling out just 20 feet above the sea. There was no need for alarm, however, as Grey had simply spotted one of the Royal Navy's then small fleet of submarines, submerged at periscope depth.

From the practical aspect, the most significant achievement at Portland was Samson making the first flight from a ship under way, flying an S27 from *Hibernia*'s ramp while the battleship steamed at 10½ knots into the wind in Weymouth Bay – an event watched by His Majesty who invited Samson to dine with him aboard the royal yacht at the end of the review. Media interest in the armed forces was considerably greater than today and there were many journalists present throughout the review. 'Good, good, but we shall do better,' they quoted Samson as saying.

Into the Royal Flying Corps

The Committee for Imperial Defence (CID) set up an Air Committee as early as April 1912, and the need for coordination and strengthening of Britain's air services was clearly in mind, for, after such a bold start, it seems almost an anti-climax that the Royal Navy's aviation wing was then merged into the Royal Flying Corps, formed in May 1912. The RFC had a Naval Wing and a Military Wing, but it was not an autonomous air service as it was controlled by the War Office, the department of state for the British Army. This provoked a reaction from the Admiralty which was concerned that its interests should be protected, even though the merger was intended to strengthen and coordinate British service aviation. The RFC was not without some benefit to the naval airmen, however, as squadron commanders, flight commanders and flying officers now received an extra eight shillings a day – generous money for the time. For those who learnt to fly privately, there was a grant of £75, and on agreeing to transfer from the Royal Navy or the Army into the RFC, there was a grant of £40 towards the cost of special clothing. By April 1913, the first ten naval officers had qualified as pilots. These were all volunteers who had to be at least the rank of lieutenant in the RN, or captain or a lieutenant in the RM, with two years' or more service in the rank, and subject to the approval of their commanding officers. The courses were also open to RNR or RNVR officers, with preference given to those who had undergone a period of training in a warship or naval establishment. Those awarded the sum of £75 for private instruction were informed that it was liable to be repaid if they left the service within four years, and, subject to prior approval, they would receive full pay with lodging and other allowances. Once qualified, naval airmen were liable to be allocated to airships or aeroplanes as required, and had no choice in the matter.

Despite War Office control, when the RFC opened its Central Flying School at Upavon on Salisbury Plain, the first commandant was a naval officer, Captain G.M. Paine. Nevertheless, there were rumblings of discontent at the Admiralty. The creation of a distinct naval aviation service was largely at the instigation of Captain Murray Sueter, first inspecting captain of naval aviation and at the time Director Air Department, Admiralty, who wrote a paper dated 24 February 1914.

In looking forward to what would become the Royal Naval Air Service (RNAS), the conditions of service were once again considered. It was first proposed that officers were to have one year's seagoing experience in a commissioned rank, and would not be away from the fleet for more than four years. Ratings were also expected to have seagoing experience early in their service and certainly before attaining the rank of petty officer. In practice, many of these requirements were later dropped, so that on its formation civilians could join.

By July 1914, Admiralty documents were discussing a Royal Naval Air Service, but strictly speaking it remained part of the RFC until after Churchill had left the Admiralty in 1915. Nevertheless, all army airships were transferred in 1914 to the RFC's Naval Wing.

Storm Clouds Gather

Meanwhile, the storm clouds were gathering over Europe, with the British and German navies engaged in an unspoken but nevertheless effective arms race. The service that had once been established as the equivalent of any other two navies in the world had effectively relinquished its lead when the new battleship HMS *Dreadnought* had made all other capital ships obsolete. As the British government dithered over whether defence or welfare reform should have priority for expenditure, the Admiralty struggled for the funds for the ships it needed. In the end, it boiled down to which nation had the superior shipbuilding capacity and, fortunately at the time, the United Kingdom was the world's leading shipbuilder. The debate over whether welfare or defence should have priority had been given an edge by the rumblings of discontent in a number of countries, especially Russia.

Just months after the 1912 fleet review at Portland, the fears of those who foresaw war with Germany were heightened by a new threat. The German airship *L.1*, commanded by none other than its designer, Count Ferdinand von Zeppelin, made a record 1,000-mile flight from its base at Friedrichshafen, ascending at 08.35 on Sunday, 13 October, and arriving at Johannisthal, near Berlin, on Monday, 14 October at 15.43. This was a notable achievement in itself, but more to the point, it raised a hue and cry in England because it was claimed that the *L.1* was heard over Sheerness during the night. Questions were even asked in Parliament. No one had heard the Zeppelin – they only thought that they had done so – but the threat posed by these large craft was all too obvious.

The real problem was that the British were having some difficulty in building a true rival to the German Zeppelins. On returning to the Admiralty as First Sea Lord during the first winter of the First World War, the redoubtable 'Jacky' Fisher, by this time Baron Fisher of Kilverstone, found that the Royal Navy had toyed with the idea of inserting balloonets into an airship envelope and putting the fuselage and engine of a Royal Aircraft Factory BE2c under the envelope, creating non-rigid airships. When Fisher demanded to know how quickly a prototype could be completed, he was told three weeks. The maiden ascent of the first, *SS-1* (for Submarine Scout 1) was on 18 March 1915, at Kingsnorth on the River Medway. Encouraged by this, Fisher demanded forty such airships. This was a tall order for what was not only a new technology, but also a new industry, but by the following year, sixteen airships were in service. The SS series were not the only RNAS airships, and on 31 May 1915, the first coastal patrol airship, *C1*, made her maiden ascent.

Earlier, starting in 1912, a chain of seaplane stations was being built, with the first on the Isle of Grain on the other side of the Medway Estuary from Sheerness. The following year, the light cruiser HMS *Hermes* was converted to act as a seaplane carrier for the 1913 naval review. Although *Hermes* was later converted back to her original form, a collier was converted to take her place and named HMS *Ark Royal*. The conversion of these two ships was caused by the arrival of the new Short Folder biplane, the first to have wings that would fold (albeit backwards) so that the aircraft could be stowed inside a hangar aboard a ship.

When formed on 1 July 1914, the Royal Naval Air Service had no less than fifty-two seaplanes and flying boats, thirty-nine landplanes and six (soon to be increased to seven) airships, as well as 828 officers and men – not many given the number of aircraft. There were some differences between the uniform of the RNAS and that of the Royal Navy, with an eagle replacing the anchor on badges and buttons, as well as on epaulettes and sword belts. The pilots' wings were also moved from the chest to the cuff, with commissioned pilots having them above the executive curl. The Central Air Office was the heart of the RNAS, and in August 1914 it was headed by Wing Commander Francis Scarlett, who was the Inspecting Captain of Aircraft.

By July 1914, there were six naval air stations: at Dundee, Calshot on Southampton Water, the Isle of Grain, Felixstowe, Fort George and Great Yarmouth; there was also a naval flying school at Eastchurch on the Isle of Sheppey. There was an airship section at Farnborough, still shared with the RFC until the RNAS assumed responsibility for all airships, and an active station at Kingsnorth on the River Medway. The practice adopted later of giving all naval air stations ships' names so that they had dual designation, as with, for example, RNAS Lee-on-Solent, HMS *Daedalus*, had still to be adopted, but for all administrative purposes these units and their personnel were on the books of HMS *Pembroke* at Chatham.

In May 1914, it had been proposed that further air stations would be prepared at Scapa Flow and Peterhead, on the Humber and near Newcastle, while plans were laid for an airship shed at Cromer. Squadrons of fighting aeroplanes were also proposed for a number of air stations, including Eastchurch, for which ten aircraft were proposed, although elsewhere squadrons initially consisted of eight aircraft in two flights. At the time, the Naval Wing consisted of fifty-five seaplanes and forty landplanes, of which thirty-five were biplanes; another forty-five seaplanes were on order along with four biplanes. Airships were in service, and one Parseval and one French Astra Torres were on order, while the Military Wing's airships were being transferred as the Naval Wing was to assume development of all lighter-than-air craft. Seven non-rigid airships were in service and another seven on order, as was a single rigid airship. Eight squadrons were earmarked for expeditionary service.

The RNAS enjoyed a degree of autonomy within the Royal Navy. At the top was the Admiralty Air Department, while there was also the Central Air Office, the Royal Naval Flying School and the Royal Naval Air Stations. Ranks included: wing captain instead of captain; wing commander; squadron commander instead of lieutenant commander, or a lieutenant with at least two years' seniority for a smaller unit; flight commander instead of lieutenant; and flying sub lieutenant. Already one could see part of the future rank structure of the Royal Air Force, and interestingly, once the Fleet Air Arm returned to the Royal Navy in the late 1930s, it was the standard naval ranks and cap badges that were used.

The concept of the flight, squadron, wing and group was already understood by the outbreak of the First World War, as indicated by the ranks of the Royal Naval Air Service. Nevertheless, when it came to allocating designations to these units, there was still some uncertainty. Should they be referred to by their base or the part of the fleet to which they belonged? Should there be numbers or letters? How many aircraft should a squadron have? Initially, the RNAS squadrons were far larger than would have been the case in later years, with as many as sixty-six in No. 1 Squadron at one time, while flights were provided for many of the Royal Navy's main bases, including air defence flights at Dover, seen as vulnerable because of its proximity to France. There were difficulties at first in identifying squadrons, since the temptation was to describe them as being part of a particular naval unit, including their home base. It was not until 1916 that a logical and consistent system was introduced and even then there were many exceptions. The eventual formation of the Royal Air Force in 1918 meant that the new service found itself with many squadron numbers duplicated in the RNAS and RFC, and resolved this problem by simply adding 200 to all of the naval air squadrons.

The RNAS was in many ways ahead of the RFC in the development of the aeroplane as a weapon of war. It undertook much of the pioneering work, not just with torpedoes, as one would expect of naval airmen, but also with bombs and fitting aircraft with machine guns. Once war broke out, the RNAS was volunteered by the First Lord of the Admiralty, Winston Churchill, for the air defence of the United Kingdom, while the RFC was employed generally in support of ground forces. Nevertheless, in practical terms, on the outbreak of war in August 1914, the RNAS had two aircraft and one airship fitted with machine guns, while the 'bombs' were often simply shells fitted with crude fins. It soon became all too apparent that the seaplane suffered severe limitations in the air-defence role, with too much drag and weight from its floats to be able to climb above a Zeppelin quickly enough to be able to destroy it from above – the safest and most effective point from which to attack.

In 1914, there were many in the Royal Navy who saw the aeroplane simply as a means of reconnaissance and for observing the fall of shot. Nevertheless, naval aviation as we know it was to evolve during the war that followed. Even so, as late as 1930, one captain was to muse that: 'In peacetime, it may be frankly admitted, seaplanes available for picnics, shooting parties, or as substitutes for captain's galleys when lying at anchor far from shore, would be fun.' Fortunately, there were others who were wiser and more far-sighted.

On 5 June 1914, Admiral Sir Percy Scott managed to bring the wrath of the establishment down upon his head when he wrote to *The Times*: 'Submarines and aeroplanes have entirely revolutionised naval warfare; no fleet can hide itself from the aeroplane eye, and the submarine can deliver a deadly attack even in broad daylight ... As the motor vehicle had driven the horse from the road, so has the submarine driven the battleship from the sea.'

Chapter 2

Defending the United Kingdom

On 3 September 1914, the Cabinet decided that the Royal Navy would undertake the aerial defence of the UK since the Army had neither the guns nor the personnel for this work. On the other hand, nor had the Navy! It is hard to escape the conclusion that the decision was driven to some extent by the enthusiasm of one man, Winston Churchill, the First Lord of the Admiralty. This replaced the ad hoc arrangements that had been hastily assembled prior to the declaration of war; nothing had been done about AA defences ashore, although on 8 August, the Royal Garrison Artillery had mounted three 1-pounder pom-poms in Whitehall to protect the Admiralty and the War Office. The Admiralty had made provision for the defence of ships from air attack, but its armaments were needed for the protection of the ships. The Admiralty assumed control of Britain's AA defences before the end of the month, establishing the Royal Naval Volunteer Reserve Anti-Aircraft Corps.

The attraction to the British government of having the RNAS provide air protection was that it freed the RFC from air-defence duties and enabled it to concentrate on offensive and defensive patrols over the front line, as well as providing aerial reconnaissance for ground forces – it was the latter role that had been behind the Army's interest in aviation. Yet the RNAS had just 128 officers and 700 ratings, who flew in or maintained thirty-nine airships and fifty-two seaplanes, with just half of the latter operational. It had just one seaplane carrier until other ships could be taken up from trade and converted – it was found that Channel and Irish Sea packet vessels were best suited for this role.

Royal Naval Volunteer Reserve Anti-Aircraft Corps

The RN resolved the problem of manning anti-aircraft guns ashore by raising part-time reservist forces, the Royal Naval Volunteer Reserve Anti-Aircraft Corps, based initially in London. The RNVR AA Corps came into existence there on 9 October 1914 and was not demobilized until

15 February 1919. At one stage, in 1916, members of the RNVR AAC were sent to Ireland. Initially under the control of the Admiralty Air Department, the Army finally became responsible for air defence on 16 February 1916, when RNVR AAC units were put under Army control, and a number of them were later disbanded as Army units took their place. The decision to create a special reserve force for AA defence is interesting, as the Royal Naval Division, which was sent to Europe to fight alongside the Army, was created because of the surplus of manpower over that needed to man the Royal Navy's warships early on in what was soon to become known as the Great War.

The RNVR AAC had an unhappy existence. In some cases, its members had been special constables. They were initially committed to four hours every other night, then the Admiralty increased this to six hours, thereby losing many men who could not meet the increased commitment. Eventually, many units were worked twenty-four hours on, twenty-four hours off, receiving standard naval pay if worked full time, and half pay if working part time. In some cases, twelve-hour shifts were worked. The RNVR AAC seems to have been the victim of much confusion of constant change and reorganization, with the constant doubt over whether it would stay with the Navy or be transferred to the Army. Meanwhile, many members were no longer serving ashore but had gone to sea with the fleet.

There was such a constant shortage of equipment that one training exercise at Shoeburyness saw those men with previous firing experience not being allowed to fire, and those with no experience being allowed to fire a single round on an obsolete Nordenfelt gun! The more modern Hotchkiss machine guns had mountings so badly designed that they could not be loaded above an angle of 55 degrees, and could not be fired at an angle of more than 70 degrees, or less than 43 degrees – so much for air defence!

The Cuxhaven Raid

Attack is often the best means of defence, and in this spirit the best counter to the Zeppelin threat was to attack their bases, the nearest of which was the Nordholz airship station 8 miles south of Cuxhaven, which had been the headquarters for the German Naval Airship Division since October 1914. The base consisted of a single large shed accommodating two 518ft long Zeppelins. The term 'shed' did not do the structure justice as it weighed 4,000 tons and was mounted on a large turntable that could turn into the prevailing wind, so that the Zeppelins inside were not trapped by wind blowing across the door of the shed. The two Zeppelins represented exactly half the naval airship fleet suitable for operations over the North Sea, with the other two based at Hamburg.

The raid was prepared by the then Commodore Roger Keyes, while the force was commanded by Commodore Reginald Tyrwhitt, both of whom were based at Harwich. Originally, the raid was scheduled for 25 October 1914, but while the raiding force, including two seaplane carriers and their escorts, sailed from Harwich in a flat calm on 24 October, by dawn the next day, when the six seaplanes were hoisted over the sides of the ships, heavy rain prevented four of the frail aircraft from taking off. Of the two that did become airborne, one had to turn back after flying just 12 miles because the engine had stopped twice due to the heavy rain. The sixth aircraft went a little further, flying 20 miles before poor visibility forced it back.

On 23 November, a further attempt was due to be made, and Jellicoe even went so far as to move the Grand Fleet into the North Sea to support the operation. However, even before an aircraft was shipped over the side of a seaplane carrier, the Admiralty cancelled the operation.

With good weather forecast for the Christmas period, on 23 December, the Admiralty ordered that the operation take place on Christmas Day. This time three seaplane carriers, *Engadine*, *Riviera* and *Express*, were used, escorted by three light cruisers and eight destroyers, again under the command of Tyrwhitt, who believed that a small force had a better chance of remaining undiscovered. Keyes sent eleven submarines, mainly to keep watch in case German ships should emerge, in which case they were also to try to attack them. Some of the submarines were positioned at the launch and recovery points to protect the seaplane carriers, and also to rescue the crews of any aircraft that might get into difficulties taking off or returning to their ships. To aid recognition, especially in poor visibility, red and white checkerboard stripes were painted around the submarines' conning towers, making the exercise exceptionally hazardous for any submarine caught on the surface by German warships. Despite Tyrwhitt's belief in small forces, he was overruled by Admiral Jellico and the Grand Fleet was once again to be brought south, just in case.

Tyrwhitt sailed from Harwich at 05.00 on Christmas Eve, without warning and reputedly leaving behind on the quaysides a number of stewards landed to obtain extras for Christmas Day. Entering the Heligoland Bight at 04.30 the following day, they came across four German patrol vessels, and *Aurora* picked up German wireless transmissions soon afterwards. At this point, Tyrwhitt, aboard *Arethusa*, considered abandoning the operation, fearful that the seaplane carriers might be sunk while waiting for their aircraft to return, but after two previous attempts had come to nothing, he was reluctant to turn back.

Just before daybreak, *Engadine*, *Riviera* and *Express* stopped engines and each put three seaplanes onto a calm sea, with a light breeze and no sign of fog. The seaplanes were to take a total of twenty-seven small bombs, with about three pounds of explosives each, to bomb the airship sheds at Cuxhaven, before flying over the Cuxhaven and Wilhelmshaven anchorages to carry out a reconnaissance of the German warships present, and then fly along the coast to Norderney island before turning north to rejoin the carriers. The aircraft each had enough fuel for three hours.

The aircraft were in the water at 06.30, their wings were unfolded, and their engines started and run up to their normal operating temperatures. Tyrwhitt signalled take-off at 06.59. Nine aircraft started, but two soon suffered engine failure and were hoisted back aboard the seaplane carriers, while the other seven, in the light breeze, had to make an extended take-off run lacking lift and, in the calm sea, having difficulty in taking off, or, in hydroaeroplane parlance, 'unsticking'.

It took an hour for the aircraft to reach land, by which time fog had come down covering the land, although as it drifted and thinned before coming down again, it allowed the Zeppelin *L.6* to take off on patrol. The seven pilots desperately tried to find their target. One thought he saw the airship shed and dropped three bombs, one of which hit a fish-drying shed. Another discovered the airship shed but in the fog failed to recognize it for what it was, and instead attacked some anti-aircraft guns. One managed to miss the airship station and instead found the Jade estuary, only to be fired at by a battlecruiser, seven light cruisers and many destroyers. One of the observers in the aircraft was none other than Lieutenant Erskine Childers, who before the war had written *The Riddle of the Sands*, predicting a future war with Germany. Childers spotted seven battleships and three battle-cruisers in Schillig Roads. Such targets were immune to anything a First World War aeroplane could do to them, but the pilot who tried to attack the light cruisers *Graudenz* and *Strasland* failed to drop any of his bombs closer than 200 yards from *Graudenz*.

The operation was over by 09.30, and by 10.00 the fog had thickened, encouraging the Germans not to risk sending their ships to attack Tyrwhitt's force, which in any case they believed was probably only the vanguard of a far more powerful force. *L.6* had already located Tyrwhitt's ships little more than an hour after the seaplanes had taken off. At 09.00, two German seaplanes attacked the seaplane carrier *Empress* with 10- and 22-lb bombs, some of which fell within 20 to 40 feet of the ship, by this time suffering from boiler problems and trailing behind the rest of the force. *Empress* was then attacked by *L.6*, although her commanding officer, Captain Frederick Bowhill, quickly discovered that it was much easier to outmanoeuvre a Zeppelin than an aeroplane, which was just as well as *L.6* dropped three 110-lb bombs.

Around 10.00, two seaplanes landed close to *Riviera* off Norderney, cut their engines and after their wings were folded, were hoisted safely aboard. A third landed close to the destroyer *Lurcher* seeking directions, but as the aircraft had little fuel left, Keyes, who was directing his sub-marines from the destroyer, took the pilot on board and the aircraft in tow.

Tyrwhitt's ship, *Arethusa*, was attacked by two German seaplanes at 10.30, although again their bombs missed. By this time, Tyrwhitt realized that his four remaining seaplanes must have run out of fuel, if they had managed to survive the attack, and turned his force back to Harwich.

In fact, three of the four were already down near Nordeney and had been picked up by the submarine *E11*, commanded by Lieutenant Commander Martin Nasmith, who had spotted a seaplane landing through his periscope while submerged and had immediately surfaced. He had agreed to give the aircraft a tow to the nearest seaplane carrier when he spotted the Zeppelin *L.5*, but then saw a submarine on the surface and, believing it to be German, prepared to dive. The other submarine also dived because it saw the Zeppelin, which confirmed its intentions in Nasmith's view, but he couldn't dive as two more seaplanes splashed down beside him. He quickly drove his submarine so close to one of them that its crew didn't get even their feet wet as they stepped out of the aircraft and on to the deck casing, while the other two crew of the third seaplane were less fortunate and had to swim to the submarine. Quickly getting a seaman to destroy the three seaplanes with machine-gun fire, Nasmith then crash-dived with *L.5* directly overhead. His submarine was shaken by bombs, but was undamaged. Nasmith was to become one of the Royal Navy's greatest submariners during the war.

Meanwhile, the other submarine was in fact *D6*, another British submarine that had been approaching to offer help to the seaplane crew.

The seventh seaplane had a more mundane recovery. Its crew were picked up by a Dutch trawler and spent some time aboard while it completed its fishing trip and returned to the Netherlands. Rather than be interned for the duration in what was, during the war, a neutral country, they were repatriated as shipwrecked mariners.

The frailty of the early seaplane and the difficulty of operating from seaplane carriers meant that successful sorties were difficult to achieve. Later in the war, on 25 March 1916, five seaplanes were sent from seaplane carrier *Vindex*, from a point 40 miles off the enemy coast, in an unsuccessful attempt to bomb the airship shed at Hoyer on the coast of Schleswig-Holstein. Operating in bad weather with snow and gale force winds, three aircraft developed engine trouble and had to land in German territory so that their crews were captured. One pilot found that there was in fact no Zeppelin shed at Hoyer and bombed what he believed to be a factory instead, while the fifth aircraft flew on to Tondern and actually found a Zeppelin shed, but when he dived down to bomb it, his bomb-release cable had jammed.

The cost of mounting these operations continued to be enormous. Lacking the speed of an aircraft carrier, having to stop to hoist seaplanes over the side for take-off, and then do the same to recover any that returned afterwards, meant exceptional measures to protect *Vindex*.

The first airship to be destroyed on the ground was the Zeppelin *LZ.38*, found in her shed by shore-based RNAS aircraft on 7 June 1915. A little more than a year later, *L.48* was shot down and yielded that most precious of gifts, the German naval signals book. Before this, however, the German submarine *U-21* had made a daring sortie into the Irish Sea and, on 29 January 1915, shelled the airship shed at Walney Island, close to Barrow-in-Furness.

Maritime-Reconnaissance

Initially what would today be described as maritime-reconnaissance was conducted by captive balloons, which were confined to the observation role and known as 'kite-balloons', and airships.

Unlike the Germans, the RNAS did not use its airships for offensive purposes because they were far more vulnerable than the robust German Zeppelin to both aerial attack and anti-aircraft fire. Compared to German airships, the British ones, with their slightly squashed shape, were less manoeuvrable and often had difficult access to engines. Payload was limited compared to German airships, as was endurance, while accommodation consisted of modified aircraft fuselages. One wartime naval aviator described the craft as 'a botched up job of half an aeroplane and half an airship'. If an engine began to overheat, water had to be taken by hand from the water ballast, with the mechanic walking along rope ladder walkways to the engine, where he would take off the radiator cap and pour in whatever water hadn't been spilt on the way.

Nevertheless, the role that did show these craft in a worthwhile light was that of reconnaissance and convoy protection, with airships patrolling above convoys to give advance warning of U-boats and minefields. Initially, such duties were undertaken by the C-class or 'coastal' airships, and the SS-class, with the C-class having an endurance of up to twelve hours. The later NS or North Sea-class had an endurance of up to twenty hours and much more comfortable accommodation for the crew, which was divided into two watches.

Anti-submarine operations were based on Felixstowe in Suffolk and were augmented in 1917 by the arrival of the first large Felixstowe flying boats – the large Curtiss America flying boats such as the H12. Initially these large aircraft enjoyed considerable success against German submarines, as they surprised some U-boat commanders.

Nevertheless, their score of successes was soon hampered by two factors. First, the Germans developed 'altiscopes', upward-looking periscopes that enabled them to search the sky for approaching aircraft before surfacing. The second problem was a lack of development, as the First World War aircraft and airships did not carry depth charges and instead had to rely on bombs. Nevertheless, the U-boats were compelled to keep as much as 50 miles offshore, making the coastal convoys safer, and it soon became clear that convoys with protection from the air were seldom attacked. Unfortunately, the flying boats still lacked the endurance to provide the cover needed, while air cover was still affected by bad weather. Operations at night were also difficult, so this became the favourite hunting time for the U-boats.

Flying boats were more manoeuvrable than airships and could cope more easily with adverse winds. They were generally more economical with manpower, having a crew of four – a pilot, who was usually the captain, an observer, a wireless telegraphy operator and an engineer – while airships required a substantial number of men for ground handling, especially as wind speeds rose.

British involvement with the flying boat had dated from before the outbreak of war, when Lieutenant Commander J.C. Porte had cooperated with the American, Glenn Curtiss, in the design of the Curtiss America large flying boat. Curtiss had flown the first practical flying boat in 1912. On the outbreak of war, the Curtiss America was purchased by the RNAS. During the war years, the Curtiss H12, H16 and HS1 flying boats were operated by both the RNAS and the USN, and a factory was established at Felixstowe to produce the famous Felxistowe series of flying boats. On 20 May 1917, *UC-36* was sunk by a RNAS flying boat in the North Sea, the first U-boat to be sunk by the RNAS.*

By 1 April 1918, the RNAS resources devoted to anti-submarine or maritime-reconnaissance operations totalled 291 flying boats and seaplanes, twenty-three landplanes and a hundred airships. Unfortunately, Admiralty hopes of increasing this force in the final six months of the war were dashed as the former RNAS units were scoured for aircraft and aircrew for the RAF's newly formed Independent Air Force for bomber operations over Germany. There can be little doubt that during the First World War, given the capabilities of the aircraft of the day and the numbers available, strategic bombing was a waste of time and had nothing other than symbolic value.

*There is a bitter footnote to this. Porte had been invalided out of the Royal Navy in 1911, and after flying for the British subsidiary of Deperdussin, he later joined Glenn Curtiss in the United States to work on flying-boat development. The two men designed and built the *America* flying boat which Porte intending to fly across the Atlantic. The First World War meant the end of this plan, but Porte returned to England to build Curtiss flying boats. A flying-boat factory was established at Felixstowe, on the Suffolk coast. Towards the end of the First World War, Porte was accused of receiving money from Curtiss from the licence fees paid to the American and he was prosecuted, but after a long trial he was acquitted and a guilty government granted him the Order of St Michael and St George, which he received from King George V. He died in 1919 from tuberculosis.

Chapter 3

The Search for Air Power at Sea

In August 1914, the Royal Navy was one of just three navies that had ships converted to carry aircraft. Yet the seaplane carriers in service early in the war were far from satisfactory, and although most were conversions from Irish Sea and cross-Channel packets, which were faster than most small or medium-sized merchantmen of the day, they were still too slow to keep up with the fleet. Worse still, they had to stop to place their aircraft in the water as they lacked catapults, and then stop again to recover them.

The limitations of the seaplane carriers were as nothing to the shortcomings of the aircraft themselves. Naval aircraft at the time did not have to be floatplanes – even before the outbreak of war the RNAS knew that it needed landplanes as well, especially for fighter defence ashore and then, later, for bombing missions, but those that accompanied the fleet to sea did have to be hydroaeroplanes, that is seaplanes (known initially as floatplanes) or flying boats. It soon became clear that as fighters, the seaplanes were hampered by the drag of their floats, could not climb quickly and were completely outclassed by the ability of a Zeppelin to climb at up to 2,000 feet a minute simply by dumping its water ballast. Getting in a position above a Zeppelin to attack took time and skill; attempting to attack from below was simply asking for trouble as Zeppelins had considerable machine-gun defences, as indeed did many of their British counterparts, some of which even had a machine gun mounted on top of the envelope. The situation with bombers was little better. The seaplane struggled to get a worthwhile payload off the water.

There were other problems with the seaplane as well. If the water was too rough, operations became hazardous or simply impossible. Dead flat calm was little better, as seaplanes and flying boats tend to 'stick' to the surface of the water in a calm, and need at least some small waves to help them 'unstick'.

At the outbreak of war, the mainstay of the RNAS was the Short Type 184 seaplane. The type number came simply from the fact that the first aeroplane was allocated the number 184 by the RNAS. This used inline engines for the most part, including those manufactured by companies such as Sunbeam and Renault, powerful for the day at 260 hp and 240 hp respectively. An unusual feature was that this aeroplane was a tail-dragger in every sense, with a third float for the tailplane, while most seaplanes had longer floats without any need to support the tail. More than 650 Short 184s served with the RNAS.

There were attempts to improve the seaplane carrier as the war progressed. The Cunard liner *Campania*, 18,000 tons, was requisitioned and joined the fleet in 1915 with a 200-foot wooden deck built over the ship's forecastle, so that Fairey's new Campania seaplane could take off from the wooden deck using wheeled trolleys placed under the floats, so at least the ship did not have to stop to launch the aircraft. The following year, the ship's fore-funnel was divided so that the take-off platform could be lengthened. Despite her pedigree, the ship was still too slow to keep up with the fleet. Performance of the Fairey Campania was far from what was needed, as cruising speed was a sedate 80 mph and the operational ceiling was 2,000 feet, but the three-hour endurance was useful for reconnaissance and observation.

The Fairey Campania was another tail-dragger, and must have been the only aircraft to have been named after a ship. It had in-line engines, such as the Rolls-Royce Eagle 345 hp or, because of the shortage of Eagle engines, the Sunbeam Maori of 275 hp, but could only manage 85 mph at sea level and took seven minutes to climb to 2,000 feet. This does not invite comparison with the Camel, for example, as the Campania was a strike aircraft with bomb racks under the wings. Only sixty-two aircraft were completed.

During April 1916, the submarine *E22* conducted 'float-off' trials with two Sopwith Schneider seaplanes, with the intention of discovering whether these aircraft could intercept Zeppelins over the North Sea. The tiny seaplanes were, of course, still burdened with the drag of their floats, and the trails were not a success. Had such been available, an aircraft carrier operating landplanes might have had a chance to catch the Zeppelins before they could reach the East Coast, albeit at a heavy cost in protection for itself, but a seaplane stood very little chance at all. The so-called 'Schneider' was in fact no sluggard as it was the Sopwith Tabloid, the same type that had won the 1914 Schneider Contest, but with a speed of just 86.78 mph.

Reconnaissance and observation duties were to become an important part of the role of the RNAS. After some initial difficulty, aircraft were used for spotting the fall of shot during the Gallipoli campaign, and were also used by some of the submarine commanders for what almost amounted to an aerial orientation before taking their submarines through the Dardanelles. Aerial spotting was used in the destruction of the German light cruiser *Konigsberg* in mid-1915, with Lieutenant John Cull and his observer continuing to spot even after a shell had destroyed the water jacket of their aircraft engine and they were gliding back to the relative safety of one of their own ships.

Many other solutions were tried. One of the most promising was to launch aircraft from lighters towed behind destroyers at high speed; this got landplane fighters into the air over the fleet or any escorted merchant vessels, but risked sacrificing the aircraft as the pilot had to ditch when the sortie ended. A number of experiments followed, ending on 31 July 1918, during which it was discovered that the lighters could be towed at up to 30 knots without throwing up spray, but that men needed to sit on the bows to keep the lighters level. On 18 August, Lieutenant S.D. Culley took off from a lighter flying a Sopwith Camel to destroy the Zeppelin *L.53*. Afterwards, he landed alongside his towing destroyer, HMS *Redoubtable*, which actually managed to pick up his landplane using a special derrick in the hope of salvaging it.

The Camel was one of the more powerful aircraft available to the RNAS, or perhaps one should say the RAF, as by this time the RNAS and RFC had both been merged into the new Royal Air Force. Another biplane, the Camel had a 130-hp Clerget rotary engine and could manage the then high speed of 115 mph at 6,500 feet. The term rotary engine referred not to the late twentieth-century Wankel engine but to one with the cylinders arranged in a circle around the camshaft and spinning around it. As power increased, the gyroscopic forces generated by having so much weight spinning around soon made this concept impractical and it was superseded by the radial engine.

Meanwhile, a more practical solution had been achieved, with each major ship in the Grand Fleet carrying two aircraft. These were an anti-Zeppelin air-defence fighter that could be launched from a platform on one of the after turrets, and another two-seat aircraft for reconnaissance, that could be launched from a platform on one of the forward turrets. The aircraft were still likely to be lost at the end of their missions, but the ships did not have to stop to launch them, and indeed could rotate the turret into the wind to avoid the need to change course. These landplanes had a better performance than the seaplanes. Picking up the pilot was done by a destroyer that could then transfer the pilot, or pilot and observer in the case of a reconnaissance machine, to the battleship or battlecruiser. Such aircraft even flew off cruisers, such as on 21 August 1917, when a Sopwith Pup was flown off from a cruiser to shoot down the Zeppelin *L.23*, the first time that a landplane flying from a cruiser had managed this, which would have been beyond a seaplane.

Just as it seemed that the Royal Navy was never to be offered ships that were large enough and fast enough to match the aspirations of the naval airmen, and meet the objectives of naval aviation, the situation changed with what was virtually the gift of a major warship. The battlecruiser HMS

Furious was the last of three ships of what had became known in naval circles as the 'Outrageous'-class. The First Sea Lord, Admiral of the Fleet Lord Fisher, recalled from retirement to make the British fleet ready for war with Germany and her allies, had pressed ahead with an ambitious plan to land British and Russian forces in Pomerania, on Germany's Baltic coastline, as close as possible to Berlin, and then advance inland. Central to this plan were three battlecruisers, with a heavy armament and a shallow draught making them ideal for operations off the coast. Two of these, *Glorious* and *Courageous*, had four 15-inch guns in two turrets, but *Furious* had two massive 18-inch guns. The direct attack on Germany was a non-starter. The British element of the invasion would have been easy targets sailing through the narrow straits between Denmark and the rest of Scandinavia, and could so easily have been bottled up in the Baltic. And it was soon clear that the Russian Army, ill-equipped and infiltrated by revolutionary activists, was going nowhere.

The three battlecruisers had an unhappy reception from the rest of the fleet. To the wits on the lower deck, *Courageous* was known as *Outrageous*, *Glorious* as *Uproarious*, or alternatively the three ships were *Helpless*, *Hopeless* and *Useless*. These unfortunate nicknames soon proved well deserved, when on the night of 8 January 1917, in the undemanding weather conditions of a sea state 4 – barely choppy water – *Courageous*, her stem lifting by 3ft, broke her back.

An embarrassed Admiralty was faced with making the best of a bad job. Seeking a worthwhile role for the new ships, it was decided to convert *Furious*, still on the slipway, to launch aircraft. The fleet's misfortune was to be good fortune for the naval aviators. Her forward turret was replaced by an aircraft hangar with the flight deck running from the roof of the hangar to the bows, although the after turret was initially retained. This soon proved useless, as one of her officers later recorded that when the massive 18-inch gun fired, her lightly built hull rippled and rivets flew out of the plates across his cabin.

Landplane operation required that aircraft could land on the ship, and on 2 August 1917, Squadron Commander (the RNAS equivalent of Lieutenant Commander) E.H. Dunning flew a Sopwith Camel fighter past the superstructure of the ship to land safely on the forward deck, just 228ft long, helped by his fellow officers who dragged the aircraft down on to the deck by grabbing hold of the toggles placed under the lower-wing trailing edges. This was risky, since the deck was only suitable for taking off. So it happened a few days later that a second attempt by Dunning resulted in his frail aircraft being blown over the side of the ship, and the unfortunate pilot drowned before he could escape from the cockpit.

The following year, *Furious* emerged from a further rebuild having lost her after turret and gained a separate platform, 300ft long, for 'landing on', as naval terminology describes a deck landing. Aircraft could be manhandled on decking running on either side of the funnel and superstructure connecting the landing and take-off platforms. In this form, she could carry up to twenty aircraft, and had the high maximum speed of 32.5 knots. Landing was helped by arrester wires running fore and aft catching hooks under the undercarriage spreader bar, with a net to catch any aircraft missing the hooks. Alternatively, the landing platform could carry an airship.

Furious was the only aircraft carrier, or 'aerodrome ship', to see operational service before the war ended, but even before the Tondern raid, another aircraft carrier had entered service. The *Argus* was converted on the slipway from the Italian liner *Conte Rosso*, and her design was a complete contrast to that of *Furious*, as she lacked any superstructure at all, being the first ship to have a through deck. Admiralty hesitation to select this as the shape of all future carriers was understandable, however, as the boiler- room smoke escaped through two large ducts at the stern, making an approach uncomfortable and with visibility affected by smoke and heat haze. Two other ships were also at an advanced stage: another conversion, *Eagle*, originally laid down as the *Almirante Cochrane*, a battleship for Chile, and the first purpose-built aircraft carrier, *Hermes*. The urgency for these two ships having gone with the Armistice, their completion was delayed while the ideal layout for deck and superstructure was fully considered. The fact that most, although by no means all, aircraft carriers built over the next eighty or more years followed the eventual layout, is evidence that the time spent in solving these problems and finalizing the design was indeed well spent.

Before the war ended, *Argus* underwent deck-landing trials with eighteen Sopwith Cuckoo fighter biplanes on the Firth of Forth in October 1918. The Cuckoo was a significant step forward, for at exactly the right time, it was the first landplane torpedo bomber that could operate from the flight deck of an aircraft carrier. Credit for this goes to Murray Sueter, by this time a commodore, who in late 1916 suggested such an aircraft to Tommy Sopwith. The aircraft first flew in June 1917, powered by a 200-hp Hispano-Suiza engine, but later versions used the 200-hp Sunbeam Arab. The Cuckoo could climb to 2,000 feet in four minutes and at this height manage 103 mph. After an initial order for 100 aircraft, 350 were eventually ordered from a variety of manufacturers, as Sopwith's own production was fully committed at the time, but many were cancelled at the Armistice, when ninety were in service. Post-war, further orders were placed, but with the Wolseley Viper engine.

Tondern

By the time the first bomber operation was flown from an aircraft carrier, HMS *Furious*, the Royal Naval Air Service was but a memory. On 1 April 1918, the Royal Naval Air Service and the Royal Flying Corps had been merged into the world's first unified and truly autonomous air service, the Royal Air Force. From the RNAS, the new service received 55,000 men and 2,500 aircraft. Despite the fact that this was undoubtedly no longer the RNAS, those who took part in the successful operation against the German airship sheds at Tondern were all ex-RNAS personnel.

In March 1918, *Furious* had had the second stage of her long conversion from battlecruiser to aircraft carrier. She now had a separate landing deck aft, but turbulence from her superstructure and the fact that an aircraft could, and therefore did, run out of space from the central superstructure meant that landing on was still hazardous. During trials, all but three of the attempted landings had been failures, ending in crashes.

Known in the terminology of the day, not as an aircraft carrier but as an 'aerodrome ship', *Furious* was the flagship of Rear Admiral Sir Richard Phillimore, Admiral Commanding Aircraft.

On 19 July 1918, seven Sopwith Camel landplanes were flown off *Furious* to bomb the Zeppelin sheds at Tondern in northern Germany. On the way to the target, one Camel was forced down with engine trouble. The remaining six aircraft reached the sheds where one was completely destroyed, and with it Zeppelins *L.54* and *L.60*. On the way back, three of the Camels had to divert and land in Denmark, where aircraft and airmen were interned until the end of the war; the other two managed to return to *Furious*, but were unable to land, so the aircraft were ditched and the aircrew rescued by a destroyer.

Smaller and slightly slower than *Furious*, *Argus* was 15,775 tons, had a maximum speed of 29 knots and joined the fleet in September 1918, just a couple of months before the Armistice. Even with the landing-on deck, experience with *Furious* had shown that turbulence from the superstructure was a problem, so the new carrier lacked any superstructure. The bridge and wheelhouse were mounted on the starboard side on a lift that had to be put down during flying operations, making manoeuvring difficult. Instead of funnels, boiler-room smoke was expelled through ducts at the stern, making landing difficult and unpleasant.

Chapter 4

On the Western Front

Shortly after the outbreak of the First World War, what was still known as the Eastchurch Squadron of the RNAS was posted to Ostend in Belgium under the command of Commander Charles Rumney Samson. At the time, military squadrons did not operate a single aircraft type and the unit had ten aircraft of assorted types. The purpose was to operate anti-Zeppelin patrols for the protection of the British Expeditionary Force which was facing fast-moving German forces sweeping through Belgium and into France. While crossing the English Channel on its way to the Continent, the BEF had benefited from the protection of the airships *Astra-Torres* and *Parseval*.

The RNAS's first forward base was at Antwerp and on 22 September, four aircraft of the Eastchurch Squadron were sent to attack the Zeppelin sheds at Cologne and Dusseldorf. Only the aircraft flown by Flight Lieutenant Collet actually reached a target – his was one of two assigned to attack the Dusseldorf sheds – but his bombs failed to explode. The 20-lb bombs dropped over the side of the aircraft by the observer were simply artillery shells fitted with stabilizing fins. All four aircraft returned safely to base. A second base was established in south-eastern France at Belfort, from where, on 21 November, three Avro 504s flew 250 miles over enemy territory and attacked the Zeppelin sheds at Friedrichshafen, again using 20-lb bombs.

Nevertheless, the BEF in Belgium was soon being forced back into France and towards the Channel coast. In the eyes of the Royal Navy, Samson's unit had not covered themselves in glory either. What was perceived as the ill-disciplined activities of his unit resulted in them being ordered home again within a few days, but on the way back, Samson claimed to have lost his bearings and landed at Dunkirk in northern France. Once there, he maintained that adverse weather prevented his unit from flying across the Channel and eventually a new base was established at Dunkirk. By this time lacking any form of bomb at all, Samson had boiler plates welded to civilian vehicles and created an armoured car squadron so that he could continue to attack the Germans. The following year, he was sent to Gallipoli.

The very real difficulty in mounting effective bombing operations was matched by a similar difficulty in providing an effective air defence against the Zeppelin menace. The weight and drag of the floats meant that seaplanes were vulnerable to the heavy defensive fire of a Zeppelin as they climbed towards it, and then took a long time to climb above it to attack. The slow and lumbering Zeppelins also had a far faster rate of climb than a seaplane as they carried a large volume of water ballast which, when jettisoned, meant that a Zeppelin could out climb the seaplanes.

The difficulty of tackling the Zeppelin menace meant that the RNAS insisted that it needed landplanes as well as hydroaeroplanes. Nevertheless, it was not over the UK but over Belgium that the first Zeppelin was shot down by an aircraft. Early on 17 May 1915, Flight Sub Lieutenant Reginald Warneford was flying on patrol with his commanding officer, Squadron Commander Spenser Gray, when they sighted the Zeppelins *LZ.37*, *LZ.38* and *LZ.39* off Dunkirk, heading east on a reconnaissance flight, at around 03.30. Both aircraft attacked *LZ.39* with machine-gun fire, coming in from below as it would take too long to climb above the airship. The Zeppelin immediately jettisoned its water ballast, which allowed it to soar at 1,000 feet a minute out of range. All three Zeppelins returned safely to the shed.

The same three Zeppelins bombed Calais on the night of 6/7 June. Wing Commander Arthur Longmore sent Warneford with another pilot to intercept, but the other pilot's aircraft suffered engine trouble and had to return. Warneford, flying a Morane-Saulnier Type L parasol monoplane, armed with a Vickers machine gun firing forwards through the propeller, and six 10-lb bombs that could be released through an improvised toggle and release wire, continued towards the Zeppelins. At around 01.05, he saw *LZ.37* north of Ostend at about his altitude. His problem became one of how to approach without the Zeppelin jettisoning her ballast and ascending out of reach, a problem that was made more difficult by the fact that hunter and hunted were moving at roughly the same speed. At 01.50, near Bruges, the Zeppelin opened fire with her Maxim machine guns and Warneford turned away, whereupon the airship gave chase. This continued until 02.15, by which time Warneford had climbed to a higher altitude and, once the firing stopped, turned to found himself behind the Zeppelin and well above it. He switched off his engine and dived towards the Zeppelin from 11,000 feet. At 7,000 feet and just above it, he released his bombs – even as the last one was released, the first one exploded and rolled his aircraft over. He struggled to regain control, but once he had done so and had time to look around, he found that the Zeppelin was on the ground in flames.

LZ.37 had crashed on top of a convent just outside Ghent, killing two nuns and two orphans, while many more were injured. Only the coxswain survived, falling through the roof and onto a bed!

Unable to restart his engine, Warneford landed to make repairs, finding that a joint on a petrol pipe had fractured. He fixed the pipe, managed to restart the engine and took off again at 03.15. He lost his way and had to land for fuel, but eventually rejoined his unit at 10.30.

This was the first success against the dreaded scourge of the Zeppelins that had already attacked east coast towns and a week earlier had made the first attack on London. Warneford heard of his Victoria Cross from King George V himself by telegram on 8 June, with the official citation on 11 June – the shortest interval between deed and award in the entire history of the VC.

The acclaim that followed Warneford's action was largely the result of the feeling of public helplessness over what had become the Zeppelin menace. As early as 19 January 1915, two of these airships had bombed Great Yarmouth, King's Lynn and Cromer on the East Anglian coastline. A hero figure overnight, Warneford was visited by the American journalist Henry Needham for an interview. On 17 June 1915, Warneford took Needham for a flight in a Farman biplane, but both men were thrown out when the aircraft turned over and fell to their deaths.

Chapter 5

Gallipoli

In late 1914, the idea of a naval campaign in the Dardanelles gained increasing favour, especially with Winston Churchill. From the outset, it was conceived as a joint operation with land forces who would occupy the forts overlooking the Dardanelles, to allow the warships an unrestricted passage. The problem was that there were no less than fourteen forts, and of these six dominated the Narrows, a nautical bottleneck less than a mile wide. The guns in the forts varied between 4-inch and 14-inch calibre, and while many were old, they were still capable of inflicting severe damage on any passing warship as even in the widest part of the Dardanelles, the channel would never be more than 3 miles from the shore. Between the forts, batteries of howitzers had been established, which could make survival difficult for the minesweepers that would have to accompany any forcing of the Dardanelles.

Gallipoli was devised as a means of ending the stalemate that had arisen on the Western Front. It was one of two such schemes, but the only one to actually proceed, the other being the plan devised by none other than Fisher himself for the Royal Navy to enter the Baltic and land a substantial army on the shores of Pomerania, the closest point to Berlin.

The Royal Navy was likely to be faced with the difficult situation that its battleships would not be able to get close enough to the forts to be able to destroy them until the minefields in the Dardanelles had been cleared, while the minesweepers would not be able to clear the mines until the guns in the forts, and the howitzers in between, had been silenced. Even so, trawlers were requisitioned for minesweeping duties. Given the strong currents, these ships would struggle to move as fast as 3 knots, making them easy targets for the howitzers. The civilian crews eventually turned their ships round and returned to port, only to be replaced by naval crews.

The officer in command, Rear Admiral Sackville Carden, planned to force the Dardanelles by destroying the outer forts using naval gunfire and, if necessary, by landing demolition parties. The minesweepers would then sweep the minefields, allowing the battleships to move within range of the forts guarding the narrows, which would be destroyed, allowing the combined British and French squadrons to enter the Sea of Marmara, anchor off Constantinople, and under the threat of their heavy guns, the Turks would surrender.

At first, all seemed to go to plan. On 19 February 1915, the pre-dreadnought battleships *Agamemnon, Cornwallis, Triumph* and *Vengeance,* with the battlecruiser *Inflexible,* the cruiser *Amythyst,* destroyers and the French battleships *Bouvet, Gaulois* and *Suffren,* started a heavy bombardment of the forts at Sedd-el-Bahr and Kum Kale at the lower end of the Dardanelles. While the bombardment had relatively little impact on the heavily built forts, a second bombardment on 25 February was more successful as it was followed up the next day by landing marines and seamen, who found little opposition once ashore, who spiked any guns that had survived the bombardment. Nevertheless, the warships had taken damage and suffered casualties in the exchange of fire with the forts.

The seaplane carrier *Ark Royal* had arrived at Lemnos with her six aircraft. These were to be used to provide reconnaissance and also to report back to the squadron on the fall of shot – as long as the aircraft could get airborne, which required good weather. This early attempt to provide what amounted to an aerial observation post for the surface fleet was a fiasco, largely due to frequent equipment failures, but also the complete inexperience of the observers in the aircraft and the gunnery direction officers aboard the ships being unable to work together. It was also discovered later that an aircraft providing observation for more than one ship often had difficulty in knowing which ship was firing, so reducing the value of its reports considerably. On the plus side, these aircraft also took a number of the submarine commanders on reconnaissance flights over the Dardanelles, both helping them to find targets, but also showing them the danger spots from minefields and shore batteries.

The landings went in on the morning of 25 April 1915. The RNAS put as many as six aircraft a day into the air on aerial observation duties, and one of the veteran naval airmen, Charles Rumney Samson, even paid great credit to the battleship *Prince George,* which 'used to do exactly what we told her . . . One day with her, the shells were getting too close to the Turks . . . we could see them running away . . . We signalled, "Salvoes, 100 yards more range", and to our delight, within 20 seconds, two beautiful bursts were right among them.'

The kite-balloon ships, *Monica* and *Hector,* were deployed to the Dardanelles for naval gunnery and spotting, but suffered from some problems with the launching and recovery of the balloons, which had difficulty until at least 200 feet above the water due to the tail fouling the superstructure of the ships, and difficulty with the gas production plant. The balloons could not be launched in high winds, and suffered acute problems in the summer heat when seams and patches started to come unstuck. The gas production plants were a hazard to the balloon ships when under fire.

Some of the first Short 184s with the RNAS were deployed to the Dardanelles aboard the seaplane carrier *Ben-my-Chree*, a former Isle of Man steam packet, and were in the area from July 1915.

The campaign saw the first attempt by an aircraft to bomb a battleship, but the bombs had little effect on the *Heireddin Barbarossa*, although she was not to survive for much longer. Rather more successful was the torpedo attack by Flight Commander Charles Edmonds on 12 August, flying a Short 184 from the Gulf of Xeros, when he sunk a 5,000-ton Turkish supply ship, dropping down to 14 feet and launching his torpedo at 300 yards. Five days later, he attacked three steamers and left one of them a burning wreck. A fellow pilot, Flight Lieutenant D'Acre, suffered from engine trouble and landed his Short seaplane, then taxied towards a large steam tug, firing his torpedo to sink her. Freed of the torpedo, his aircraft managed to take off again and return to the *Ben-my-Chree*.

Problems with aircraft were commonplace. Using water as a coolant, engines tended to overheat in the high temperatures of the eastern Mediterranean.

For most of the campaign the Short 184s were used on reconnaissance and spotting duties, as well as bombing Turkish harbours. The spotting sorties were flown for a monitor that shelled enemy shipping. On 8 November 1915, the railway bridge over the River Maritza was bombed. On 27 August 1916, after British and Australian troops had been withdrawn, an air strike led by the *Ben-my-Chree*'s commanding officer, the redoubtable Commander Charles Rumney Samson, attacked the Chikaldir Bridge.

Even after the final evacuation from Gallipoli, the RNAS continued operations in the eastern Mediterranean. Mudros was kept on as a base, and from there on 14 April 1916, two aircraft bombed Constantinople, doing little damage but boosting morale and earning both pilots the DSO. More successful on 26 July 1916, the Turkish destroyer *Yadighiar-i-Milet* was badly damaged by bombing by RNAS aircraft in the eastern Mediterranean. Again, on 9 July 1917, RNAS aircraft from Mudros bombed the *Sultan Selim* (ex-*Goeben*) and the *Midilli* (ex-*Breslau*) at Constantinople.

Often portrayed as a disaster, which ultimately it was, Gallipoli suffered from poor leadership, with the initial landings in some cases being unopposed. Despite this the troops were not allowed to advance inland – if they had they would almost certainly have cut the peninsula in two.

Chapter 6

A Lighter Shade of Blue

The decision to merge the Royal Flying Corps and the Royal Naval Air Service could be described as a bold and forward-looking move, or as a disaster. It was a mixture of both. It was certainly forward-looking to consider a new autonomous air service that recognized the strategic importance of air power as an element of war in its own right. The British innovation was to be copied around the world.

The RNAS and RFC had competed and overlapped, with much wasteful duplication of effort. The British government asked the South African statesman Field Marshal Jan Smuts to report on the matter and he recommended a single, autonomous, integrated, air service. This was initially to become the Air Service, although legislation laid before Parliament was drafted as 'The Air Force (Constitution) Act' in October 1917, so the service emerged as the Royal Air Force on 1 April 1918. It included some 360,000 personnel, including around 25,000 members of the Women's Royal Air Force, which disbanded in 1920, although not before a substantial number had served with the occupation forces in Germany.

It was not a happy birth. Trenchard, in command of the RFC units in France, believed in a unified air service, but wanted it to be created later, not while the country was fighting a war of unprecedented ferocity. In the event, when he was recalled from France to prepare for the creation of the Royal Air Force and to be its first Chief of the Air Staff, he found Lord Rothermere, the Secretary of State for Air, so difficult to work with, and devious, that on 19 March, he resigned. Nevertheless, for the sake of appearances, his resignation did not take effect until 13 April. The future 'Father of the Royal Air Force' did, nevertheless, eventually return to his duties.

Naturally enough, the new service was finding its way at first, while playing its part in the greatest conflict thus far. A new rank structure was needed, and while that of the RNAS provided the basis of officer ranks up to and including Air Commodore, for other ranks and very senior officers, a much modified form of army ranks was chosen. Even so, when the most senior, five-star, rank was being decided, it was initially going to be 'Marshal of the Air'. As the Sovereign automatically held the most senior rank in each of the armed services, this proposal was put to him and rejected, with the response that the Almighty had this already. So, Marshal of the Royal Air Force became the most senior rank.

This may have seemed academic to the former members of the RNAS and RFC trying to find their feet in the new organization. Once the ranks were announced along with a new uniform, many paid for these out of their own pockets, hoping to ensure that in the much-slimmed-down post-war service, there would still be a place for them. The new uniform was pale blue, reputedly using material ordered by the Tsar for his troops before the Bolshevik Revolution. This, the classic 'frustrated export order' was to prove frustrating in other ways as it was thought to be too pale and impractical, so something darker was chosen. Having changed their uniforms once, the would-be first generation of RAF officers then had to change them yet again.

Despite this, even in the British Empire, when new air forces were formed, they remained part of the Army initially – as in Canada. Even at home, the new service was controversial when it became clear that it included all military and naval aviation. In the end, a compromise was agreed. The fleet's spotting aircraft flown from battleships and cruisers would continue to be flown by naval officers, and RAF squadrons attached to the fleet would include a small number of naval aircrew. In this respect, the French managed the creation of their autonomous air force, the *Armée de l'Air*, rather better, as they transferred a number of shore-based fighter squadrons, but left everything else with the Navy, the *Marine Nationale*, including maritime-reconnaissance. Of course, it could be argued that maritime-reconnaissance was a suitable case to become part of an autonomous air service as the aircraft were to become so heavy that carrier operation would be impossible, and the aircrew would be a distinct breed, better attuned to mixing with the transport and heavy bomber units of an air force than with the seagoing carrier men who, after all, were sailors who flew rather than airmen who went to sea.

It is worth looking at the order of battle for the RNAS on 31 March 1918, on the eve of the service merging with the Royal Flying Corps into the new Royal Air Force:

1 Wing (Dunkirk): 2, 13 & 17 Squadrons.
2 Wing (Mudros): A, B, C, D, E, F, G, Z (Greek) Squadrons.
3 Wing disbanded 1917.
4 Wing (La Panne): 4 & 8 Squadrons.
5 Wing (Malo-les-Bains): 7, 11, 12, 14 & 15 Squadrons.
6 Wing (Otranto): 1 & 2 Squadrons.
10, 11, 13, 22 & 41 Wings under RFC control.

Towards the Armistice and Beyond

The newly formed Royal Air Force continued to fight the war. In France, the units were known collectively as the Independent Air Force, and continued to operate effectively over German lines as resistance began to crumble, undermined by the blockade of German ports.

When the Armistice came into effect, the RAF had around 360,000 men and women with 23,000 aircraft spread over more than 200 squadrons. The bulk of the personnel and aircraft had come from the RFC, with the RNAS contributing a relatively modest 55,000. The 200-squadron strength of the RFC had been a nominal figure in that many of the squadrons with numbers above 150 never became operational.

Post-war, the government soon embarked on a programme of cut-backs. Reductions in defence spending follow the end of any major conflict, but the nation's dire financial state, to be followed by the years of recession and depression, lent a particular severity to these. In one sense, the cuts helped to submerge the old RFC and RNAS rivalries and create a completely new service with its own traditions and *esprit de corps*. The RAF was quickly reduced to just twelve squadrons, with one in Germany with the occupying British Army of the Rhine, two at home and the remaining nine in the Middle East and India.

Despite being autonomous, the new Air Force saw its own ministry merged with that of the Army, and after the post-war general election, the new Secretary of State for War and Air, Winston Churchill, immediately invited Trenchard to return. He accepted and stayed for ten years, earning the title 'Father of the Royal Air Force'. Having been conceived in haste, the new RAF took some time to settle down. Both the British Army and the Royal Navy were pressing for their own air power and as early as 1921, the former stated that aircraft were auxiliary arms to the two traditional services. Lord Balfour, chairman of the Standing Sub-Committee of the Committee of Imperial Defence in 1921, investigated, and strategic significance was emphasized when Balfour was forced to produce an independent report because of the intransigence of the older services: Balfour accepted that, while the new service must either work in close co-operation with the older services or even be subordinate to them, it had to be autonomous in such matters as fighter defence or long-range bombing.

There were many who saw the autonomous RAF as likely to neglect the interests of the Royal Navy. On 20 July 1918, Admiral Sir David Beatty, Commander-in-Chief Grand Fleet, wrote to the Admiralty:

> In the torpedo-carrying aeroplane we have a weapon of great potential value ... [that] may be able to exercise a profound effect ... In February 1918 the Admiralty informed me that by the end of July one hundred torpedo-carrying aeroplanes would be available. On 18 July I am informed that instead of the 100 the number will be 12. Actually there are 3. As late as 18 July the Admiralty stated 36 pilots would be trained by the end of August. Actually there will be none ... Under the new organisation and the setting up of an independent Air Ministry,

the essential requirements of the fleet in aeroplane construction will only be met if urged with vigour by the Naval Air Division ... Through failure to present the facts to the Air Ministry, machines will be diverted to less important roles and the main fleet will suffer.

The return of peace was to see naval air power in demand. Allied participation in the Russian Civil War, initially to keep Russia in the war against the Central Powers, and then in support of the White Russians, saw aircraft from the seaplane tender HMS *Vindictive* bombing the Red Fleet in Kronstadt Harbour on 18 August 1919.

The end of the First World War saw the collapse of Turkish rule in the Middle East and then revolution within Turkey itself. In 1920, Turkish nationalists fought Greek forces in European Turkey, and then came face to face with British occupation forces in Constantinople, now Istanbul, and Chanak. The seaplane carrier HMS *Ark Royal* was dispatched from Egypt with five Fairey IIID seaplanes. The ship evacuated army units in Chanak and then its aircraft flew spotter patrols, until HMS *Argus* arrived with Nieuport Nightjars and additional Fairey IIIDs.

In 1924, the Fleet Air Arm was created for the first time, comprising those RAF units operating from aircraft carriers. This was largely a reaction to the recommendations of the Balfour Committee. The Fleet Air Arm was part of what had become known as RAF Coastal Area, being under naval control whilst the units were at sea, and under RAF control when ashore. Rather than form as squadrons, at first the carrier units were organized as flights in the 400 series, with numbers 401–439 as spotter flights attached to battleships and cruisers; 440–459 as reconnaissance flights, and 460 onwards as torpedo flights. It was not until 1936 that these were reorganized into squadrons, and numbers in the 700 series were given to second-line or support units, and in the 800 series to combat squadrons.

It was clear that in solving many of the problems inherent in the early conversions of *Furious*, fresh problems had been created with *Argus*. The third aircraft carrier was also to be a conversion. HMS *Eagle*, 22,600 tons, was based on the Chilean battleship, *Almirante Cochrane*, incomplete as work had been suspended on the outbreak of war. This was the first ship to meet with modern ideas for the appearance and layout of an aircraft carrier, with the now familiar starboard-side 'island'. She also introduced the cambered 'round down', in a further attempt to minimize turbulence. *Eagle* was not commissioned until February 1924.

The fourth carrier was the first in the world to be designed from the keel up as such, HMS *Hermes*. Although laid down in January 1918, and displacing just 10,850 tons, her construction was delayed while decisions were taken on the ideal layout for an aircraft carrier. With her hull plated up to flight deck level, her starboard island and single large funnel, *Hermes* appeared as the classic aircraft carrier.

The starboard island was set to become the standard, although the Japanese were also to experiment with port-side islands on two ships. Many suggest that the starboard island was chosen for traditional reasons, in that before the advent of the wheel, ships were steered by a large oar on the starboard, or 'steerboard' side. But experience had shown that pilots in trouble tended, for reasons that are still not fully understood, to veer to port, and a starboard position for the island was the safest. The Japanese *Akagi* and *Hiryu*, had port-side islands so that they could operate in pairs with ships with starboard islands, allowing aircraft to operate on different approach patterns without congestion. Reports suggest that they had double the number of serious flight-deck accidents as a result.

The Struggle for Control of Naval Aviation

While there were few serious campaigns afloat for the Fleet Air Arm, a campaign for control of naval aviation was being waged ashore. The decision to create the Royal Air Force was one of those taken without any benefit of hindsight, and possibly also without a true understanding of the different requirements of naval and army aviation, organic air power or strategic air power. There was an inability to consider the consequences, largely because so few understood the potential of air power. In terms of creating a strong strategic air service, the decision was right. In denuding the Royal Navy and the British Army of air power to fit their requirements, and in failing to force senior officers in both services to understand air power, the decision was wrong.

Aircrew and maintainers aboard the aircraft carriers, and seaplane carriers or tenders, all became members of the Royal Air Force, co-existing alongside the general service officers and ratings that formed the ships' companies of the carriers. The sole exception to this arrangement was those concerned with the operation of seaplanes and flying boats operated from battleships and cruisers, who remained naval aviators. These provided the reconnaissance and spotter role for the guns of the fleet. Aboard the carriers, however, there was a demarcation line between the seafarers and the aviators. This was emphasized to a great extent by the system under which RAF stations in the Mediterranean and Far East included flights that could operate from aircraft carriers visiting those areas.

Reconstruction and expansion of the RAF was inhibited by the austerity measures of the Depression years. Struggling to find a role, the RAF discovered the concept of air control, helping and to some extent relieving ground forces of much of the work needed to maintain order in Mesopotamia, in what is now Iraq. This was accorded a higher priority than maritime aviation.

The debate over who should control naval aviation continued. There was frequent lobbying by the Royal Navy which wanted control of its own aviation and had the examples of the United States, France and, of course,

Japan with which to push its case. A further investigation took place under the auspices of the Committee for Imperial Defence, chaired by Sir Thomas Inskip, which recommended a transfer of the Fleet Air Arm to Admiralty control. This became known in the service as the 'Inskip Award'. The recommendation was accepted and in 1937, it was decided to return naval aviation to the Admiralty, although the formal transfer did not follow until 1939. The exception to this transfer was that long-range maritime reconnaissance remained with the RAF, in contrast to the practice in France and the United States.

Members of the Royal Air Force serving with the Fleet Air Arm had a choice: to remain in the Royal Air Force or transfer to the Royal Navy. Some 1,500 opted to transfer and, with those few naval airmen serving aboard battleships, battlecruisers and cruisers, or as token naval representation on the carrier squadrons, provided the skeleton on which future naval aviation could be fleshed out.

Creating the Carrier Fleet

International efforts to guarantee peace and end the arms race that had culminated in the First World War resulted in several initiatives, including the creation of the League of Nations in 1920. The Washington Naval Treaty of 1922 attempted to restrict the size of warships, with an upper limit of 27,000 tons on new construction, while limits on armaments as well as on the total tonnage were allowed for each of the signatories for each type of warship, and for their overall fleets. The upper tonnage for a cruiser, for example, was set at 10,000 tons. The Royal Navy and United States Navy were both allocated a maximum aircraft-carrier tonnage of 135,000 tons, out of a maximum fleet tonnage of 525,000 tons each.

The high proportion of aircraft carriers in the total tonnage suggests that at least some foresaw the significance of this new arrival on the naval scene. More significantly, the Treaty provided an indirect, unintentional, stimulus to aircraft-carrier construction by its limits on the size of the battlecruiser fleets, requiring the United Kingdom, the United States and Japan to cut their battlecruiser tonnage. Each of these three nations converted two battlecruisers into aircraft carriers, the Royal Navy taking the two sister ships of HMS *Furious* – the 15-inch gun HMS *Courageous* and *Glorious*.

HMS *Furious* herself had undergone extensive reconstruction by this time, having rejoined the fleet in 1925 as a flush-decked aircraft carrier with a separate take-off deck leading from the hangar deck. Her two sisters reflected changed ideas on aircraft-carrier design, having the separate take-off deck from the hangar, but with the more conventional starboard island. Both ships had a displacement of 22,500 tons and a maximum speed of around 30 knots. *Courageous* entered service in May 1928 and was joined by her sister in March 1930. These were the first aircraft carriers to have lateral arrester wires. During their short lives, their take-off decks fell into disuse as aircraft sizes grew.

The British wished to see the maximum size for aircraft carriers reduced from the 27,000 tons of the Washington Treaty to 22,000 tons. This was a strange decision, since many of the participants at the London Naval Conference of 1930 had been in favour of raising the limits. The British approach meant that her next aircraft carrier, only the second to be laid down as such, had to be limited to 22,000 tons displacement. The designers of the new HMS *Ark Royal* went to considerable lengths to ensure that the ship made good use of the available tonnage – weight was reduced through the use of welding, through reducing armour, except for some around the hangar, and by the flight deck being extended beyond the hull fore and aft to provide the maximum length. The hull was plated up to flight-deck level at both the bow and the stern. She was fitted with two accelerators, and, unusually in a British carrier, three lifts. Her designed aircraft capacity was seventy-two, although for operations, sixty was more realistic, and this was reduced as the size of aircraft increased. The *Ark Royal* had a good turn of speed, being capable of 32 knots.

Nevertheless, the 'Ark' had a potentially fatal weakness: her thin flight deck. On one occasion a 20-lb practice bomb fell off an aircraft as it landed and punched a hole in the flight deck, killing two of the ship's company. Many senior officers expected her to be sunk by aerial attack, so it was the supreme irony that she was later sunk by a torpedo fired by a U-boat.

By the time the new carrier joined the fleet in November 1938, the first ships of a new class were under construction: fast, armoured, carriers.

Four of the new carriers were ordered in 1936, intended as replacements for *Argus, Furious, Eagle* and *Hermes*. Two more were ordered in 1937 and it was soon realized that the new ships would not be replacements, but instead they would be additions to the fleet, which would need every ship as war loomed closer.

The new carriers introduced the armoured flight deck and hangar deck, providing an armoured box capable of withstanding heavy punishment. They were unusual in having triple screws. Despite the heavier displacement of 23,000 tons, their aircraft capacity was well below that of the *Ark Royal*. The six new ships, HMS *Illustrious, Victorious, Formidable, Indomitable, Implacable* and *Indefatigable*, differed in many important features. In addition to having accelerators, they also introduced the barrier landing system to the Royal Navy, so that aircraft missing the arrester wires were stopped before reaching the deck forward, which could seldom be kept empty as aircraft returned from their missions.

A seventh ship, the maintenance carrier HMS *Unicorn*, had just two screws, and increased headroom in her hangars, pointing the way to a future design of light fleet carriers.

When, in 1937, it was decided that the Fleet Air Arm be handed over to full Admiralty control, it was clear that war in Europe was inevitable. Although the Admiralty did not formally take control until 24 May 1939, in 1938, the Admiralty was authorized by Parliament to implement a 300 per cent increase in Fleet Air Arm personnel. One of the first moves was to introduce a ratings' pilots' course at RAF Leuchars in Scotland, but it was later decided that most RN pilots and all observers would be commissioned, although the wartime commissions took effect only after the successful candidates had completed their post-training leave. While Germany and Italy were preparing for war, it was also clear that Japanese ambitions in China were running far in excess of what the democracies could tolerate.

War had nearly broken out in 1935 when action against Italy was contemplated after that country invaded Abyssinia, present-day Ethiopia, and plans had been prepared for an air strike against the port by aircraft flown off the Mediterranean Fleet's carrier, HMS *Glorious*. Showing considerable foresight, the Commander-in-Chief of the Mediterranean Fleet pre-war, Admiral Sir Dudley Pound, feared that an attack on Taranto would be the carrier's one opportunity to strike at the enemy before air power made her position untenable, and the ship would either have to be withdrawn or would be lost in action. At the time, *Glorious* was commanded by Captain Lumley Lyster, who, some years later, was to return aboard the new aircraft carrier *Illustrious* as the Mediterranean Fleet's first Rear Admiral, Carriers.

The ships and the authority for expansion may have given the impression that the Royal Navy was finally equipping its Fleet Air Arm for war, but the reality was different. There were few naval aviators and maintenance personnel, hardly any naval air stations, and large numbers of these were to be built from scratch, with some, in unsuitable sites for the bombers and fighters of the RAF, transferred to naval control. There were no high-performance naval aircraft. For offensive purposes, the Fairey Swordfish biplane was to be the mainstay of the fleet, and for defensive purposes, there were two aircraft: the monoplane Blackburn Roc and the Gloster Sea Gladiator, another biplane.

In short, the outbreak of war found the Fleet Air Arm with an inadequate range of aircraft. The Fairey Swordfish was outdated. Its successor, the Albacore, was yet another biplane, and one with an engine so troublesome that the Swordfish soldiered on. The Gloster Sea Gladiator fighter was the last biplane fighter built for the RAF, and it is amazing that production of this antique continued for so long. The Fairey Fulmar looked modern, but the need to carry a two-man crew made the aircraft too heavy, its performance was barely adequate to counter a bomber and it was vulnerable to enemy fighters. An oddity was the Blackburn Skua, another monoplane and officially a fighter/dive-bomber/reconnaissance aircraft, but to those who had to cope with it, 'more dive-bomber than fighter'. All of this was partly the neglect of the Fleet Air Arm's aircraft procurement needs whilst under RAF stewardship, when the RAF's priorities with scant funding lay elsewhere, but also partly because many senior naval officers believed that high-performance aircraft could not operate safely from aircraft carriers.

The Swordfish

Having control of all British service aviation at the time, it was the Air Ministry that was responsible for the specification of the Fairey Swordfish, issuing its requirement in October 1930. The winner of the resulting contest was Fairey Aviation, whose prototype was designated S9/30, and which was given the go-ahead in late summer of the following year. The prototype S9/30 made its first flight in February 1934.

The Air Ministry was sufficiently impressed with the aircraft to order eighty-nine, a large order given the straitened circumstances of the day, and the first aircraft reached the RAF in July 1936. Production aircraft had the Pegasus II engine and a three-bladed constant-pitch propeller. Swordfish replaced Fairey Seals in No. 825 Squadron aboard HMS *Glorious* in the Mediterranean, and No. 811 aboard *Furious*, which had been flying Blackburn Baffins while serving with the Home Fleet. By 1940, with all financial restraints on arms procurement gone before the outbreak of war, Fairey had delivered 692 Swordfish, and turned to concentrate on the aircraft's supposed successor, the Fairey Albacore. The original Swordfish I continued in production with Blackburn, which built a further 300 before introducing the Swordfish II. Operating from a variety of decks, many of which did not have catapults, or 'accelerators' as these were known at the time, the Swordfish II introduced a strengthened lower mainplane for rocket-assisted take-off, known as RP or rocket-projectile assistance. Blackburn built 1,080 of this version, many of them having the more powerful Pegasus XXX engine which also powered a further development, the Pegasus III, nicknamed the 'pregnant Stringbag', of which another 320 were built.

Later versions didn't simply have stronger mainplanes and more power, they also introduced airborne radar, making the Swordfish the only biplane to be so fitted – a museum piece with the latest technology. The radar helped in the search for surface vessels, the most significant of which to a Stringbag were to be enemy submarines caught on the surface, either cruising or charging their batteries. First in use in May 1941, the radar was a big improvement in capability, but it had its limitations. While early versions could detect a large surface vessel at distances of up to 25 miles and pick up a coastline, so that it was an aid to navigation as well as to attack, the low-lying shape of a U-boat could not be detected beyond 4 or 5 miles.

Mk III Swordfish lost their guns, doubtless those in authority finally appreciating that there was no way that the single machine gun in the hands of the telegraphist/air-gunner – or TAG in naval parlance – let alone the single forward-firing machine gun, could protect the aircraft.

It was not simply the biplane configuration that marked the Swordfish down as an anachronism – other features added to the impression, including the three open cockpits, one for the pilot, another for the observer, as the Fleet Air Arm designated the navigator, who in truth had to do much more than simply navigate, and a third for the TAG, with communication between the crew being by means of a simple tube known as a Gosport tube, dating from before the First World War. In the early versions the TAG even had to communicate via the observer in the middle cockpit by shouts and gestures. Instruments were primitive for the pilot, little better than the basics of compass, altimeter and air-speed indicator (ASI), although the aircraft could home in on the carrier's beacon for a safe return. Checking the fuel in the air meant the pilot staring through a hole in the instrument panel to see the fuel indicator, which was situated some distance ahead over the engine. It was not always reliable and the best method of actually being sure of how much fuel remained was to use a dipstick, something that could only be done on the ground or on the deck. Later aircraft did have blind flying panels for operations at night, but flying through cloud in formation remained risky.

The Spartan open cockpits may well have saved one Stringbag. One pilot wishing to give his aircraft a test flight after repairs offered his rigger what would today be called an 'air experience flight'. Wearing only his cotton overalls, as the aircraft gained height the rigger slunk down inside the cockpit to avoid the cold, only to discover that the floor of the cockpit was sticky from leaking oil – he immediately alerted the pilot and they were able to make an emergency landing back on the carrier before the engine seized up. On another occasion, Gerald Woods, an observer, recalls flying off from *Ark Royal* on an anti-submarine patrol in a brand-new Blackburn-built Swordfish, but returning after fifteen minutes as a main oil line had broken leaving him in his rear cockpit 2 inches deep in oil. As the crew got out for a replacement aircraft, they left a trail of oily footprints along the deck.

If communication between the crew was primitive, on the early versions so was that with the ground or ship. There was no voice communication for Stringbags for the first couple of years of wartime flying, when Morse transmissions remained essential, so perhaps it was a blessing that radio silence was often ordered. Communications between aircraft were often by means of an Aldis lamp, especially at night when a gesture from a pilot or observer could not be seen. By 1944, nevertheless, radio was available.

The Swordfish was also amongst the last service aircraft not to have an automatic cartridge starter, but instead was started by a manual starting handle, sometimes known as a 'Hucks', that was inserted into the engine and wound furiously by two mechanics until a flywheel had gained sufficient momentum to start the airscrew revolving.

'When, as often happened, the engine misfired,' recalled Woods. 'The ground crews' cursing would have made an Irish navvy blush as this tiring performance recommenced.'

Range of the Swordfish could be increased considerably using an additional fuel tank, usually slung under the aircraft on a bombing mission, but for torpedo dropping it needed to be inserted into the observer's cockpit as the torpedo was always mounted under the fuselage. On some missions, this meant dispensing with the observer, especially if enemy fighters were expected, but usually the observer was decamped into the TAG's cockpit, no easy move given that it was less spacious and the observer had to take with him his Instruments, plus the bulky 'Bigsworth' chart board. Operating with an additional fuel tank in the middle cockpit had another drawback, as fuel tended to overflow into the rear cockpit during take-off and whenever the aircraft climbed. Flying into heavy AA fire up to one's ankles, or even one's knees, in aviation fuel was not to be recommended – it certainly did nothing for peace of mind!

In many ways the Swordfish was intended to be a 'maid of all work', and in line with this a floatplane version was also developed to operate from battleships and cruisers. A few floatplane versions also served with the Royal Air Force at Gibraltar. Stringbags could easily be converted from floats to wheeled undercarriage, and vice versa, but there was never an amphibian variant.

To those from other navies seeing the aircraft for the first time, it came as a shock. An American naval officer is said to have stared in disbelief at the aircraft. 'Where did that come from?' he asked.

'Fairey's', came the reply from a British naval officer standing nearby.

He stroked his chin thoughtfully. 'That figures,' he replied.

Yet, altogether, 2,392 were built before the aircraft was finally taken out of production in mid-1944, and it remained in service until July 1945. In the final year of the war, the Swordfish was absent from the British Pacific Fleet, as indeed was the Barracuda, effectively sent home in disgrace after its performance in tropical conditions failed to impress.

Fighters or Dive-bombers?

The other aircraft available to the Fleet Air Arm in September 1939 were uninspiring and included the Blackburn Roc, a monoplane encumbered with a two-man crew, with the second man being a telegraphist/air-gunner, and with the first power-operated turret of any British naval aircraft. It was meant to be a naval version of the RAF's Defiant, and while Winston Churchill favoured fighters with a rear-gunner, the concept failed in practice because the aircraft became heavier, slower and less manoeuvrable, and enemy fighters soon learned how to avoid the rear-gunner. The Roc served briefly aboard carriers.

Yet it was another uninspiring design, also from Blackburn, the Skua, a two-seat carrier-borne fighter/dive-bomber, that gave the Fleet Air Arm some of its first triumphs in the air. Powered by a 890-hp Bristol Perseus XII radial engine, and with a maximum speed of just 225 mph, it was a Skua that shot down Britain's first German aircraft of the war when, on 25 September 1939, one of No. 803 Naval Air Squadron's aircraft, flying from HMS *Ark Royal*, accounted for a Dornier Do18 flying boat off Norway. After the invasion of Norway on 10 April 1940, Skuas of Nos 800 and 803 Squadrons, at this time based ashore at Hatston on the mainland of Orkney, dive-bombed and sank the light cruiser *Konigsberg* in Bergen Fjord. This was the first major operational warship to be sunk by aerial attack.

The Battle Fleet, and Submarine!

It became the practice in most navies to base one or two aircraft aboard cruisers and three or four aboard battleships and battlecruisers, and the Royal Navy was no exception to this. Between the wars, each 'fleet' or overseas 'station' would have a squadron in the 700 series allocated to it, but shortly after the outbreak of the Second World War, all aircraft operated by warships other than aircraft carriers were grouped into No. 700 Naval Air Squadron for administrative convenience – the Squadron did not have a commanding officer and at one time operated almost a hundred aircraft. The importance of No. 700 steadily diminished as the war proceeded because of the growing number of aircraft carriers of all classes. A carrier-borne landplane had more speed, range and manoeuvrability than a seaplane or amphibian and could be operated in much harsher conditions.

Nevertheless, between the wars, three navies experimented with submarine-based aircraft: the Royal Navy, the French *Marine Nationale* and the Imperial Japanese Navy. The Royal Navy used a modified M-class submarine, *M2*. The M-class had consisted of just three boats, each complete with a 12-inch gun salvaged from a Majestic-class battleship; the idea was that such submarines would surface close to a target and attack with the gun rather than use the more expensive torpedoes, of which most submarines simply carried one plus a reload for each tube. *M1* sank after a collision in 1925, *M3* was converted to become a minelayer, but *M2* was converted to carry an aircraft and was commissioned in 1927.

Aboard *M2*, a hangar was built in place of the 12-inch gun forward of the conning tower or 'fin', and on surfacing, the hangar door would open downwards, unfolding flat so that a catapult could be hastily assembled over the hangar door and deck casing while the aircraft was brought out of the hangar and its wings unfolded. The whole operation was supposed to take minutes. After landing, the aircraft could be picked up by a crane, also on the forward end of the conning tower, swung aboard and, with wings folded, pushed back into the hangar. All of this required an aeroplane specially designed for the purpose: the Parnall Peto, a two-seat biplane built of stainless steel and with such a limited performance that its crew supposedly flew in plimsolls rather than heavy flying boots if any extra equipment needed to be carried. Standard equipment included a radio so that reconnaissance sorties could be flown, but the aircraft was unarmed.

To convince the sceptics, much was made of safety precautions, including those taken to prevent the inner door of the hangar being open at the same time as the outer door, but there was no actual mechanism to prevent this from happening. Trials started in 1927 with a flight by Lieutenants C.W. Byron and C. Keighley Peach, who had the distinction of receiving both flying pay and submarine pay. Several years of successful trials and exercises followed, but on 26 January 1932, tragedy struck when *M2* dived off Portland, never to surface again, with the loss of more than sixty officers and men. Several attempts to salvage *M2* nearly succeeded, but failed because of bad weather. The conclusion that was reached was that she had shipped a large sea through the outer hangar door while the inner door was still not secured and the submarine was swamped.

Chapter 7

A Bad Start to the War

British folk history often recalls the so-called 'Phoney War', the period between the outbreak of war and the invasion of Denmark and Norway, and then France and the Low Countries, that marked the real beginning of hostilities. There was no phoney war at sea. No sooner had the Prime Minister, Neville Chamberlain, finished broadcasting to the nation on 3 September 1939, than the Admiralty sent the signal, short and to the point: 'Total Germany'. The Royal Navy was engaged in operations from the outset, and this continued beyond the surrender of Japan as it fell to British warships to take the surrender of Japanese forces in Hong Kong, Singapore and Malaya. The Fleet Air Arm was involved from the beginning to the end.

The point was made in no uncertain terms on the first day of war in Europe. That evening of 3 September 1939, the liner *Athenia* was torpedoed off the Hebrides without the warning required by the Hague Convention. No less than 128 of those aboard lost their lives, and twenty-eight of them were Americans. Completely unashamed by this, Hitler accused the Royal Navy of sinking the ship to bring the United States into the war.

In home waters, the Fleet Air Arm's shore-based aircraft provided cover for convoys from the beginning of the war in Europe on 3 September 1939 until the German surrender on 8 May 1945. At times Fleet Air Arm squadrons were placed under RAF Coastal Command control to ensure better integration. The FAA complemented the work of the RAF, with the latter using larger twin-engined, and in due course, four-engined, long-range aircraft, while the FAA operated over shorter ranges, all that was necessary for the North Sea and English Channel.

The Fleet Air Arm started the Second World War with 232 aircraft and 360 qualified pilots, with another 332 under training. The Royal Navy had seven aircraft carriers, of which four, HMS *Argus*, *Eagle*, *Furious* and *Hermes*, had officially been due to retire, but had been retained in service as the war clouds gathered over Europe. This meant that, while the first of the Illustrious-class carriers was awaited, the best ships were the converted battlecruisers, HMS *Courageous* and *Glorious*, and the new *Ark Royal*. Not one of these three ships was to survive the first two years of war.

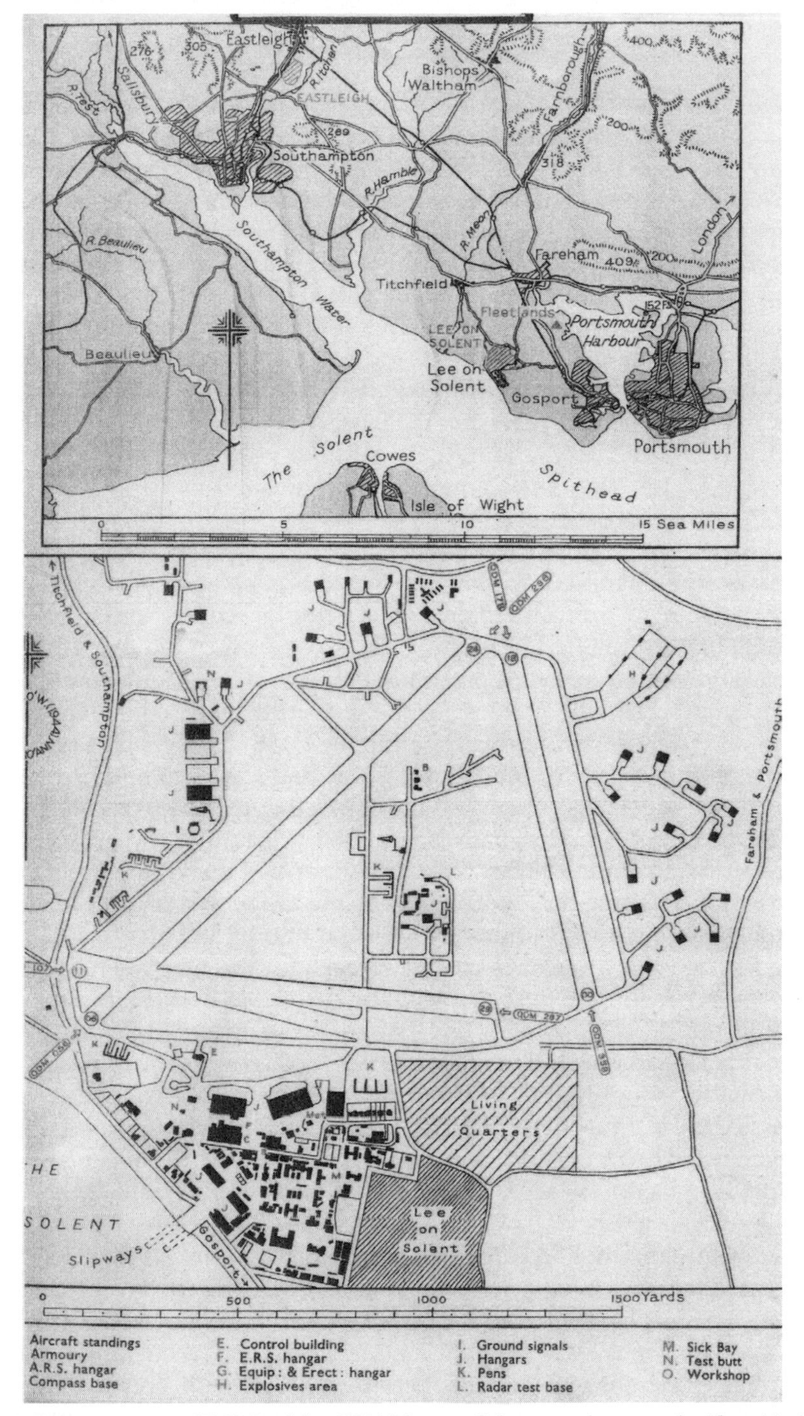

Map 1. For many years, HMS *Daedalus*, RNAS Lee-on-Solent, was home to the Fleet Air Arm, conveniently situated for aircraft carriers based on Portsmouth and also having a slipway as well as three runways.

There were few Royal Naval Air Stations at the outset. HMS *Daedalus* at Lee-on-Solent, on the Hampshire coast opposite the Isle of Wight, roughly halfway between Portsmouth and Southampton, was one of them. Not only was 'Lee' convenient for the ships of the fleet based at Portsmouth, it also had a slipway for seaplanes and amphibians. Yeovilton was under construction. For the most part, at this time Fleet Air Arm depended on lodging facilities at RAF bases, at home and aboard, with Hal Far in Malta, for example, not passing from the RAF to the Fleet Air Arm until after the war. It also depended on the RAF for basic and intermediate training, while ground crew were trained by the RAF as well. It was to be one of the achievements of the war years that the Fleet Air Arm established itself with complete self-sufficiency, and in the meantime, as we will see later, it was the United States Navy that came to the rescue.

Early Losses

In contrast to the First World War, the Royal Navy was quick to instigate a convoy system to protect Britain's vital supply routes from Germany's substantial and growing U-boat fleet and from surface raiders. The initial approach was to deploy ships on anti-submarine sweeps, an operation that could be compared with looking for the proverbial needle in a haystack. It was on one of these sweeps that the carrier HMS *Courageous* was lost, on 17 September 1939, a fortnight after the war had started. Poorly protected, with just two escorting destroyers, the ship's Swordfish aircraft had spent the day on anti-submarine patrols over the Western Approaches, to the south-west of Ireland. The last aircraft had landed on for the night, when *U-29* fired a salvo of three torpedoes at the ship, two of which hit her, sinking her in just twenty minutes with the loss of 500 men.

The loss of such a major fleet unit so early in the war was only partly compensated for by the loss of the German pocket battleship, or *Panzerschiff*, *Admiral Graf Spee*, after the Battle of the River Plate, scuttled in Montevideo Roads on 17 December 1939. The German ship proved to be insufficiently armoured to withstand shellfire from the British heavy cruiser *Exeter* and her two supporting light cruisers during the battle on 13 December. The Fleet Air Arm was, of course, limited to a reconnaissance role for this operation, with catapult-launched aircraft of 700 Squadron playing their usual part.

When Germany invaded Denmark and Norway on 9 April 1940, it was clear that Denmark was a lost cause as German forces swept over the border, while a landing force sailed into the harbour at Copenhagen. Norway, however, was a different matter. The size of the country and the inhospitable terrain, high mountains interspersed with fjords, with deep snow still on the ground, meant that German forces could be challenged. Despite landings by air and from the sea, German forces could not seize enough of the country quickly, while the loss of the troop transport *Bhicker* at Oslo, with the German headquarters staff, gave the King and the Norwegian government the opportunity to flee the city and organize resistance. Britain and France quickly assembled an initial expeditionary force of 13,000 men, supported by air and naval forces, although it was estimated that an army of 50,000 would be needed to liberate the country.

Difficult terrain and the shortage of good air bases ashore meant that the Norwegian campaign was ideal for the aircraft carrier, had the Royal Navy been equipped with high-performance aircraft. Initially, aircraft were provided by HMS *Furious*, which also acted as an aircraft transport. But she lacked any fighters and the Fleet Air Arm at that time had nothing heavier than 500-lb bombs. During the campaign, six Supermarine Walruses from 701 Squadron were based ashore at Harstad.

At first, all went well. Successful actions by destroyers and the battleship *Warspite* were matched on 10 April by twenty Blackburn Skuas of 800 and 803 Squadrons operating from Hatston on Orkney, sinking the cruiser *Konigsberg* at Bergen; these aircraft had been left behind in March, when *Ark Royal* had been sent to the Mediterranean.

Ark Royal and *Glorious* were hastily recalled and sent to operate off Norway. *Ark Royal* sent Swordfish of 810, 820 and 821 Squadrons to attack targets ashore, bombing the airfield at Vaernes, as well as maintaining anti-shipping and anti-submarine patrols. Nevertheless, despite these successes and the basing ashore of RAF Hurricane and Gladiator fighters, the battle ashore went against the Allies. Eventually, after the invasion of France and the Low Countries, it was decided to evacuate Norway to reinforce France, now under heavy attack by fast-moving German forces.

The evacuation was covered and then assisted by the two carriers, HMS *Ark Royal* and *Glorious*. Ashore, the RAF had been told to destroy their aircraft and join the evacuation, but conscious of the need to save as many aircraft as possible, especially the Hurricanes, it was decided to fly these to the carriers. Despite her shorter deck, *Glorious* was chosen for the Hurricanes because her larger lifts meant that the aircraft, which did not have folding wings, could be struck down into her hangars without having their wings removed, which would take time. The alternative was to leave the aircraft to obstruct the flight deck, which could prevent further operations by the ship's aircraft. It was a brave decision since the Hurricanes lacked arrester hooks and their pilots were not carrier trained – they used sandbags to weight down the tail wheels and successfully landed on the carrier.

Short of fuel, *Glorious* sailed from Norway on 8 June, steaming at a stately 17 knots, considered fast enough to protect her from submarine attack. Aircraft were struck down into the hangar and patrols were not flown, while torpedoes and other munitions were also removed. The ship lacked radar, but a watch was not maintained from the crow's nest. At 16.00, the two German battlecruisers, *Scharnhorst* and *Gneisenau*, amongst the few enemy ships to be fitted with radar, opened fire at 28,000 yards with their 11-in guns. The carrier was outgunned. Frantic attempts were made to range her aircraft on the deck and five Swordfish were on the deck by 16.15 when the first German shells scored their first hits, destroying the aircraft. Further shells then penetrated the flight deck and exploded amongst the Hurricanes on the hangar deck, detonating fuel and ammunition still in the aircraft. Within an instant, the hangar deck was an inferno. Although the ship increased speed to 27 knots, by 17.00, when a salvo destroyed the bridge, she was a pillar of smoke. Her escorting destroyers, *Ardent* and *Acasta*, were lost making a valiant torpedo attack on the *Scharnhorst*.

Glorious finally sank at 18.00. Some believe that as many as 900 of her ship's company and embarked RAF aircrew of 1,500 might have survived the sinking, but of those who did, just thirty-nine survived two days in the cold water, without food or drink, before they were rescued.

Xmas Menu.
1940

Breakfast.
Cornflakes.
Fried Bacon, Egg.
Marmalade.

Dinner.
Giblet Soup.
Roast Turkey & Stuffing.
Roast Potatoes.
Fresh Runner Beans.
Christmas Pudding & Sauce.
Figs, Dates & Nuts.
Oranges.

Tea.
Wholemeal Bread.
Christmas Cake.

Supper.
Cream of Tomato Soup.
Cold Ham.
Pickles.

There were undoubtedly many hardships in being at sea during the Second World War, but clearly efforts were made to ensure that Christmas Day was suitably festive aboard HMS *Ark Royal*. Nevertheless, during prolonged periods at sea, rice had to be substituted for potatoes.
(The late S.H. Wragg)

In an act of retaliation, on 13 June, Skuas of *Ark Royal*'s 800 and 803 Squadrons were sent to attack *Scharnhorst* and *Gneisenau* in the harbour at Trondheim. The aircraft came under heavy attack from defending fighters as well as intense AA fire, so that eight of the fifteen aircraft were lost and their crews either killed or taken prisoner. This operation, likened to the Charge of the Light Brigade by one of the participants, did not inflict any damage as the only bomb to hit *Scharnhorst* failed to explode, possibly because it was dropped at too low an altitude to arm itself.

France Becomes a Potential Enemy

A number of Fleet Air Arm squadrons provided cover for the evacuation of the British Expeditionary Force from Dunkirk, helping to ensure that the vulnerable vessels bringing back the troops were not exposed to German warships. A shortage of aircraft enabled the Fleet Air Arm to second pilots to the RAF for the Battle of Britain. Fifty-six naval airmen flew with RAF Fighter Command during the Battle of Britain, including Sub Lieutenant (later Lieutenant Commander) Dickie Cork, who was wingman to the great fighter ace, Douglas Bader.

Meanwhile, the squadrons embarked in the carriers were involved in disarming that part of the Vichy French fleet based in North Africa and West Africa. On 3 July 1940, aircraft from HMS *Ark Royal* augmented the guns of the Mediterranean Fleet's battleships at Mers-el-Kebir, helping to blow up the old battleship *Bretagne*, and cripple the battlecruiser *Dunkerque* and the battleship *Provence*, both of which had to be run aground to save them from sinking. Some ships managed to escape to Toulon, including six destroyers and the battlecruiser *Strasbourg*. Five days later, aircraft from HMS *Hermes* supported two heavy cruisers attacking Dakar in West Africa, damaging the battleship *Richelieu*. There was little enthusiasm for an attack on a navy that had so recently been an ally, but it was recognized that these major fleet units would have been invaluable to the Germans. At this stage of the war it was not clear whether Vichy France would attempt to remain neutral or become an ally of the Germans.

Chapter 8

The USN Comes to the Aid of the FAA

The pressures that the Fleet Air Arm found itself under at the outset of the war in Europe in September 1939 were not just those of rapid expansion, but of how to achieve it. The Royal Navy was in the unwanted situation of not being in control of its own aviation training, yet needing to expand rapidly. It was to be from the still neutral United States that a solution was to come.

Traditionally, British regular officers had joined as early as the age of thirteen years, spending four years at the Royal Naval College at Dartmouth, which operated as a fee-paying public school. Those who had attended other schools joined at seventeen or eighteen years, and spent a term at Dartmouth. In both cases, after graduating from Dartmouth, they would spend eighteen months as a midshipman. Despite the officer's cap badge, midshipmen were not regarded as being officers in the full sense, being addressed as 'mister' and not joining their seniors in the wardroom, the naval term for the officers' mess, but instead being confined to the 'gunroom mess'. In peacetime, a midshipman who wanted to fly would undergo most of his training with the RAF, with the Royal Navy providing catapult training so that he could fly seaplanes and amphibians from battleships, battlecruisers and cruisers. Training for pilots and observers that had taken two years in peacetime was compressed into ten wartime months.

Pilots

During wartime, all adults under a certain age had to register for National Service and as people could be ordered into certain work, those who were interested in naval aviation couldn't leave matters to luck, but would instead present themselves at a recruiting office. There was chaos at first. One man ended up in the Fleet Air Arm because he had been told that he would have to wait until he was called, unless he wanted to short-circuit the system by volunteering for the Royal Marine Commandos or the Fleet

Air Arm. Even then, they had run out of forms. He thought that he might become an aircraft mechanic, but when the forms eventually arrived, they were stamped 'PILOT OR OBSERVER'. Another volunteered for the RAF, but was told that there was a waiting list of almost a year, but if he tried the Fleet Air Arm he would be flying within a couple of months.

There was a substantial proportion of RNZNVR personnel in the FAA during the war. This was because the Royal Navy had a recruitment office in New Zealand, while those wishing to join the RAF had to make their own way to the UK to volunteer.

This first hurdle surmounted and the forms submitted, the applicant would be summoned to HMS *St Vincent*, the barracks at Gosport, the small town across the harbour from Portsmouth. Here, groups of forty or so were medically examined, the whole process taking a couple of hours. An interview board followed, a triumvirate chaired by a senior officer, up to and including a rear admiral, supported by an instructor lieutenant commander and an engineer, usually a lieutenant commander or commander. At this stage, the candidate would be offered the choice of becoming either a pilot or an observer. If successful, he would be sent home until he could be accommodated on a course.

For the aspiring naval airman in wartime, training started with a return to HMS *St Vincent*, although sometimes nearby HMS *Daedalus*, RNAS Lee-on-Solent, had to be used as well for a week or so until accommodation was available. Here, the recruits joined in batches of fifty or sixty every four weeks, forming into courses, with those for observers given even numbers and those for pilots odd numbers. They were kitted out with standard naval ratings' uniform, as Naval Airmen 2nd Class, including bell bottoms. In wartime, ratings' cap ribbons no longer showed the name of their ship, but just the simple 'HMS'. Some found a supplier able to produce ribbons showing 'FLEET AIR ARM', but this was unofficial and could only be swapped for the correct ribbon once away from base.

Pay for the new recruits was just 14 shillings (70p) per week, but a cup of tea in the NAAFI cost just an old penny, and bed and board was free. Cigarettes were a shilling a hundred, traditionally duty free for naval personnel.

Recruits spent seven weeks at *St Vincent*, learning to march, salute and look after their kit, become capable of handling a machine gun, and learn navigation, Morse, semaphore and meteorology. They would also have become familiar with naval terminology and know that whenever they left a shore station, they were still officially 'going ashore'. At the end of their basic training, an examination would have to be passed before starting elementary flying training, which initially was handled by the RAF, at either Elmdon, now Birmingham International Airport, or Luton, now London Luton Airport. These were additional training facilities set up by the RAF in an attempt to increase the flow of pilots, but a further stimulus came with additional training bases overseas, at first in Canada and then at Pensacola, where training was provided by the United States Navy. This was known as the Towers Scheme, set up by Admiral Towers of the USN, initially planned to train thirty pilots a month for the Fleet Air Arm, and another 100, mainly flying-boat crews, for the RAF.

Training overseas not only increased the output of pilots and observers, it often enabled training to become more concentrated, with better flying weather. Most important of all, the vulnerable training aircraft were away from the threat of being bounced by a Luftwaffe fighter. The RAF also had many of its pilots trained abroad, often in southern Africa under the Empire Flying Training Scheme.

Graduating from *St Vincent* as Leading Naval Airmen with anchors on their sleeves, it was either the train to London for those going on to Elmdon or Luton, or a troopship to the United States for those on their way to Pensacola. At Luton, basic training was given on Miles Magisters, streamlined monoplanes, while at Elmdon, the training was on de Havilland Tiger Moths. Here, the RAF instructors believed that they could tell whether or not someone was pilot material within a week. On the Tiger Moth, some went solo after as little as five hours, and few took more than ten hours; on the Magister, 'Maggies', it took longer, but anyone taking twelve hours started to worry about his chances. This stage of training usually took eight weeks and the student pilots would spend between fifty and sixty hours in the air. Pay at this stage was 6s 6d (32.5p) a day, of which 3s 6d was flying pay, but being based on an RAF station, cigarettes now cost 6d for ten, and a half pint of bitter was also 6d.

On graduating from Luton or Elmdon, still as Leading Naval Airmen, the next stage was the RAF's No. 1 Service Flying Training School at Netheravon. Here, the student pilots were streamed to become fighter or bomber pilots. The former continued their training on Fairey Battles as a prelude to Skuas and Fulmars in the early days, although later they would have graduated to Sea Hurricanes, Seafires, an American fighter or, towards the end of the war, Fireflies. The latter were trained on Hawker Harts and would expect to fly Swordfish or Albacores, and later, Barracudas or Avengers. Despite their lowly rank, at this stage the student pilots were accommodated in the officers' mess, had WAAFs to make their beds and had white cap ribbons to show that they were future officers.

There was another difference between the two services. Most naval pilots and observers were commissioned, while the RAF had a substantial number of sergeant pilots and navigators. One way of becoming a rating pilot in the Fleet Air Arm was to blot one's copybook. One example was of two student pilots who were caught stealing petrol from the aircraft and selling it. The fuel was eventually dyed red to stop such activities, the two who were caught were imprisoned for six months, and emerged to complete their training and fly as petty officer pilots.

Those who were sent to the United States for training were in so many ways the lucky ones, as their counterparts at Netheravon suffered from a shortage of aircraft. It was not unknown for half-a-dozen keen would-be fliers to arrive at dispersal to find just one aircraft, and sometimes none at all. The weather could also play a part in reducing the number of hours flown, so that sometimes the new pilot would have as little as eighty-eight hours of solo flying instead of the hundred plus expected. This was where they were supposed to learn formation flying and aerobatics, night flying, navigation and instrument flying, with dive-bombing for the bomber pilots and fighter tactics for the rest. They also shot at towed targets. On leaving Netheravon, the new pilots received their wings. The pass rate must have varied, but it seems that on average about half failed, or 'dipped' in naval slang. There were also casualties from accidents and, occasionally, from enemy action.

Newly qualified pilots went on leave for a week, their first since joining, their commissions dating from the end of that leave. They were all commissioned into the RNVR. Those over twenty-one years of age became Temporary Sub Lieutenants, those under twenty-one, Temporary Acting Sub Lieutenants, and those under twenty became Temporary Midshipmen. They then returned to the Royal Navy for their operational training. They would learn how to fly naval aircraft and how to fly from aircraft carriers or from the catapult of a cruiser, or other major fleet unit. Here they would come across another FAA/RAF difference. The RAF had operational training units, the Fleet Air Arm treated theirs as naval air squadrons, with numbers in the 700 series, along with squadrons handling a miscellany of other supposedly non-operational tasks.

Training in the USA

Those selected to train in the United States had first to get there, taking passage in a troopship, often boarding not in one of the pre-war liner ports such as London, Liverpool or Southampton, but in some point convenient for convoy assembly, such as Gourock on the Clyde. Accommodation aboard was Spartan, but they did at least known how to sling the hammocks with which they were issued, unlike their RAF counterparts. Food, on the other hand, seems to have been good.

On arrival, usually via Canada, the early students found that the US Naval Air Station at Pensacola was under the command of the famous pioneer, Captain A.C. Read, who as a lieutenant commander in 1919 had led the famous flight of flying boats across the Atlantic via the Azores. They also found what amounted to a self-contained town of 16,000 people, with recreational facilities that few major cities in the United Kingdom could match. This superior setting extended to their accommodation, comfortable dormitories with eight beds each, and a spacious dining room with negro stewards. Then there was the climate, for Pensacola was in

Florida and on the Gulf of Mexico. Liaison officers were appointed to look after the British cadets – these took no part in their training but were there to represent their interests and look after their welfare. Not surprisingly, given its facilities, which included four airfields and many emergency strips, Pensacola was known to the USN as the 'Annapolis of the Air'.

For those training at Pensacola, there was also the attraction of rationing and blackout-free USA. Petrol cost just 11 cents a gallon at a time when there were 4 US dollars to the pound sterling, and serviceable old cars were also easily and cheaply available. Many bought cars and enjoyed a spell of independence during their time off that wouldn't have been possible with strict rationing in Britain.

Naval cadets at Pensacola found themselves integrated into classes with USN and USMC cadets. Destined to be fighter pilots, for the first six weeks they attended ground school, studying navigation, including celestial navigation, meteorology, theory of flight, and fuel, oil and hydraulic systems. There were instructional films and a compulsory period of physical training lasting two hours every day. They had a written test every Friday afternoon. Everyone had to undergo a spell in a decompression chamber, so that they could appreciate the effects of a lack of oxygen at altitude. This extended to them sitting at desks inside the chamber and taking written tests while pressure was reduced to the equivalent of an altitude of 18,000 feet. Only once this altitude was reached were they fitted with oxygen masks, while pressure was reduced to the equivalent of 30,000 feet – and then they took more tests.

Just as those trained by the RAF soon discovered differences in practice between the two services, so too did those trained by the USN. Being on parade in the Royal Navy was far more demanding than in the USN, but the drill for taking over the two-hour watch as 'Mate of the Deck' in their living quarters had evolved into a ceremony taken very seriously by the USN, but not by their RN guests.

Following ground school, flying training started. Basic training was in a Naval Aircraft Factory N3N-3 biplane with dual controls, and unusually for such aircraft, the instructor sat in the front seat. The student pilot was expected to be able to fly solo at around ten hours. One pilot who went through the process remembers a steady stream of his classmates being dropped from the course and returned to the UK for medical reasons, including air sickness, which USN doctors maintained would never disappear given time. Another was poor depth perception, which could result in the student pilot attempting to land 50 or 60 feet above the runway!

After more than thirty hours of flying solo, the training extended to flying in bad weather. This started with many hours under the hood of a ground-based Link trainer, the crude predecessor of today's flight simulators, where the students practised 'flying' along radar beams, timed approaches to airfields and let-downs in simulated bad weather. The next stage was to fly in a Harvard dual-control trainer, with the student sitting in the rear cockpit under a hood so that he did not have so much as a chink of light. The instructor sat in front, also acting as safety pilot. The instructor would fly the aircraft to within radio distance of a small civil airfield, before turning on the radio and leaving the student pilot to fly the approach. This entailed the student finding the beam, tracking it down to the right altitude and speed, and finally positioning the aircraft to land on the duty runway. Even harder than it sounds, the student achieved all this by listening to the radio signals and interpreting them, while also reading the instruments and using a stop watch correctly, while at the same time controlling the aircraft. At the end of this exercise, the instructor would snap up the hood so that the student could see whether or not the airfield was ahead.

The next stage was flight in a Vought-Sikorsky O3U-1 biplane, similar to a Swordfish, before moving on to a landplane version of the Vought OS2U-3 Kingfisher, with more sophisticated flying controls, to start formation flying and aerobatics. After which, it was time to be commissioned and move on to the fighter course, at Miami, further south and almost at the other end of the state.

Fighter training took place at the USN's Fighter Training School at Opa Locka, 14 miles north of Miami. Training here was intensive, working eight days without a break before a night and the following day at liberty. Their new aircraft was the North American Harvard, known to the USN as the SNJ-3, marking a considerable advance in sophistication compared to the aircraft previously flown, and equipped with radio. The only real worry for the aspiring aviator was that so much of the training took place over the Everglades, the vast areas of swamp and scrub around Miami. The training included ground strafing, air-to-air firing at drogues and gun-camera attacks on simulated bomber formations or individual aircraft flown by other students.

After the Harvard, the students moved on to the Brewster Buffalo, fighters that had only just been discarded by the USN, and which did not have a good reputation. At this stage, the Royal Navy resumed responsibility for their training, and not only did they have to become accustomed to a fighter, but they also had to start learning the Fleet Air Arm, as opposed to the USN, way of doing things. This meant not only learning British flying methods and phraseology, but also map reading, flight information, patrol formations, simulated forced landings and dummy deck landings, known as ADDLs, aerodrome dummy deck landings, as well as navigation exercises over the sea, anti-submarine bombing and night flying. ADDLs meant landing on a runway marked out like a carrier deck, and of the same size. By now they would soon be ready to convert to their operational aircraft. Lacking dual-control aircraft for conversion training, pilots adapted to new aircraft types by studying the handbook and spending time in the classroom and the cockpit before attempting a first flight.

Apart from the climate and vastly superior accommodation, with higher performance aircraft on which to learn, training in the United States had other advantages compared to war-torn Britain. At first, many Americans resented the presence of the Britons, jeering and shouting not just off base, but on it as well, because many felt that Churchill was attempting to draw the United States into the war. Attitudes changed overnight, of course, with the Japanese attack on Pearl Harbor.

Specialist Training

While these were the standard training programmes, the system was capable of variation. Initial training took into account any previous significant experience. Airline pilots, for example, were sent on a conversion course with 780 Squadron at Eastleigh, now the airport for Southampton, to familiarize themselves with the very different conditions of naval flying, using a variety of aircraft, including Hart Trainer, Nimrod, Shark, Gipsy Moth, Hornet Moth and Tiger Moth, Proctor, Swordfish and Vega Gull. From this, the younger recruits would go on to carrier or catapult training. In some cases, conversion training was unnecessary, as with the former Jersey Airways pilots who signed up for naval commissions, and flew airliners conscripted into the Royal Navy on communications duties.

Carrier deck-landing training was given when needed, with refresher training after any lengthy period spent flying from a naval air station. For those trained in the United States, the USN also helped with deck-landing training. After using a runway marked out as a carrier deck, the new pilots would have a chance to learn on the real thing. For most, this meant using the USS *Challenger*, an escort carrier originally intended for the Royal Navy, but retained by the USN for just this purpose. A small number were able to use the USS *Wolverine* or *Sable*, two riverboats converted to training carriers to avoid using an operational carrier.

Fighter training for those being taught in the UK was no less intensive. The fighter school was initially at RNAS Yeovilton, where the circuit became so congested and overcrowded with inexperienced pilots that an unacceptably high number of accidents occurred. A second training airfield was soon established at Zeals.

Other bases provided specialized training for different types of naval aviation. In the UK, the deck-landing school was at RNAS Arbroath, HMS *Condor*, known to some as Aberbrothock, where there was also an observers' school. Torpedo training took place at RNAS Crail, in Fife, HMS *Jackdaw*. Advanced instrument training took place at Hinstock, HMS *Godwit*. Those destined to operate from MAC-ships also had their own special training centre at RNAS Maydown, which was initially a satellite of

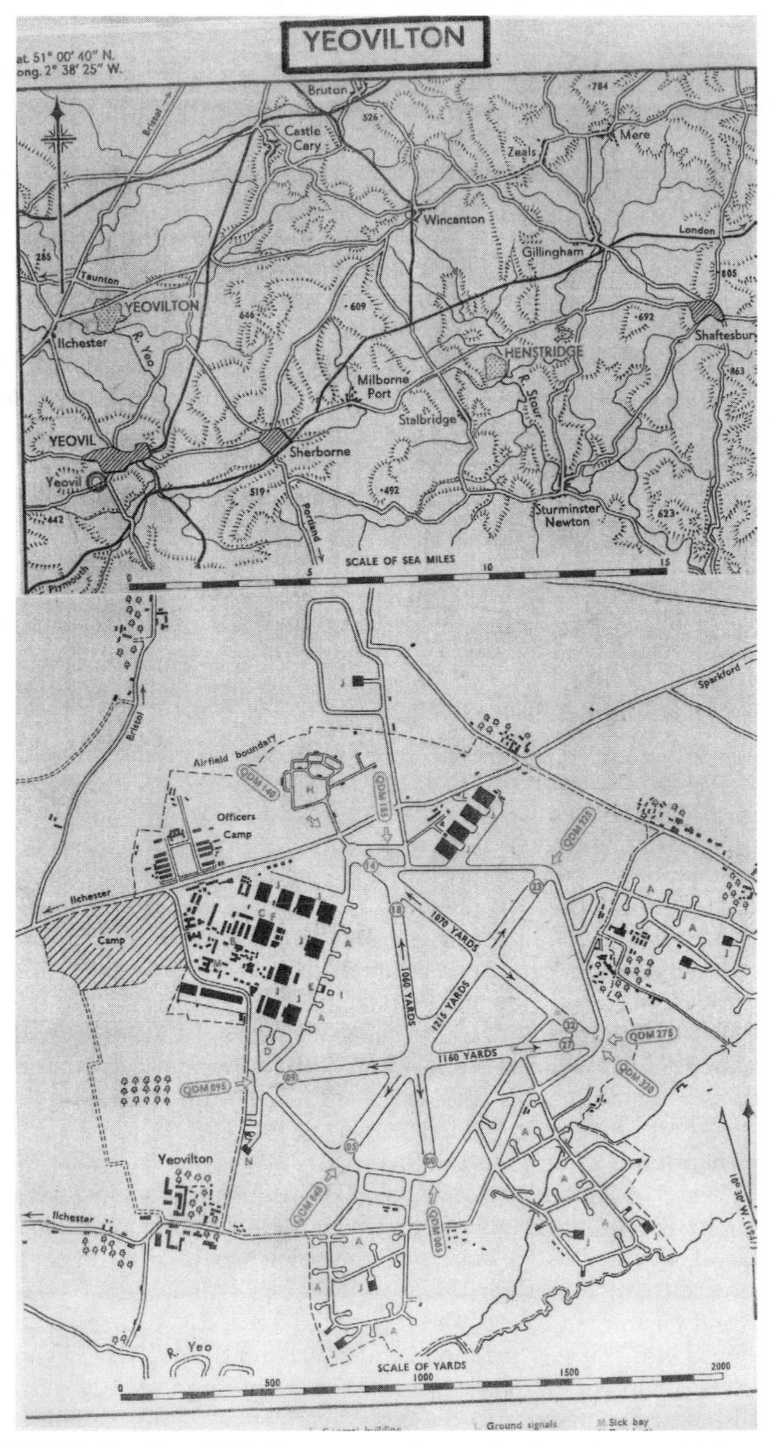

Map 2. RNAS Yeovilton, HMS *Heron*, was under construction when war broke out, but rapidly became so important and busy that it had satellite airfields at Henstridge and Zeals.

Eglinton before becoming HMS *Shrike*. It housed the anti-submarine school as well.

Catapult training for the flights embarked in major warships passed to 700 Squadron in 1942. After initial and advanced training, seaplane and amphibian pilots would have three weeks at Donibristle learning aerodrome circuits, wireless telegraphy, water landings, photography, anti-submarine attacks and dive-bombing. This was followed by three weeks at Dundee, with crew training, navigation and night landings. Then a week of catapult training aboard HMS *Pegasus* in the Irish Sea, before a week at Donibristle and two weeks at Twatt in Orkney before embarkation. As the war progressed, catapult training ceased.

There were other specialized courses, with one of the more unusual being that for maintenance test pilots. Early in the war, this was a course of just four weeks, but later extended to ten weeks, and was held at RNAS Worthy Down, HMS *Kestrel*. On the extended ten-week course, the pilot had a minimum of five weeks flying on the main types of aircraft in service, which by this time included the Avenger, Barracuda, Corsair, Firefly, Hellcat, Seafire and Wildcat. This was another task that fell to 700 Squadron in October 1944, after catapult training had ceased, with eighty-four test pilots trained in the following eleven months.

Observers

Much of the initial training for observers was similar to that for aspiring pilots, including the spell at *St Vincent*. The role of the observer was especially significant for naval aviation, since it was felt that even fighter aircraft needed an observer given the greater problems of finding a fast-moving carrier at sea. This, of course, also affected the performance of the aircraft, having two seats instead of one. At the same time, the work of an observer was more than just that of a navigator. The observer did observe, often took photographs and, in the catapult flights, could be called on to help relay the fall of shot in a naval gun battle. It was also important that the observer could handle the radio, especially in aircraft without a telegraphist air-gunner, or TAG, or when the TAG was replaced by a fuel tank, as happened often with the Swordfish.

There were two main observer schools. The first was No. 1 Observer School, initially based at Ford and then Yeovilton, before moving to Piarco in Trinidad, where 749, 750 and 752 Squadrons provided training using a variety of aircraft, including Percival Proctors, Albacores, Barracudas, Walrus and Grumman Goose. The second, based at RNAS Arbroath, HMS *Condor*, was No. 2 Observer School, and consisted of 740, 741, 753 and 754 Squadrons, again with a mixture of aircraft, including Proctors, Walruses, Swordfish and Kingfishers. In the early years some Seafoxes, Sharks and Seals were also operated there. At one point, 754 Squadron operated a substantial number of Lysander target tugs.

Deck Landing Control Officers

Deck landing control officers, DLCOs, or batsmen, as they were known, trained at East Haven, which also had the Deck Landing Training School. They were all experienced naval pilots. Initial training consisted of aircraft from the training squadron, 731, flying circuits involving dummy deck landings. This routine gave rise to the nickname 'clockwork mice' for the pilots, and not surprisingly, the pilots sometimes relieved the tedium by occasionally making an irregular approach to make life more difficult for the aspiring batsmen. At least at this stage, they were in no danger of getting wet.

The unfortunates chosen for this demanding role, sometimes spending hours standing upright directing aircraft, with a stiff breeze over the flight deck added to the carrier's movement, and with the risk of injury or worse if a landing was botched, were rewarded by a generous Admiralty with the loss of their flying pay.

Telegraphist Air Gunners

Telegraphist air gunners, TAGS, were naval ratings, with the highest rank on a squadron usually being a chief petty officer. Training took six or seven months, during which they would be expected to accumulate sixty hours' flying time. Initial training was at Worthy Down, home of No. 1 Air Gunners School, where 755 Squadron provided the early part of their wireless course and 757 did the same for air gunnery, with 756 providing the more advanced element of the wireless course, including cross-country flying and beacon flying. The advanced element of the air gunners' course was provided by 774 Squadron, with live firing at St Merryn in Cornwall.

These arrangements were augmented by training in Canada, when a second school opened in 1943, at Yarmouth, Nova Scotia, an RCAF base handed over to the Fleet Air Arm. Confusingly, while the RN referred to this as No. 2 Air Gunners' School, the RCAF referred to it as No. 1 Naval Air Gunners' School.

Naval Anti-aircraft Gunners

Naval anti-aircraft gunners were not part of the Fleet Air Arm, but the FAA was involved with their training. The prime task of aircraft in the fleet requirements unit squadrons was to provide practice for anti-aircraft gunners, usually by towing target drogues, as well as helping to calibrate ships' radar. One squadron, 723, dived towards fleet units whose gunners fired back using live ammunition, although with gun sights offset 15 degrees to port – an interesting life for the pilots!

Air Mechanics and Artificers

The Royal Navy operated a two-tier system for technical personnel, which was not unique to the Fleet Air Arm. The skilled tradesmen were known as 'artificers', and their work was supported by the less-skilled naval air mechanics. This was a system designed to both increase the manpower available in the shortest possible time, and make the best use of the more highly skilled. The less-skilled air mechanics were often at leading rank, but could advance to the senior rates. Artificers were normally petty officers (POs), or chief petty officers (CPOs), and had either served an extended service apprenticeship, at this stage provided at RAF Halton, or were reservists bringing their civilian skills with them. To encourage volunteers, skilled men were usually paid their pre-war civilian rates. Heading the artificers and mechanics on any squadron would be an air engineer officer.

Recruitment of the desperately needed technical personnel started well before the outbreak of war. The Admiralty knew that it not only needed to allow for dramatic wartime expansion, it also had to replace the many RAF personnel looking after the aircraft of the fleet. An Admiralty Fleet Order in the late spring of 1938 sought volunteers for the FAA from those already serving. Many volunteered in the belief that promotion would be quick. After some waiting, the applicants were interviewed by senior officers. One applicant, who wanted to be a naval air mechanic (E), working on aircraft engines, was told: 'You are an AB (able seaman), so you know about knots and spicing, so you'll be better off as an air mechanic (A), a rigger.' This was an apt reflection of the needs of aircraft such as the Swordfish and Sea Gladiator. He heard nothing more that summer. In September, when the Munich crisis broke, he was drafted to a destroyer, but as he prepared to join his ship, the First Lieutenant asked for all volunteers for the FAA to assemble outside the drafting office.

As with the rest of the Fleet Air Arm, the new recruits were dependent on the Royal Air Force for their training. The RAF, accustomed at worst to training relatively raw naval recruits, thought these experienced seamen to be a motley crew, since they didn't understand them and their adherence to their own routines. They were divided up by specialization – airframes, engineers, electrical and ordnance – with training at RAF Henlow, St Athan, in South Wales, and Eastchurch, on the Isle of Sheppey, respectively. Training took about a year and for the naval air mechanics (A) was divided between six months at Henlow and then four months at RAF Locking, near Western-super-Mare.

For the naval air mechanics (A), training included the theory of flight as well as aircraft repairs and general maintenance, including work on the fabric covering of many airframes, and studying aircraft hydraulic and pneumatic systems.

There was no automatic promotion to a higher rate on completing the courses. The naval air mechanics of all kinds were posted to HMS *Daedalus* at Lee-on-Solent to await drafting to their squadrons. In contrast to modern practice where special training is regarded as vital for working on different types of aircraft, no special training was given in most cases, although usually handbooks were available. Even when the FAA introduced the relatively sophisticated Sea Hurricane, the Royal Navy's first high-performance aircraft, no special training was given. The first time this was thought necessary came with the all-metal Seafire, where the air mechanics went to Supermarine at Eastleigh for two weeks. The Seafire also introduced hydraulically operated folding wings to the FAA, a marked advanced on the mechanically folding wings of the Swordfish. When American aircraft joined the fleet later, their greater sophistication was compensated for by their being much easier to work on, and by having standardized layouts for the positioning of components.

Chapter 9

The Forgotten Victory

During the Abyssinian crisis in the late 1930s, when Italy attempted to colonize the country, now known as Ethiopia, the League of Nations had considered intervention. One obvious course would have been simply to close the Suez Canal to Italian ships, which would almost certainly have led to war in the Mediterranean, putting the British Mediterranean Fleet and its main base at Malta in the front line. HMS *Glorious* was the aircraft carrier with the Mediterranean Fleet at the time, and it was one of her officers who conceived the idea of an attack on the Italian fleet and its base at Taranto, in southern Italy. This would have been a daring raid, especially since at the time the ship carried nothing more potent than the Fairey Seal. It was thought that the operation would be best carried out by the RAF flying from Malta and if the Fleet Air Arm had to do it, it would be the one big blow before the carrier had to be quickly withdrawn from the Mediterranean or was sunk by the Italians.

These plans were revived and revised after Italy had entered the Second World War on the side of Germany, a few days before the fall of France in June 1940.

The amended plan was for two aircraft carriers to be used for the operation, HMS *Illustrious* and *Eagle*, attacking on 21 October 1940, the anniversary of Nelson's great victory at Trafalgar. The newly commissioned *Illustrious* had completed a working-up voyage to the Caribbean and on her return was almost immediately sent to the 'Med' to reinforce the Mediterranean Fleet, whose flag officer was none other than Admiral Sir Andrew Cunningham, known as 'ABC' to his men. Not only was an additional aircraft carrier welcomed, but aboard *Illustrious* were not just additional Fairey Swordfish but also Fairey Fulmar fighters. The Fulmar was outclassed as a fighter as even its Rolls-Royce Merlin engine couldn't provide the sparkling performance of a Supermarine Spitfire when forced to carry a second crew member, but it was a step up from the handful of Gloster Sea Gladiators that had been the fleet's fighter protection up to that time.

'I want you,' the First Sea Lord, Admiral of the Fleet Sir Dudley Pound, explained succinctly to Captain Denis Boyd, commanding officer of

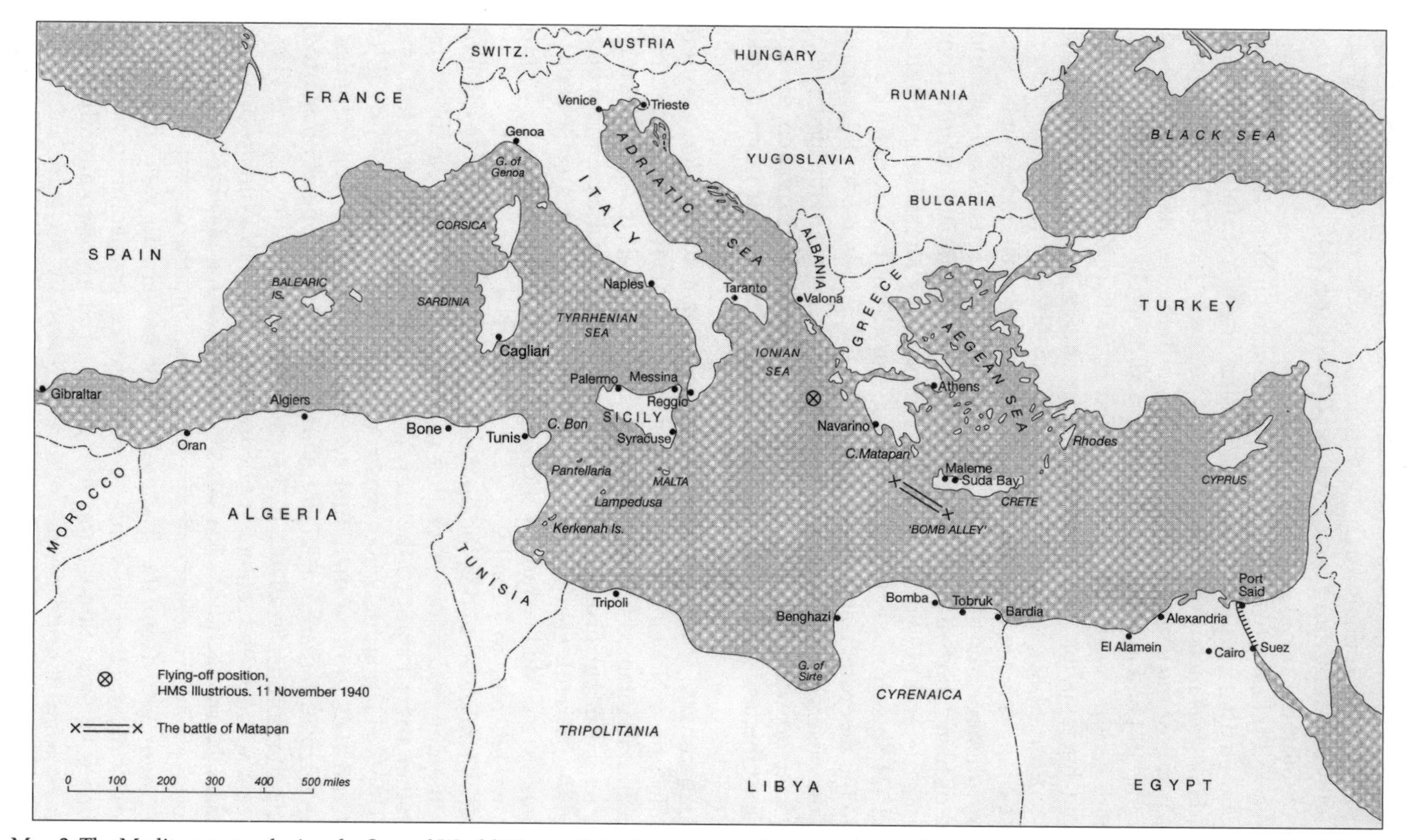

Map 3. The Mediterranean during the Second World War, with Malta roughly halfway between Gibraltar and Alexandria, about 1,000 miles from each, but just 80 miles from the coast of Sicily and Axis air bases.

Illustrious, 'in view of the desperate situation, to take *Illustrious* through the Straits of Gibraltar and join Andrew. He needs you badly out there.' Boyd sailed with his ship from Scapa Flow on 23 August 1940 and cleared the Straits of Gibraltar on 30 August.

All seemed set for a two-carrier force to operate together and mount the long-planned attack on Taranto, but fate intervened. A serious hangar fire aboard *Illustrious* meant that she could not be ready for 21 October. While the fire had cost the ship just two of her aircraft, the rest had been doused with water and had to be completely stripped down before any operation. Still more serious, *Eagle* had been attacked by Italian aircraft, which had damaged her aviation fuel system, as near misses had exploded in the water and forced her to remain at Alexandria for repairs.

These changes meant that the date of the operation had to be put back to the next full moon, the night of 11/12 November, using just *Illustrious*, and instead of using thirty aircraft, twenty-four were assembled, mainly from the ship's 815 and 819 Squadrons, but reinforced by aircraft from Eagle's 813 and 824 Squadrons. For the attack these squadrons had extra fuel tanks fitted to the Swordfish, and in the case of the torpedo-bombers this meant taking the observers' cockpits and forcing the observers, with their bulky 'Bigsworth' boards (on which charts and maps were displayed during flight) into the less spacious confines of the telegraphist/air-gunner cockpits.

Using a convoy of reinforcements to Greece as a cover, *Illustrious* left Alexandria on 6 November with a cruiser and destroyer escort. Secrecy was further maintained by successful combat air patrols (CAPs), flown by the carrier's 806 Squadron, operating Fairey Fulmar I fighters, and whose total tally of twenty enemy aircraft during the Squadron's spell aboard *Illustrious* in the Mediterranean included Italian reconnaissance aircraft shot down en route to Taranto.

Bad luck continued to dog the operation. One Swordfish had to ditch in the sea the day before the attack due to engine failure, and the following day another aircraft suffered the same problem. It was discovered that one of the ship's aviation fuel tanks was contaminated by sea water, so all of the aircraft had to have their fuel systems drained and then refuelled. Another aircraft suffered a failure shortly before the operation started, reducing the number available to just twenty-one.

The raid was led by Lieutenant Commander Kenneth Williamson, with Lieutenant Norman 'Blood' Scarlett-Streatfield as his observer, and consisted of two waves: the first with twelve aircraft and the second with nine. Finding their way from the flying-off point to Taranto was simplified, despite cloud, once the port's anti-aircraft defences opened up to shoot at a patrolling RAF Short Sunderland flying boat. The first two aircraft of the first wave were flare droppers, followed closely by Swordfish carrying torpedoes so that they could strike at the Italian warships while these were silhouetted against the light of the flares. The second wave carried bombs and concentrated on shore installations, including fuel storage tanks.

Everything seemed to be going smoothly, but then, as the last aircraft on the starboard side moved out, its wing tip caught that of another aircraft, tearing the fabric and, worse, breaking several of the ribs inside the wing. Without delay, the aircraft was taken out of service and struck down into the hangar for repairs. Inevitably, given the damage, it was not ten minutes later but thirty minutes before L5F could rumble down the flight deck. Few aircraft could have been repaired so quickly. A Swordfish could fly with almost all of its fabric gone, but it would have been foolhardy to have attempted to take off with damaged ribs.

The second-wave aircraft also seemed to be fated. In one aircraft, the external fuel tank had broken loose twenty minutes after leaving the ship, falling into the sea and leaving loose fittings banging on the fuselage. Then the engine cut out and the aircraft began losing height; although the pilot managed to restart it, he had no choice but to return to the carrier while they still had sufficient fuel, nursing a sickly engine.

Meanwhile, the aircraft of the first strike had found thick cloud, hazardous in its own right, as aircraft could, and sometimes did, collide when flying in cloud. It was also very cold in the open cockpits. Most of the formation broke up at this point.

Unknown to the attackers, fate had played a hand and there had been a stroke of good fortune during the day. That morning, the Italian fleet had readied for sea for gunnery exercises. The crews of the warships had spent much of the morning in the tedious chore of removing the torpedo nets that surrounded the ships. Then, for some unknown reason, the Admiral had called off the gunnery exercises, but no one had given the order to re-rig the nets again.

Even so, the Italians were not caught completely off their guard. A succession of alerts and all-clears had broken up the evening, but this was not unusual in a major target area in wartime. At around 19.55, a report had been received that the sound of aircraft engines had been heard off the coast. This was assumed to be just another reconnaissance flight. Shortly after 20.00, there were further reports of aircraft engines from listening stations and the alarms were sounded, with gun crews rushing to their posts while the civilians ashore raced for the air-raid shelters. Further noises came later, most of which were caused by a Short Sunderland patrolling dutifully in the Gulf of Taranto, always watchful for any movement by the Italian Fleet. The alarm went off for a second time. There was no immediate action until after a further twenty-five minutes had elapsed, it was clear that something was happening as the noises became louder.

Richard Janvrin was on the flare-dropping mission:

> We had a grandstand view so we didn't go down to sea level. We dropped our flares at about 8,000 feet. And in fact we were fired at

considerably. We had a fair amount of ack-ack fire and most extraordinary things that looked like flaming onions ... one just sort of went through it and it made no great impression. One didn't think that they would ever hit you.

... there was always fear but I think in the same way one always had butterflies in the tummy beforehand, but when things were actually happening you don't seem to notice the butterflies much.

... the torpedo aircraft went down and they attacked in two sub flights. The leader took his sub flight of three and attacked. And he ... attacked a Cavour-class battleship, launched his torpedo, which hit and was shot immediately afterwards ...

... we had bombs as well, and we dive-bombed some more fuel tanks ... and then we returned to the carrier.

Williamson had swept through the barrage-balloon cables, later maintaining that neither he nor Scarlett-Streatfield had noticed them, heading for the destroyers *Lampo* and *Fulmine*, which welcomed him with a barrage of machine-gun fire, before turning towards the massive outline of a battleship and dropping to just 30 feet before releasing their torpedo. In fact, they felt the splash as the torpedo hit the water, so it is likely that they were even lower. There was no time to wait and see as they had to escape the intense AA fire, but a few minutes later the night was shattered by a massive explosion. Their torpedo had found its mark and they had sunk the *Conte di Cavour* in shallow water. Struggling to get away, in turning in the middle of the harbour to escape, the Swordfish crashed, although even those on board the aircraft were later not sure whether this was caused by Italian AA fire or an accident.

Many compared the scene over Taranto with the eruption of a volcano, because the AA fire was so intense and the Italians favoured tracer shells, known to the aircrew as 'flaming onions'. Italian AA gunnery seems to have been very inaccurate, but from the point of view of the attackers, the use of tracer was welcome, simply because they could see it coming and take evasive action. The bombers were also busy.

Charles Lamb was another flare-dropper. He saw aircraft 'flying into the harbour only a few feet above sea level – so low that one or two of them actually touched the water with their wheels as they sped through the harbour entrance. Nine other spidery biplanes dropped out of the night sky, appearing in a crescendo of noise in vertical dives from the slow moving glitter or the yellow parachute flares.'

The dive-bombers had the task of striking at the lightly armoured cruisers and the destroyers, many of which were in the inner harbour or Mar Piccolo, in which space was far tighter and AA fire continued to be intense. Dive-bombing has been credited with almost miraculous accuracy and effectiveness over the years as a result of the German blitzkrieg, although the need to pull out of the dive in time to allow the aircraft to climb away safely meant that the pilot could not see his bomb hit the target. Even so, while there was no doubt that it could be accurate, against well-drilled and experienced AA gunners with the nerve to withstand the attack, dive-bombing could be a very hazardous occupation. The torpedo-bombers could keep very low and produce a difficult target, indeed, they had to do this otherwise if dropped from too high, their torpedoes risked breaking up on impact with the water. One advantage of a torpedo, as an American admiral famously put it, compared to bombs, was 'that it is much easier to get water into a ship from the bottom than from the top'. The dive-bombers had to dive from a height and release their bombs whilst still high enough for the bombs to arm themselves before hitting the target. It was not unknown for a Swordfish to have its wings ripped off in a dive.

The cloud that had hampered the formation flying of the first wave had gone as the second wave got into formation. The second-wave pilots could see the fires started by the first wave's bombs while they were still 60 miles away.

Counting the Cost

Aboard *Illustrious*, Lyster and his staff, Boyd and the rest of the ship's company were waiting anxiously both for news of the attack and to see just how many of the lumbering Swordfish might return. Tension rose as the time for the first strike to have been completed came and then passed. There was no signal from Williamson. There couldn't be. Those aboard the carrier realized that the first strike should have been leaving the target by this time. As they continued waiting for the aircraft of the first strike, eventually the longed-for signal was received from the second strike: 'Attack completed'.

It was the radar officer, Lieutenant Schierbeck of the Royal Canadian Naval Volunteer Reserve who first noticed the returning planes on his set. Shortly afterwards, two aircraft arrived, their navigation lights switched on, glowing dimly in the dark to reassure those waiting below. One after another the aircraft hooked on, jerked abruptly in the air a few feet above the flight deck and then dropped down on to the deck. Then they taxied forward to await their turn to have their wings folded before being struck down into the hangar. Almost before they stopped, excited observers had jumped down and ran to the ready room for debriefing. Their excitement told the team on deck all that they needed to know. The pilots, staying with their aircraft until they were struck down, were surprised to find that they were riddled with holes, with torn fabric flapping around the fuselage and wings. Later that morning, one of them was able to count seventeen shell holes in his aircraft.

The raid had been a complete success. At a time when the RAF was suffering unsustainable losses on its bombing raids over enemy held

Lots of struts in all directions,
Curved and cut-out centre-sections –
Stringbag the Sailor's had his day,
But in his own inimitable way
He's left his mark on history's page,
The champion of the biplane age!

The Swordfish, or 'Stringbag', may have been an aircraft from another age, but it inspired genuine affection and respect from its aircrew. (The late Lord Kilbracken)

territory, the Fleet Air Arm had indeed done well to lose just two aircraft. Williamson and Scarlett were fortunate to have escaped with their lives having been shot down, and from the wild Italian fire afterwards.

Jubilant

The crews were jubilant as they returned to *Illustrious*. Yet Cunningham, renowned for taking acts of great bravery as being nothing much more than what was to be expected of naval officers, showed remarkable understatement even for him. As the carrier and her escort rejoined the fleet on the morning of 12 November, a hoist of flags was raised aboard *Warspite* saying simply, '*Illustrious* manoeuvre well executed'.

Tired and exhausted – it was three in the morning – when the escorting cruisers rejoined the fleet at daylight on 12 November, the crews were surprised to be told that they would be going back that night. Their maintainers had been told to 'do a major' on the aircraft during the day, to get them ready for another attack. 'Even the Light Brigade was only asked to attack once,' as one wit put it.

Descending to the wardroom, they found that the stewards had painted a large 'Welcome Home' sign which was hanging from the deckhead – entirely their own idea.

One of the most spectacular aerial operations of all time, the raid has never been given the recognition it deserved, as senior officers failed to appreciate just how successful it had been. The ship's company tore down the notices announcing the first list of awards because just six medals were awarded, and the highest of these was a DSC for Scarlett-Streatfield. The sailors could be excused for believing that something better was deserved, such as a VC!

The German Revenge

Despite inflicting so much damage on the Italian fleet, secure in a well-defended harbour, *Illustrious* emerged completely unscathed from the operation. Nevertheless, the Germans were shocked that a single ship could do so much damage when ships were supposedly safe in harbour rather than engaging in battle on the high seas. They wasted little time. Over the New Year, the Luftwaffe moved General Geissler's X Air Corps, *Fliegerkorps X*, from Poland to Sicily. This was a battle-hardened force, numerically far smaller than the Regia Aeronautica's 2,000 or more aircraft, but it had considerable experience in anti-shipping operations earlier during the Norwegian campaign. The Luftwaffe had its weaknesses. These included the absence until late in the war of heavy bombers, and although an autonomous air force, it was also committed, like the Russians, to close support of ground forces rather than true strategic air power as understood by the Royal Air Force and the United States Army Air Force. Nevertheless, the Luftwaffe, with its professional and experienced commanders, understood and believed in the concentration of power: X Air Corps, situated in Sicily, just 60 miles from Malta, was more powerful than the combined RAF and Fleet Air Arm strength in the Mediterranean, scattered over more than 2,000 miles from Gibraltar to Alexandria.

Geissler had 150 Heinkel He111 and Junkers Ju88 twin-engined medium-bombers and the same number of Junkers Ju87 Stuka dive-bombers, as well as fifty Messerschmitt Bf109 fighters. Many have suggested that it was moved primarily to attack Malta, but its first priority, agreed with the Regia Aeronautica, would be British shipping, and especially the Mediterranean Fleet, with *Illustrious* as the prime target. Malta was second on the list, followed by the base at Alexandria. In addition, both air forces would sow mines in the approaches to the Suez Canal and the Grand Harbour, as well as mining both.

It was this force that was to do so much to make the British presence in the Mediterranean barely tenable. Pound had been remarkably prescient in his predictions for the lifespan of an aircraft carrier in the Mediterranean once hostilities had started.

Operation Excess

The convoy, known as Operation Excess, left the UK for Gibraltar in company with a far larger convoy for the Cape, dividing at Gibraltar. There were five fast cargo ships, of which one was for Malta. The others were intended for Alexandria. The convoy sailed from the UK in December. On Christmas Day, while the convoy was still on its first stage, the passage to Gibraltar, the German heavy cruiser *Hipper* was sighted and the convoy scattered. Force H left Gibraltar to provide support. Meanwhile, one of the heavy escorts, the elderly battleship *Renown*, was damaged by the heavy seas and was delayed in Gibraltar for repairs. The convoy reached the safety of Gibraltar without any interference from the Germans, but one of the ships for Alexandria had been driven ashore in the bad weather and had to be abandoned.

It was not until 6 January 1941, that the small convoy was finally able to steam eastwards from Gibraltar, a delay that was to have serious consequences. As with the arrangements made for the arrival of *Illustrious*, Operation Excess was to involve both Force H and the Mediterranean Fleet, with Force H covering the convoy as far as Sicily, after which protection would pass to the Mediterranean Fleet.

On 7 January 1941, the Mediterranean Fleet sailed from Alexandria to meet the convoy. Convoy protection was at its best when enemy ships could be kept well away, and to discourage the Italian Navy, Malta-based Wellington medium bombers raided Naples on 8 January, finding two battleships, the *Guilo Cesare* and the *Vittorio Veneto* there, and managed to damage the former, persuading the Italians to withdraw both ships northwards.

The handover date was fixed for dawn on 10 January 1941, although in reality this meant most of Force H leaving the convoy at dusk on 9 January, with the exception of the cruisers *Gloucester* and *Southampton* and two destroyers, which were detached from the main force and sent with the convoy through the Sicilian Narrows in brilliant moonlight. Had the convoy been able to keep to its original schedule, all might have been well, with a safe handover a couple of days before the end of 1940. The arrival of *Fliegerkorps X* in Sicily was known to British Intelligence, largely due to the signals-monitoring station at Lascaris in Malta. What was not immediately apparent was that *Fliegerkorps X*'s prime target was not Malta, which could wait, but *Illustrious*. It was clear to the Germans that the ship and her aircraft would be a menace to Axis shipping in the Mediterranean.

Many had been concerned that *Illustrious* would be exposed when operating within range of enemy aircraft. Cunningham, nevertheless, was insistent that the carrier should be with the main body of the fleet, mainly because of the beneficial effect her presence always had on morale aboard the rest of the ships. He had also concluded that aircraft carriers were at their safest when able to benefit from the protection of other ships, something that was to be proven later during the war in the Pacific.

Around 12.30, two Italian torpedo-bombers made an unsuccessful attack on the carrier, missing her as her Commanding Officer, Captain Denis Boyd, successfully 'combed' the torpedoes, manoeuvring his ship so that they raced past. The attack had the effect of drawing the patrolling Fulmars down to low level. Relief Fulmars were being readied for take-off on the carrier's flight deck, so that the earlier patrol could return to the ship, when the carrier's radar spotted two large formations of aircraft flying from the direction of Sicily. Even as the Fulmars struggled to get off the flight deck, the Germans attacked, with forty-three Junkers Ju87 dive-bombers, the dreaded *Stuka*, giving the Mediterranean Fleet its first taste of the deadly accuracy of dive-bombing.

The first bomb narrowly missed the ship, one of three near misses that day, but over the next ten minutes, no less than six 1,000-lb bombs struck *Illustrious*. Of all the aircraft carriers operational during the Second World War, only *Illustrious* and her five sisters could take such punishment with their armoured flight decks and hangar decks, but the armour plating was meant to resist 500-lb bombs, the lifts that moved the aircraft between flight deck and hangar deck were not armoured, and bombs fell through these. The hangar deck contained aircraft, many armed and with fuel in their tanks. It was also the action station for all off-duty aircrew and many of them had assembled there. The bombs exploded in this space, the effect enhanced by the armoured top, sides and bottom of the hangar deflecting the blast through the aircraft and the naval airmen. Within seconds of the first bomb entering the hangar, it was a blazing inferno.

Despite the ship being a blazing, crippled wreck, Boyd refused permission to flood her magazines while the threat of bombing remained. Had a bomb exploded in the magazines, or had one penetrated her aviation fuel system with its high-octane gasoline, or had the pipelines carrying aviation fuel been damaged by the mining effect of near misses, the ship could have been blown apart.

It took three hours before *Illustrious* was able to head for Malta, proceeding at just 17 knots, a little more than half her usual speed. Those of her aircraft in the air either headed for Malta or ditched. The fighters were welcome additions to those based ashore on the island and their arrival was the first clue to most people that something had gone wrong.

Meanwhile, the crippled carrier was attacked again by another twenty-five dive-bombers, and here Boyd's refusal to flood the magazines was fully vindicated as her AA guns flashed into life. Her Fulmar fighters had refuelled at Hal Far, and returned to provide air cover, shooting down at least six Stukas.

It was not until 21.45 that evening that *Illustrious* finally limped into a darkened Grand Harbour.

Cunningham was probably one of the few naval commanders to appreciate so early in the war the value of having major fleet units operating with an aircraft carrier, so that she could benefit from the collective force of their AA fire. The truth may be either that the aerial attack really was so overwhelming that nothing could be done, or that tactics were still evolving and that the major fleet units were not close enough to provide the necessary cover. But there is the inescapable feeling that aircraft-carrier deck layouts of the day meant that two capable carriers would have been needed to provide the required level of fighter cover, something that was beyond the resources available to the Royal Navy so early in the war.

The *Illustrious* Blitz

Illustrious was to spend two weeks in Malta. The first two days were overcast with low cloud that kept the Axis aircraft away. The raids started on 13 January and became a daily occurrence after that, with the Luftwaffe and the Regia Aeronautica operating jointly to provide what became known in Malta as 'the *Illustrious* blitz'. At first, once the air-raid sirens sounded ashore, the ship's company uncovered the guns, while the dockyard workers and those of the ship's company not needed scrambled from their working place to the caves, in nearby Senglea, being used as air-raid shelters. Getting from deep in the bowels of a large warship to safety ashore was no easy task.

The air raids reached a new peak for Malta on 16 January, described by many as the first really heavy bombing raid. The Luftwaffe sent forty-four Stukas, seventeen Ju88s and ten Messerschmitt Me110s, escorted by ten Regia Aeronautica Fiat CR42 and some Macchi 200 fighters. The Stuka pilots dived through intense anti-aircraft fire, with many flying below the high fortress walls of Valletta to deliver their bombs accurately. This first attack took just a few minutes, but was followed within fifteen minutes by a second wave. *Illustrious* suffered yet another hit during the first attack, but near misses left the dockyard around her burning and cratered.

Aboard the carrier, the blasts of exploding bombs swept away the ladders, scaffolding and tarpaulins shrouding the ship. It was not just the intensity of the attacks, the bombs were heavier too, with the Stukas struggling to lift 2,500-lb bombs and taking ninety minutes to reach 10,000 feet. The bomb that hit the ship caused further damage, and three near misses fell into French Creek, flinging her against the Parlatorio Wharf.

The attack was not without losses for the Luftwaffe, which had ten aircraft shot down, with honours equally divided between the AA defences and the fighters.

After the raid, it was decided to take all non-essential personnel, about a thousand men, off the ship, leaving a skeleton crew aboard. Even the AA gunners went to the temporary accommodation at RAF Hal Far as the

Army wanted to test a new box barrage system, and found that the ship's AA fire got in the way.

There was some consolation that some ten aircraft had been shot down, without any corresponding losses amongst the Malta-based Hurricanes and Fulmars.

Away from the ship, those ashore had no idea of the progress being made in getting *Illustrious* seaworthy. It was not until the ship's company was recalled during the afternoon of 23 January that they realized she was ready. Under cover of darkness, with the ship darkened and some repair stages still hanging over her sides, she left the Grand Harbour quietly and secretly. The Governor, Sir William Dobbie, was holding a session of the Council of Malta, the island's governing body, when a servant entered and drew the blackout curtains before switching on the lights. Someone said, 'She's off – and safe.'

Illustrious reached Alexandria on 26 January, on the first stage in her journey to the still neutral United States and a complete refit at Norfolk, Virginia.

Chapter 10

Bringing the Enemy to Battle

On paper, in 1939 the Royal Navy's surface fleet was far superior in numbers to those of Germany and Italy combined, but it was overstretched, with operations in the Atlantic, the Mediterranean and a presence in the Indian Ocean and Far East; and it had convoys to protect. In the face of U-boats and surface raiders, the advantage in the vast expanses of the oceans lay with the predators. German and Italian convoy protection was limited to Norwegian waters and the Mediterranean, which increasingly resembled a maritime crossroads. German and Italian convoys sought to supply their forces in North Africa, plying north-south in the face of British air and naval attack, often using light forces and submarines based on Malta. British convoys sought to lift the siege that was starving Malta and, at first, supply British forces in North Africa and the Suez Canal Zone. While the Italian fleet had suffered a major blow after the raid on Taranto, it still presented a threat, and was supported by German and Italian air power that was vastly superior in both quantity and quality. Eventually, British supplies and reinforcements for North Africa had to take the lengthy route around the Cape of Good Hope and through the Suez Canal.

In February 1941, Force H raided the Gulf of Genoa, with *Ark Royal* taking part, and her aircraft bombing Leghorn and dropping mines off the naval base of La Spezia.

Still in the Mediterranean, the Germans managed to convince their Italian allies that the Royal Navy had just one battleship operational, which encouraged the Italians to send the battleship *Vittorio Veneto* to sea with an escort of cruisers in early 1941. By this time, the Royal Navy had three battleships in the Mediterranean, with the *Warspite* and *Valiant* joined by *Malaya*. *Illustrious* had departed for repairs in the United States and had been replaced by another new carrier, *Formidable*. She brought a new aircraft, the Fairey Albacore, supposedly an improvement on the Swordfish, but still a biplane, and prone to engine problems. She also had Fairey Fulmar fighters. Altogether, she had just twenty-seven aircraft: thirteen Fulmars, ten Albacores (only half having long-range tanks) and four Swordfish.

As with preparations for the Taranto operation, the encounter with the Italian fleet in the Battle of Cape Matapan raised the problem of confusing enemy agents in Alexandria. On 27 March 1941, many officers were seen to be going ashore with suitcases, awnings were kept spread and guests were invited to dinner. After dark, those ashore hastily rejoined their ships, awnings were furled and dinner was cancelled. The fleet sailed at 19.00.

At sea the following morning, at 06.00, *Formidable* mounted combat air patrols, anti-submarine patrols and sent off her reconnaissance aircraft. They didn't have long to wait. At 07.20, four cruisers and four destroyers were sighted by one aircraft, and nineteen minutes later another aircraft reported four cruisers and six destroyers. In fact, at this time, a British destroyer and cruiser force was being pursued by the Italians, led by the cruiser *Trieste*.

Anticipating action, *Formidable* had six Albacores of 826 Squadron ranged on deck from 08.30, and at 09.39, Admiral Cunningham ordered these into action, to attack the *Trieste* force of cruisers. By this time, the British cruisers, commanded by Rear Admiral Pridham-Wippell, were in trouble, outgunned by Italian heavy cruisers which were gaining on them, and within range of the heavy guns of the *Vittorio Veneto*. The Albacores arrived at 11.27, escorted by Fulmar fighters which managed to shoot down one of the two Junkers Ju88 fighter-bombers that had appeared, and drive off the other one. Pressing home their attack in the face of heavy Italian AA fire, they forced the battleship to break off the attack. A second strike of three Albacores and two Swordfish from 829 Squadron was sent before the first strike returned, keeping the decks clear for the returning aircraft. *Formidable* was attacked shortly after 12.45 by two Italian S79s, but was not hit by their torpedoes.

In between the attacks by the two waves of carrier-borne aircraft, RAF Blenheim bombers from Greece made four attacks on the Italian fleet, scoring a number of near misses as they bombed from high altitude, but no hits. Then, at 15.30, Lieutenant Commander Dalyell-Stead led 829 Squadron into the attack while the Fulmars distracted the AA gunners and lookouts by machine-gunning the ships. The lead aircraft dropped its torpedo 1,000 yards ahead of the *Vittorio Veneto* as she turned to starboard, only to be hit by the concentrated fire of her AA defences, crashing into the sea just before the torpedo hit the ship. The battleship was holed close to the port outer screw 15 feet below the waterline and within minutes her engines stopped. Rapid work by her damage-control parties saw her under way again at 17.00, at the reduced speed of 15 knots. Five minutes later, Lieutenant Commander Gerald Saunt left *Formidable* with six Albacores of 826 and two Swordfish of 829, while a Swordfish seaplane from *Warspite* re-established contact with the *Vittorio Veneto* at 18.20. In the gathering darkness, the carrier-borne aircraft, joined by two Swordfish from the naval air station at Maleme in Crete, struck at the Italian fleet, seriously damaging the heavy cruiser *Pola*.

It took the Italian admiral, Iachino, an hour to appreciate just how desperate was the plight of the *Pola*. Not expecting a night battle, he sent the heavy cruisers *Fiume* and *Zara*, with four destroyers, to her aid. Cunningham, meanwhile, had mistaken the radar trace of *Pola* for *Vittorio Veneto*. Before his ships could open fire, the two heavy cruisers and destroyers of the Italian rescue party blundered across the path of the British ships, and were hit by the combined 15-inch broadsides of the three battleships. Both cruisers were sunk, along with two of the four destroyers, and *Pola* herself was despatched by torpedoes from two British destroyers.

More than 900 Italian survivors were picked up by the British ships the next morning before German aircraft forced them to retire. In an act of gallantry, Cunningham signalled their position to Rome, allowing Italian ships to take over the rescue, despite the risk of exposing his own position.

Sink the *Bismarck*!

It was to be the German Navy's turn next, with the Fleet Air Arm again playing an important role in the hunt for and destruction of the German battleship *Bismarck*.

The Kriegsmarine's small force of battleships and battlecruisers presented a serious threat to the United Kingdom for the first three years of the Second World War, but there was to be no replay of the First World War Battle of Jutland – the Germans knew that they could not win such a confrontation. Instead, the threat came from the danger these ships presented to the convoys. Despite the loss of the *Konigsberg*, the Germans were not too concerned about aerial attack once the ships were at sea, appreciating that a fast-moving ship on the open sea presented a difficult target for bombers, while torpedo-bombers were vulnerable to heavy AA fire. The *Bismarck* and her sister ship, *Tirpitz*, were to be a major pre-occupation for the British for as long as the two ships presented a danger.

The first raiding cruise of the *Bismarck* and her escorting heavy cruiser, *Prinz Eugen*, was known to the Germans as Operation Rhine Exercise. The two ships left Gotenhafen in Germany on 18 May 1941, under the command of Admiral Gunther Lutjens. Anxious to avoid any encounters with the Home Fleet, with its northern base now at Scapa Flow in Orkney, Lutjens sought a route north of Iceland, but called first at Korsfjord, south of Bergen in occupied Norway. This would have been an opportunity for the ship to fill her fuel tanks, which had not been completely topped up before leaving Germany as a hose had given way, interrupting fuelling. But the opportunity was not taken which subsequently proved to be an incredible blunder.

Once at sea, the German ships were shadowed by the heavy cruisers *Suffolk* and *Norfolk*, making good use of their radar in heavy weather. Vice Admiral Holland took the battlecruiser *Hood* and the new, and not fully operational, battleship, *Prince of Wales*, to confront the Germans. On 24 May, the British intercepted the Germans and a classic naval gun battle broke out, during the course of which the *Hood*, with Holland aboard, exploded, with the loss of some 1,500 men, leaving just three survivors. The *Prince of Wales* was forced to break off the fight after receiving several heavy hits from the two German ships. Despite these setbacks, the British had managed to damage the *Bismarck*, hitting her three times and causing a fuel leak that forced Lutjens to break company with the *Prinz Eugen* and attempt to head for St Nazaire, with Brest as an alternative, in occupied France. These problems were compounded by battle damage having severed the connections with the ship's forward fuel tanks.

Despite her damage, the *Prince of Wales* joined *Suffolk* and *Norfolk* in shadowing the *Bismarck* throughout 24 May. That evening, at 22.30, nine Fairey Swordfish of 825 Squadron from the new carrier, *Victorious*, found the Bismarck and launched a torpedo attack. As the ship increased her speed to 27 knots and zigzagged, the Swordfish launched their torpedoes so that these were heading for the ship from different directions, with at least one hitting the ship, killing a warrant officer and injuring six ratings. This was followed by a brief gunnery exchange with the *Prince of Wales*, before this was broken off in the fading light.

On 25 May 1941, Vice Admiral Somerville left Gibraltar with Force H, which included the aircraft carrier *Ark Royal*, with 800, 808, 818 and 820 Squadrons embarked; the first two operated Fulmar fighters, 818 and 820 operated Swordfish.

Contact with the *Bismarck* was lost early on 26 May, but an RAF Catalina flying boat rediscovered her later that morning. In rough weather, fifteen Swordfish took off from *Ark Royal* in the early afternoon, while the cruiser *Sheffield* shadowed the German ship. Unfortunately, the Swordfish crews had been briefed that the only ship that they would see would be the *Bismarck* and, dropping out of the clouds, initially attacked *Sheffield* before realizing their mistake. Prompt evasive action by the cruiser and problems with the magnetic detonators on the torpedoes meant that no damage was done.

Again, in low cloud and with poor visibility, a further strike by fifteen Swordfish from *Ark Royal* was launched at 19.15, with the aircraft carrying torpedoes with contact detonators. Directed to the target by *Sheffield*, the aircraft had to return for further directions in the poor visibility, but on the second occasion the sound of *Bismarck*'s heavy AA fire told those aboard the British cruiser that the Swordfish had found their target. Aboard the battleship, Captain Lindemann attempted to zigzag once more, but first two torpedoes struck the ship forward, and then one struck aft, jamming the twin rudders and forcing the ship into a continuous turn to port. All of the Swordfish returned to the carrier.

During the night, British destroyers carrier out a torpedo attack, but failed to inflict any further serious damage on the stricken battleship. During the morning of 27 May, the battleships *Rodney* and *King George V* engaged the *Bismarck*, and within ninety minutes she was burning fiercely. Two cruisers attacked with torpedoes, but a further Swordfish attack had to be abandoned because of the danger of attacking while heavy shellfire was falling on the target from the British battleships.

Eventually, the Germans were forced to abandon ship. Many of her crew reached the water, but the cruiser *Dorsetshire* was obliged to cut short a rescue attempt after one of the survivors told his rescuers that U-boats were coming, so that just 115 of the 2,200 men aboard survived.

Helping the Russians

Shortly after the loss of the *Bismarck*, Germany invaded the Soviet Union in Operation Barbarossa. Overnight, the USSR moved from the status of a pariah state, an ally of Germany and partner in the occupation of Poland, to an ally of Britain. Despite the poor performance of the Soviet armed forces, especially the Soviet Navy, during the invasion, there was political pressure on the British 'to do something'. This fell entirely on the Royal Navy, since there was no opportunity for the Army to relieve the pressure on the Russians, and suitable targets were beyond the reach of RAF Bomber Command. The reluctant Commander-in-Chief, Home Fleet, Admiral Sir John Tovey, was urged by Winston Churchill to carry out an attack 'as a gesture in support of our Russian allies to create a diversion on the enemy's northern flank'. The Russians wanted an attack on German shipping.

The most obvious targets were north of the Arctic Circle, at the ports of Petsamo and Kirkenes, since an attack on the Baltic ports was out of the question. Just two ships were available: *Victorious*, with the Albacores of 827 and 828 Squadrons, and Fulmars of 809 Squadron, which would attack Kirkenes; and *Furious*, with Swordfish of 812 Squadron, Albacores of 817 Squadron and Fulmars of 800 Squadron, which would attack Petsamo.

This was not a rerun of the raid on Taranto, taking place as it did in broad daylight on 22 and 25 July 1941. The terrain around Kirkenes forced aircraft to fly high enough to encounter anti-aircraft fire on the run in to the targets, and indeed, good targets were to be scarce. Worse still, the aircraft from *Victorious* had to fly over a German hospital ship on the way to the target, and while they couldn't attack the hospital ship, it was able to warn the shore defences of their approach. In each case, the Germans were expecting the attackers and fighters were waiting. In return for the sinking of one cargo vessel of just 2,000 tons and the setting on fire of another at Kirkenes, *Victorious* lost thirteen aircraft. At Petsamo, there were no ships, just empty wharves for the torpedo-bombers to attack, and three aircraft were brought down. Worse still, forty-four aircrew were lost, seven of them killed and the rest taken prisoner.

Loss of *Ark Royal*

At this difficult early stage of the war, the loss of any major fleet unit was a disaster. In post-war years, the Royal Navy has devoted much time and attention to damage control, and even before this, during the war in the Pacific, good damage control did much to minimize the effects of Japanese Kamikaze attack. It can be argued that poor tactics resulted in the loss of several aircraft carriers during the first two or three years of the war, but that others were lost simply due to the fortunes of war.

The loss of HMS *Ark Royal* off Gibraltar, after being torpedoed by *U-81* on 13 November 1941 could be seen as sheer bad luck. Just one life was lost. The torpedo knocked out much of her machinery and left her dead in the water, a sitting duck awaiting a tow. The 'Ark' had led a charmed life as she would not have survived the treatment that the Germans and the Italians dealt *Illustrious*.

The Channel Dash

As the war progressed, the Fleet Air Arm had gained a reputation for effectiveness. Naval air power was something that could never again be dismissed out of hand.

Surface vessels still posed a threat, including the fast battlecruisers *Scharnhorst* and *Gneisenau*. In 1940, these ships accounted for twenty-two ships, totalling 116,000 tons, as they preyed on the North Atlantic convoys. The Royal Navy had forced them to take refuge at Brest, in occupied France, with the heavy cruiser *Priz Eugen*. Here they were subjected to the attentions of RAF Bomber Command, and although the size of bombs and bombing techniques used by the RAF at this stage meant that they were unlikely to be sunk, damage was inflicted. The German Navy's natural instinct was to bring the ships home, in an exercise named Operation Cerebus, at which stage, Hitler intervened. He ruled against taking the most obvious route, into the Atlantic and around the west of Ireland, and instead ordered the ships to take the shortest route, through the English Channel.

The British expected the three ships to be moved and had prepared contingency plans under the heading 'Operation Fuller'. A close watch was maintained on the three ships. In the event, the planning failed, mainly due to intense secrecy, so that too few people who were to have an important role in its implementation even knew of its existence. There were other factors, including a number of those involved playing everything strictly according to orders, a lack of initiative, poor communication between the

Admiralty and the Air Ministry, poor weather and technical failures, many of which could be ascribed to bad luck.

Bad luck played its part in the failure of the RAF to detect the breakout as the ships sailed from Brest, with technical failures hampering operations on 11 February 1942. When RAF fighter pilots discovered the ship, one pair maintained strict radio silence, wasting valuable time, although when the other pair radioed a warning, they were not believed. Bad weather grounded Coastal Command's torpedo-bombers in Scotland until it was almost too late, while secrecy meant that when they did arrive, it was with bombs rather than torpedoes. Thick fog meant that the heavy coastal artillery at Dover was unable to engage the German force.

It fell to a detachment of six Swordfish of 825 Squadron, based at Lee-on-Solent, to face the three ships, escorted as they were by a strong CAP of thirty Luftwaffe fighters, continuously refreshed out of a force of 280 aircraft assigned to the operation. Having been moved forward to Manston in Kent, they were put on standby on the afternoon of 12 February and were promised an escort of sixty Spitfires from Fighter Command.

In the gloom of a late winter afternoon, Lieutenant Commander Eugene Esmonde took his six aircraft into the air. A breakdown in communications meant just ten Spitfires turned up. In poor light, they found the three warships and their escort of ten destroyers, several of which were larger than any of their British counterparts. The lumbering Swordfish were caught in a hail of fire from the fighters above and the warships below, but they pressed home a torpedo attack. His aircraft badly damaged as pieces were knocked off it in the heavy fire, Esmonde managed to keep the aircraft airborne long enough to launch his torpedo before crashing into the sea. His target, the *Prinz Eugen*, managed to avoid the torpedo. All six Swordfish were shot down, with the loss of Esmonde and twelve others out of the eighteen naval airmen involved in the attack. Esmonde was awarded a posthumous VC.

Having originally planned to have 300 aircraft available for Operation Fuller, the British now panicked and 700 aircraft were put on standby. The only damage suffered by the ships as they raced for home was when *Gneisenau* hit a mine as the trio approached Kiel.

Sink the *Tirpitz*

If the definition of a truly successful deterrent is one that never has to be used, the German battleship *Tirpitz* can probably count amongst the most successful. This ship was never involved in a surface action and spent most of her short life hiding in Norwegian fjords, but she was a constant thorn in the flesh of the British. She suffered the attentions of the best that the Fleet Air Arm and the RAF could put into the air.

Tirpitz sailed from Wilhelmshaven for Norway on 16 January 1942, where she was poised to threaten the Allied convoys making the long and hazardous passage round the North Cape to the Soviet Union. Her first operational sortie was on 9 March 1942, when Vice Admiral Ciliax took her to sea to destroy convoy PQ12 bound for Russia. Having missed the convoy in bad weather, *Tirpitz* and her three escorting destroyers were discovered by the Royal Navy and attacked by Albacore torpedo-bombers of 817 and 832 Squadrons flying from *Victorious*. The ship escaped unscathed, but Hitler ruled that she must stay in port if there was any risk of her encountering a British carrier.

On 4 July 1942, she moved her berth, causing Norwegian Resistance to believe that she was being readied for sea. When this was communicated to the Allies, it persuaded Admiral Dudley Pound to order the Russia-bound convoy PQ17 to scatter, with disastrous results as merchantmen were left at the mercy of U-boats and the Luftwaffe. A more effective sortie by the ship was in late 1943, when she accompanied the battlecruiser *Scharnhorst* and ten destroyers north to bombard shore installations at Spitzbergen on 6 September. After this, she was moored in the Altenfjord, where she was attacked by British X-craft on 22 September, putting her machinery and main armament out of action for six months.

In the far north of Norway, the Altenfjord was undoubtedly the safest berth any ship has ever enjoyed. The steep sides of the high mountains on either side meant that attacking aircraft could not see the ship until it was too late, by which time they were in clear view of her AA armament. During an attack, aircraft had to dive steeply and at all times were in real danger of flying into the sides of the fjord. Even so, the Fleet Air Arm mounted nine attacks against the ship and RAF Bomber Command mounted another seven, mainly flying from airfields in the Soviet Union.

The heaviest attack was on 3 April 1944, in Operation Tungsten, when aircraft were flown from the carriers *Victorious, Furious, Emperor, Fencer, Pursuer* and *Searcher*. The raid was carried out by Barracudas of 827, 829, 830 and 831 Naval Air Squadrons (NAS). A strong fighter force was sent to provide the essential cover against German fighter defences, with a mixed force of Seafires, Hellcats, Corsairs, Wildcats and Martlets provided by 800, 801, 804, 880, 881, 882, 896, 898, 1834, 1836 and 1840 NAS. Other squadrons remained close to the carriers, providing anti-submarine cover. Fourteen bombs from this force hit the ship, causing more than 400 casualties, but failed to sink her due to the maximum weight of bomb employed being no more than 500-lb. Nevertheless, the attack caused enough damage to put the *Tirpitz* out of action for three months.

With such a large ship, so well protected, different tactics were needed. On 15 September 1944, Lancaster bombers of the RAF's 617 Squadron damaged the *Tirpitz* using 12,000-lb 'Tallboy' bombs, damaging her so severely that she could not be repaired *in situ*. She was moved south to Tromsø, where bombers operating from Britain were able to reach her, and on 12 November 1944, 617's Lancasters attacked again, using 'Tallboys' once more. This time three of the large bombs hit the ship, causing her to capsize, trapping a thousand of her crew below decks. It was not until after the war had ended that it was discovered that the ship had not been taken to Tromsø for repairs, but to act as a large and supposedly unsinkable fortress.

Chapter 11

The Urgent Need for More Flight Decks

Desperation led to consideration of some measures that were clearly impractical. Early in the war, one idea investigated was the creation of a large airbase made of ice in mid-Atlantic. It was found that by mixing ice with a concoction of wood pulp, known as pykrete by its inventor, Hermann Mark, an Austrian-born chemist, the ice lost much of its brittleness. Tests proved that pykrete was weight for weight as strong as concrete, and did not shatter on being hit by a projectile. Yet the original concept of a simple iceberg had developed to the stage that the USN estimated that the volume of steel needed to freeze sufficient pykrete in a single winter was going to be greater than the amount needed to build a comparable ship of steel. The project was abandoned.

Originally intended purely as a stop-gap measure while the escort carriers were awaited, for various reasons the merchant aircraft carriers took time to arrive, despite the fact that had they been present earlier, the massive convoy losses of 1942 could have been avoided. Another interim measure was the use of catapult-armed merchant ships or CAM-ships, although, as with the fighters flown off lighters towed by destroyers during the First World War, these had the drawback that the aircraft could only make a single sortie and then had to be ditched. The other problem was, of course, that adequate fighter cover really demanded combat air patrols, or CAP, to be flown constantly above the convoy. Until the MAC-ships were available, the convoy war went badly against Britain.

The CAM-ships had aircraft provided by and flown by the Royal Air Force for the most part, but the Royal Navy did fit out four 'fighter catapult ships', and like the CAM-ships these carried Sea Hurricane fighters which were ditched after making their one sortie, with the pilot baling out and hoping to be picked up afterwards. Unfortunately, the first such launch, on 11 January 1941 from *Pegasus*, failed to down an enemy aircraft.

The irony is that some of the aircraft carriers lost in the early years might have been better used as escort carriers, rather than put into situations where they were at the mercy of enemy aircraft, as happened with the small *Hermes*.

Merchant aircraft carriers, or MAC-ships, were always either tankers or grain ships because these ships always loaded and discharged cargo by means of a pipeline, with no hatches to open. The tankers could carry three Swordfish while the grain ships could carry four as it was possible to convert one of the holds aft into a small hangar, into which aircraft could be struck down with a hoist. Once the superstructure of these ships had been cut down and converted into an island on the starboard side, with their boiler uptakes diverted to the island, a flight deck could be laid over their holds. The grain ships had a shorter flight deck – at between 413 and 424 feet – than the 460 feet of the tankers, but the extra length of the tanker deck was no advantage as it was offset by having aircraft parked on the deck, reducing the take-off run. Regardless of the type of ship, the width of the flight deck was a standard 62 feet. Aboard the tankers, the absence of a hangar naturally made maintenance work difficult, while it was unpleasant and even dangerous in bad weather, and sometimes impossible.

With the benefit of hindsight, it seems almost criminal that work on the MAC-ships did not proceed more quickly, and that such vessels were not available until early 1943 rather than within months of war breaking out. The reason for the lengthy delay was that too few at the Admiralty believed the concept would work. The Naval Air Division convinced itself that 12-knot ships would be too slow to operate aircraft. The Director of Naval Construction felt that it would take more than a year just to design such ships, obviously expecting everything to be just right. The Admiralty and the Ministry of War Transport agreed that it would be far too dangerous for aircraft to land and take off on a steel flight deck running over tanks containing thousands of tons of highly inflammable fuel.

This impasse was overcome by the director of Merchant Shipbuilding, Sir James Lithgow, member of the famous British shipbuilding family, who sketched out a rough design using the back of an envelope.

'I have two ships about to be built which can be converted without undue delay,' he claimed. 'I am prepared to do this provided I am not interfered with by the Admiralty.'

Work on converting the first two MAC-ships, *Empire MacAlpine* and *Empire MacAndrew*, started in June 1942, and by October work had started on ten more, although the original plan to have thirty-two such ships was cut back to nineteen as escort carriers started to arrive. The first two ships were both grain ships, but the October batch included the first tanker, *Rapana*. The simpler tanker conversion took much less time and ships were converted in as little as five months. This in itself seems rather long given the comparative simplicity of the conversion, and that the first American escort carrier, the USS *Long Island* underwent a more thorough conversion in three months. The tanker MAC-ships could carry 90 per cent of their pre-conversion cargo, giving up some of their hold capacity for aircraft fuel, but the figure for the grain ships was lower with one hold no longer available as it was used as the aircraft hangar.

To suit the capacity of the ships, the Swordfish for these ships were deployed as flights of three or four aircraft each, and belonged to Nos 836 and 860 Squadrons, based at HMS *Shrike*, RNAS Maydown. It had originated as a satellite of HMS *Gannet*, RNAS Eglinton, just outside Londonderry in Northern Ireland, but achieved its own independent status at the beginning of 1944. The two squadrons were known as the MAC-ship Wing, and of these 836 was the larger squadron, manned by Royal Navy personnel, while 860 was manned by members of the Royal Netherlands Navy, who operated from two Dutch MAC-ships, MV *Acavus* and *Gadila*. Each MAC-ship flight had a lettered suffix, so that the first flight to be formed within 836 was No. 836A, and so on. Eventually, when at full strength, with half-a-dozen spare flights ashore at Maydown in County Londonderry, 836 had no less than ninety-two aircraft, beating even the total of sixty-three for No. 700, the wartime parent squadron for the catapult flights aboard the Royal Navy's battleships and cruisers. Unlike No. 700, which existed for administrative convenience, No. 836 had a commanding officer, although despite the Squadron's huge size and tremendous responsibilities, Ransford Slater still only held the rank of lieutenant commander, the equivalent of a major in the Army; in the Royal Air Force, squadrons could be, and in the case of Bomber and Coastal Commands usually were, led by a wing commander, the equivalent of a lieutenant colonel. Slater himself was very much a working flight commander, leading 836A and so taking his share of time at sea.

Maydown was a convenient base, with ships' flights disembarked to the air station as the convoy approached the Clyde. On the other side of the Atlantic, the MAC-ships used Halifax, Nova Scotia, and their aircraft disembarked to the Royal Canadian Air Force base at nearby Dartmouth.

From May 1943, until VE-Day, MAC-ships made 323 crossings of the Atlantic and escorted 217 convoys, of which just one was successfully attacked. The Swordfish they carried flew 4,177 patrols and searches, an average of thirteen per crossing, or one per day at average convoy speed. Usually, the mere sighting of an aircraft was enough to force any U-boat to submerge. No confirmed kills of U-boats can be attributed to the aircraft carried by the MAC-ships, but on the other hand, and what really matters, was that there were no instances of any ship being sunk in a convoy protected by a MAC-ship. None of the MAC-ships was sunk while on duty.

The slow and lumbering Swordfish was to be the ideal aircraft for convoy protection duties, but at first it was not the only contender. The Fleet Air Arm also took a serious interest in the Vought-Sikorsky Chesapeake, a monoplane known to the wits on the squadrons as 'Cheesecakes'. The

Chesapeake looked much more like a modern warplane, with a variable-pitch propeller and a retractable undercarriage, which when lowered also acted as an airbrake, important for an aircraft originally designed as a dive-bomber. After three months being assessed for the anti-submarine role by No. 811 Squadron at Lee-on-Solent, the then home of naval aviation on the south coast between Portsmouth and Southampton, the Admiralty decided that the Chesapeake would not be suitable for operation from escort carriers. The main reason given for this decision was that the engine was not powerful enough, although at least one naval aviator who had flown the aircraft maintained that it had shown no shortcomings, and that reverting to the Swordfish was like 'trying to fly a truck'.

Aboard a MAC-ship, a flight of three aircraft would have three crews each with a pilot, observer and TAG, as well as a petty officer in charge of the maintainers, who included four riggers and fitters to look after air-frames and engines, three electricians, including one who was a specialist able to look after the ASV radar, and two air mechanics Ordnance (AMOs) to take care of the weaponry. There would also be a batsman – possibly more necessary than ever given the limitations of the MAC-ship flight decks – an air staff officer (ASO) responsible for liaison with the convoy commodore and escort commander, as well as briefing the aircrew, and usually a naval surgeon as well.

The need to keep radio silence except in extreme emergencies meant that Morse communications were the norm between aircraft and between aircraft and ships. It was important that signals were brief and so the instructions to aircrew, usually from the convoy commodore's ship, were in code with each pattern of search or reconnaissance assigned its own 'reptile' code name. This not only kept instructions brief, it also maintained some degree of security if the instruction had to be amended while the aircraft was in the air. These patrol patterns were suitable for one aircraft at a time, reflecting the reality that few aircraft were available. Even if all aircraft were fully operational, the need to rearm and refuel meant that not all could be in the air at one time. Only two patrols, code-named Cobra and Viper, could be used by more than one aircraft.

On a convoy, the merchant ships were controlled by the convoy commodore, usually a senior Royal Navy or Royal Naval Reserve officer, including many who had come out of retirement, even dropping a rank or two, to provide their experience for this demanding and important role. The commodore's ship would be a merchant ship, usually steaming as the leading vessel in the central column of the convoy. The warships providing the escort would be controlled by the senior officer (escort), known as the SOE, in close liaison with the commodore. Flags and Aldis lamps were the preferred means of communication, but VHF radio, which could not be picked up by the enemy at a range of more than a few miles, could also be used.

The difficulties of operating safely and efficiently from a MAC-ship were such that Slater insisted that all flight commanders had to have made at least one MAC-ship crossing before being appointed, although in the beginning this rule must have been breached before it could be honoured.

No. 836 and its Dutch sister squadron 860 used Swordfish IIs fitted with radar. This was not the only innovation as the aircraft were all fitted with underwing racks for the firing of rocket projectiles (RPs). Four RPs could be installed under each lower wing and a single RP was enough to sink a U-boat, with pilots trained to dive at an angle of 20 degrees towards a U-boat and fire their rockets from a height of 800 feet. The only drawback of the RP system was that it required a cloud ceiling of at least 1,000 feet, and if the cloud was lower, depth charges had to be used. This must have posed problems for aircraft actually in the air when the weather changed as the convoy made its steady progress across the Atlantic. Depth charges also remained necessary for U-boats that managed to dive before the aircraft could catch them, but many U-boats spent some time on the surface, both to recharge batteries and also because a U-boat could overtake a convoy on the surface to get ahead into a good position for an attack. A U-boat capable of 20 knots on the surface could only sustain 7 knots submerged, generally too little to keep up with a convoy, although the U-boat packs were often spread out ahead of a convoy, waiting. Part of the role of the aircraft carried aboard MAC-ships and escort carriers was to force the U-boats to remain submerged, while U-boat commanders preferred to wait until they were in a position to attack a convoy before submerging.

The first successful RP attack against a U-boat had been in May 1943, when Sub Lieutenant Horrocks flying a Swordfish from the escort carrier HMS *Archer* sank *U-752*.

The Escort Carriers

The struggle to overcome the shortage of aircraft carriers continued on both sides of the Atlantic. It is a popular misconception that the first British escort carrier, HMS *Audacity*, influenced the development of the escort or auxiliary carrier, but this is wrong. The first escort carrier, also known initially as an auxiliary carrier by the United States Navy, was the USS *Long Beach*, which was commissioned into the USN on 2 June 1941, followed shortly after by HMS *Audacity*, on 20 June. The two ships differed considerably, with the most significant difference being that the American ship had a hangar.

The origin of this new class of ship was that the American Moore-Macormick Line was building a substantial number of merchantmen on a standard hull known to them as the C3. Standardization of merchant hulls had been an innovation introduced by the United States Maritime Commission in order to dramatically increase the output of American shipyards, which between the wars had seen launchings fall to as little as fifty merchantmen a year. In 1940, after the fall off France, launching rose to 200 ships a year. These figures were to be exceeded later once the simpler utility 'Liberty' ships were introduced as the C3, and the other standardized hulls at first favoured by the MC proved to be too complex for high rates of production, especially since wartime labour was less experienced and less skilled than that available in peacetime.

Meanwhile, the United States Navy had purchased a number of Moore-Macormick Line C3 merchant vessels both for their own use and that of the Royal Navy, with the first of these, the *Mormacmail*, a break-bulk dry cargo ship, immediately put into dockyard hands for conversion to a carrier. The President of the United States insisted that the work be completed within three months, far less time than that taken for the supposedly simpler MAC-ship conversions. This was despite the fact that the ship was a 'one-off', effectively a prototype, so the use of prefabricated and standardized components that was to be a feature of the later escort carrier programme was not an option.

In the case of the *Mormacmail*, conversion consisted of removing the superstructure and building a hangar aft with a wooden flight deck over the top of this continuing forward for a total length of about 360 feet. A navigating bridge was built under the flight deck. There was no island superstructure, while the ship's diesel propulsion meant that exhaust gases could be discharged horizontally. A single lift provided access to the hangar, itself just 120 feet long, while there were arrester wires aft. For self-defence, the ship had just two single 3-inch guns provided forward and a single 4-inch aft on the quarter deck. Ample provision of tanks for 100,000 gallons of fuel was also made during the conversion, allowing the ship to provide fuel for escorting destroyers. The resulting carrier had a maximum speed of 16 knots. Aircraft capacity was originally intended to be twenty-one aircraft, but in practice this was reduced to sixteen on operations, althought as a transport a far higher figure was possible. Once in service, it was soon clear that the flight deck was far too short, especially given the lack of catapults and the low speed of the ship, so this was extended by a further 60 feet to 420 feet. The bridge was replaced by two sponsons to port and starboard, and five 20mm Oerlikon guns added to improve air defence, although twin 20mm guns were soon added and the aft 4 inch replaced by another 3 inch. After a year in service, a radar mast was added.

If the first American escort carrier was the result of a planned purchase with a programme of conversions very much in mind, by contrast the first British ship was the result of a grudging acceptance of the need for air power at sea. In March 1940, the Royal Navy had succeeded in capturing the *Hannover*, a fast refrigerated cargo ship built for the Norddeutscher Line in 1939, when she was in the West Indies. In January 1941, permission was given for her conversion to an aircraft carrier. A contrast with *Long*

Island was the provision of just 10,000 gallons of aviation fuel. The ship was capable of only 15 knots. Armament was a 4-inch gun at the stern, with four 2-pdrs forward and aft at the edge of the flight deck, while four 20mm singles were also mounted forward but behind the forward 2-pdrs. There were also a number of Hotchkiss light machine guns and, for anti-submarine protection, four depth-charge projectors near the stern.

Commissioned into the Royal Navy as HMS *Audacity* on 20 June 1941, the ship was quickly deployed on convoy escort duties on the route between the UK and Gibraltar, which included running the gauntlet of aerial attack by Focke Wulf Fw200 Condor maritime-reconnaissance aircraft based in occupied France. Six Grumman Wildcats, known initially to the Royal Navy as Martlets, were provided, with no anti-submarine protection at all. *Audacity* was to survive for just three operations, but her performance was convincing enough. On her three convoys with just six aircraft, they managed to shoot down, damage or drive-off nine Focke Wulf Fw200 maritime-reconnaissance aircraft and report nine U-boats to the escorting destroyers. No doubt the threat of aerial attack was the greater menace, but it seems entirely unsurprising in these circumstances that when the ship did meet her end while on her third convoy escort duty on 20 December 1941, escorting a UK-bound convoy off Portugal, it was to torpedoes from *U-751*.

Aboard *Audacity*, flying operations had been tough. There were just two arrester wires compared with the six on the larger British fleet carriers, of which the second had no hydraulic retardation. If caught it brought aircraft and pilot to an abrupt and brutal halt, but at least it was better than continuing down the flight deck to the crash barrier, which would damage an aircraft, at the very least wrecking the airscrew, and possibly making a mess of the pilot as well. That, of course, was assuming that the barrier was hit head on, but it was not unknown on a pitching, rolling deck for an aircraft to catch the barrier with its undercarriage and somersault over it, with fatal results. Aboard *Audacity*, of course, the forward part of the flight deck was likely always to have aircraft parked, with no hangar deck to be struck down into.

Life for the maintainers was also far from ideal. As on the MAC-ships, they had to maintain aircraft in the open without shelter from the wind and the sea, often wet from rain and spray. The damp sea air was devastating to aircraft left in the open, jamming throttles, and corroding gun wells and the electrics. It was bad enough in daylight, but at night the maintainers had to struggle to continue working with torches masked by blue filters while a shipmate shielded this tell-tale light with his coat.

On the other hand, having been converted in a hurry, the accommodation aboard had standards of comfort quite out of place aboard a warship, especially for the officers, with comfortable staterooms which there had been no time to remove.

The aircraft were quite the opposite and a revelation to British naval pilots accustomed to aircraft that were at best obsolescent. The Grumman Wildcat, known at first to the Fleet Air Arm as the Martlet until standardization of nomenclature after US entry into the war, was a thoroughbred carrier fighter, described as 'tough and tireless'. On *Audacity*'s final voyage, Sub Lieutenant Eric 'Winkle' Brown's aircraft had a bent airscrew, but he still managed to chase a Focke Wulf Fw200 Condor into thick cloud, until suddenly he found the aircraft heading straight towards him. Brown, who favoured the head-on attack to compensate for the Martlet's lack of speed, just managed to press the firing button, sending a stream of bullets into the Condor, shattering the windscreen and blasting bits off the aircraft's nose, before he had to pull up to avoid a head-on collision, only just managing to miss the aircraft's tail. He turned back to see the aircraft hit the water so hard that the port wing was torn off.

The next British escort came from the United States, where one of the six C3 hulls purchased by the US Navy was converted. Originally laid down as the *Mormacland*, HMS *Archer* was designated BAVG-1, 'British aircraft escort vessel', before her transfer under Lend-Lease and commissioning into the Royal Navy on 17 November 1941. A hangar occupied a quarter of the ship's overall length, with the wooden flight deck continued forward on open girders to a point just short of the forecastle. Another difference between *Archer* and the two earlier ships was that she had a hydraulic catapult, known to the Royal Navy at the time as an accelerator, forward, as well as the usual arrester gear aft. A small platform was fitted to the starboard side of the flight-deck well forward for navigation and air control. Although designed to carry 85,000 gallons of aviation fuel, the Royal Navy objected to the US practice of replacing used fuel with sea water and determined that permanent ballast be carried to enhance stability, so that her fuel capacity was reduced to around 40,000 gallons.

The British habit of refining the escort carrierss sent to them by the USN caused considerable irritation, as the USN estimated that there were delays of between twenty-four and thirty weeks between delivery of a ship to the RN and its operational availability. The way in which the hulls of the escort carriers were broken up into watertight compartments was also regarded as being below British standards. One result was that the Americans reproached the British for making poor use of the carriers supplied at some sacrifice to the USN's own interests. The question was, of course, whether the risk to the crews of the carriers, or the risk to merchant shipping and escort vessels on the convoys lacking air cover, was the greater.

The outcome of the British alterations to the escort carriers was that these ships were not available on the North Atlantic until March 1943. Even then the first ship was the USS *Bogue*, although she was joined by HMS *Biter* in April and by *Archer* in May. By June, there were four escort carriers operating, and even this small number sufficed to make enough of an impression on the 'Atlantic gap' that the U-boats were forced to change their tactics and start looking for victims in the less heavily patrolled waters of the South Atlantic.

Defensive armament aboard *Archer* consisted of three US-pattern 4-inch guns mounted with one aft and another on the forecastle, while there were also fourteen 20mm Oerlikon guns in single mountings in seven positions on each side of the ship, and two twin 20mm on either side of the flight deck aft. In late 1942, the 4-inch guns were replaced by British weapons of the same calibre and two twin 40mm Bofors installed the following year. Also in 1942, the flight deck was lengthened to 440 feet. The ship's Achilles heel was her machinery, a complex arrangement of four diesel engines driving a single shaft that proved cumbersome and unreliable.

While the escort carriers were awaited, convoys were being mauled by U-boats. Allied merchant shipping losses in the Atlantic and the North Sea soared from 2,451, 663 tons in 1940 and 2,214, 408 tons in 1941 to 5,366,973 tons in 1942, when these ships were so desperately needed. The German *Kriegsmarine* had entered the war at a disadvantage, having not expected war to break out until 1944–5, and was far from ready. Most important of all, it had started the war with a fairly small U-boat strength of just fifty-nine submarines, but by 1942, U-boats were coming into service at an increasing rate. The impact of the escort carriers and of improved maritime-reconnaissance aircraft could be seen the following year, 1943. After June 1943, except for July, when 136,106 tons of shipping was lost, no other month saw more than 50,000 tons lost. The year end figure was a total of 1,764,202 tons, a decrease of more than 67 per cent over the previous year. By the end of 1944, the annual total of Allied shipping lost to the U-boats had slumped to 293,624 tons.

By this time, *Archer* was in service and to her credit one of her Swordfish became the first aircraft to sink a U-boat using rocket fire in May 1943. Even so, her engine troubles remained and she was laid up as a stores ship in August 1943 and decommissioned in March 1945.

Despite considerable experience of aircraft-carrier design on both sides of the Atlantic, the right configuration was also slightly difficult to establish at first. The solution should have been clear enough: simply build a scaled-down and utilitarian version of a full-sized carrier, with arrester wires, catapults, hangars and island. The crippling and unsustainable losses of 1942 could have been much reduced, if not avoided altogether, had conversions started earlier. If a dozen of the merchantmen lost in 1942 had been taken up earlier from trade and converted, it would have eased pressure on wartime production and the condition of the civilian population in the UK, and saved the lives of countless seafarers. It could even have seen the war end up to a year earlier as Germany struggled to provide yet more U-boats, and drained the other services of supplies.

The tide began to turn with the next batch of escort carriers, known to the British as the Avenger-class. Initially this was to have been a class of five ships, *Archer*, *Avenger*, *Biter*, *Charger* and *Dasher*, but the United States Navy, struggling to meet both its own increased wartime demand for naval airmen and also much of that of the Royal Navy, understandably decided to retain *Charger* to provide carrier-deck training for the new generation of Fleet Air Arm pilots.

The Avenger-class set the pattern for succeeding escort carriers in many ways, with small starboard islands for navigation and air control, and radar for both air and surface threats. Once again, in Royal Navy service the fuel storage was reduced to 36,000 gallons primarily on safety grounds. Built on the C3 merchant hulls, the four Avenger-class carriers were commissioned into the Royal Navy between March and July 1942. Armament consisted of three 4-inch guns and nineteen 19mm. On arrival in the UK, their flight decks were lengthened to 440 feet.

The first, *Avenger*, had the distinction of escorting the earliest of the Arctic convoys to have an escort carrier, PQ18, and carried Hawker Sea Hurricane fighters as well as Fairey Swordfish for reconnaissance and anti-submarine work. The Arctic convoys needed protection from aerial attack as well as from submarines, while the new German battleship *Tirpitz*, moored for most of the time in a Norwegian fjord, was a constant threat, able to outgun and outrun any convoy escort. All three ships also supported the Allied invasion of North Africa, Operation Torch.

With so few escort carriers at first, the casualty rate was considerable. *Avenger* was sunk the month after Operation Torch on 15 December 1942, when she became yet another victim to U-boat attack. The carrier was torpedoed by *U-155* off Gibraltar, her thin merchantman hull offering little protection, for the torpedo set off a fire from which explosions followed and just seventeen of her crew of 500 survived. The disaster seems to have fitted the American cynics view of the escort carrier designation of CVE as standing for 'combustible, vulnerable, expendable', since hasty construction – it was intended that they could be converted back to merchant ships after the war – and poor armour protection meant that they were vulnerable in battle.

Yet, despite all the effort put into making the escort carriers safer for the Royal Navy, one disaster put in doubt the value of the British modifications. While the fate of *Dasher* was not as costly in lives as that of *Avenger*, it was tragic enough, especially since it was not due to enemy action. Following the North African landings and convoy escort duty in the North Atlantic, *Dasher* was blown apart by an aviation fuel explosion while in the Firth of Clyde on 27 March 1943. Her loss has been the cause of some speculation, including sabotage by German agents, but a fuel explosion caused either by a leak or during aircraft refuelling has become regarded as the most likely cause.

Once again, an escort carrier had lived up to the American jibe about being 'combustible, vulnerable, expendable'. The ship exploded into an inferno and only the bows were unaffected. The ship's commanding officer had announced shore leave over the tannoy and many of the crew were below decks washing and shaving ready for a 'run ashore' once she returned to port, when there was a massive explosion below decks, hurling the aircraft lift, weighing 2 tons, 60 feet into the air. Fires broke out detonating the anti-aircraft ammunition which in turn tore holes in her hull and in just three minutes she had sunk. Out of a ship's company of 528, no less than 379 were either killed by the explosion, trapped by the fires or died before they could be picked up.

The only one of this batch of carriers to survive the war was *Biter* which, after being returned to the USN in April 1945, was immediately passed on to the French Navy, becoming the *Dixmude*.

British shipyards were by this time busy building escort vessels for the convoys, often working under heavy air attack with those on the south and east coasts especially vulnerable. There was also much repair work to be done, especially on the west coast ports that were used for convoys to turn round. The ability of American shipyards to mass produce ships on standard hulls, using many prefabricated parts, meant that setting up a duplicate production line on the eastern side of the Atlantic was unnecessary. The Lend-Lease terms also made these ships attractive to a nation that was bankrupting itself – effectively the United Kingdom had run out of foreign exchange by the end of 1940 – by the demands of the war, but the Lend-Lease traffic was not one-way, for in what has sometimes been referred to as 'reverse lend-lease', British- and Canadian-built corvettes were transferred to the United States Navy for convoy escort duties.

There were to be a small number of British-built or converted escort carriers, because the Admiralty believed that riveted construction was better suited to the demands of the Arctic convoys to the Soviet Union than the welded construction favoured by the Americans. In fact, US-built escort carriers do not seem to have suffered unduly from the low temperatures and violent seas.

One of the first British-built ships was HMS *Activity*, converted from the fast refrigerated cargo ship *Telemachus* before she was completed. She was one of the few escorts to have a steel flight deck, but lacked catapults and also suffered from having a short hangar, less than 100 feet in length, that limited her capacity to just ten aircraft, while just 20,000 gallons of aviation fuel were carried. Commissioned late in 1942, she was used initially for deck landing training before seeing service on convoys to Russia and on the North Atlantic, while after the end of the war in Europe she ferried aircraft to the Far East.

The British received first the US Bogue-class, which became their Attacker-class, and then the similar Ameer-class, sometimes referred to as the Ruler-class. The impressive output of American shipyards, part of the 'arsenal of democracy', meant that while these vessels were being built, along with hundreds of wartime utility 'Liberty' merchant ships, the Independence-class light carriers, based on cruiser hulls and the purpose-designed and built Essex-class fleet carriers were also produced. It was not until the end of the war that the British light fleet carriers, the Colossus-class, began to appear, based on a design that could be built by yards without a tradition of warship building, but even so, a purpose-designed carrier.

The shortage of flight decks felt by the three carrier-operating navies during the Second World War resulted in some unusual compromises. One of these was that the British fast armoured carrier, HMS *Victorious*, second ship of the successful Illustrious-class, went on loan to the United States Navy. This was after she had spent much of the winter of 1942/1943 being refitted at the Norfolk Navy Yard. She then went 'on loan' to the United States Navy, being given the temporary name of USS *Robin*, until later relieved by the American interpretation of the fast carrier, the USS *Essex*, leadship of the class of the same name with no less than twenty-five large carriers in all. The *Robin*, alias *Victorious*, operated with the US Pacific Fleet, and no doubt helped to improve interoperability between the two navies, something which was a matter of some concern. In fact, for a period after the Royal Navy returned to eastern waters, HMS *Illustrious* and the USS *Saratoga* operated together for the same reason, and also to ensure that the Royal Navy could get used to the concept of massed air attacks using a combination of fighters and bombers, and with ships from more than one carrier.

There were four more all-British escort carriers, the *Pretoria Castle*, the two Nairana-class ships *Nairana* and *Vindex*, and *Campania*, the latter resurrecting a name from the First World War.

The urgency of providing more carriers must have been very much in mind when the Admiralty agreed that the *Pretoria Castle*, a pre-war Union Castle liner sailing between the UK and South Africa, which had been converted into an armed merchant cruiser, could be taken over for further conversion into an aircraft carrier. Commissioned in April 1943, she was to be the largest escort carrier in service with the Royal Navy, at 19,650 tons standard displacement, and with a full-length hangar and steel flight deck with a single catapult forward, although the design was hampered by having just a single lift forward, close to the small island, that gave problems in handling aircraft. Armament included two twin 4-inch guns aft, plus ten twin 20mm Oerlikons and four quadruple 2-pdrs – although much time must have been wasted and availability of the ship considerably reduced by the order that the 2-pdrs were only to be used while in the escort-carrier role, and that when used as a training carrier they had to be replaced by eight single 20mm Oerlikons. Aircraft totalled twenty-one, usually fifteen torpedo-bomber-reconnaissance aircraft, usually the trusty Swordfish, and six fighters.

Nairana and the similar *Vindex* were both converted from fast refrigerated cargo ships, and again had a full-length hangar and steel flight deck, although both lacked catapults, and once again there was just a single lift. Smaller than *Pretoria Castle* at 13,825 tons, they nevertheless had the same 21-aircraft capacity. Aviation fuel capacity was one of the highest for British escorts at 52,000 gallons, which enabled *Nairana* to keep her escort vessels 'topped up' when she acted in the hunter-killer, anti-submarine role in the Atlantic in 1944–5. Both ships commissioned in December 1943. It was an indication of just how adequate convoy protection had become during the last eighteen months of the war that escort carriers could be sent on 'hunter-killer' missions that had been so dangerous that the Royal Navy had lost its fleet carrier HMS *Courageous* on one such operation just a fortnight after war had broken out in Europe. The differences were, of course, that the hunter-killer operations towards the end of the war, that followed the successful US experience of this type of operation in the mid and South Atlantic, enjoyed far greater escort-vessel protection for the carrier, and constant patrols by radar-equipped Swordfish. Improved intelligence following the British breaking of the German Enigma codes coupled with high-frequency radio-direction finding also meant that information on the whereabouts of U-boats was far better than at the beginning of the war.

The final British ship, *Campania*, was similar to *Nairana*, but with a slightly longer and wider hull, despite a lower tonnage at 12,450 tons, although only eighteen aircraft could be carried. The first British escort to have an action information organization, AIO, she was commissioned in March 1944. Her early duties were on the Russian convoys, but instead of heading to the Far East after the German surrender, she was deployed to the Baltic. Unlike many of the other escorts, she remained in service post-war until going into reserve in 1952 and then being scrapped in 1955.

Having a single lift presented many problems. The one most frequently encountered was that of sometimes having to range a number of aircraft on the flight deck simply to get the aircraft needed for a sortie out from the back of the hangar deck. This was time-consuming and demanded much exhausting man-handling, often on slippery hangar and flight decks that were pitching and rolling. Worse than this, however, was the problem of having a lift motor fail. The carrier then had to operate like a tanker MAC-ship, as if there were no hangar or, more usually, operate the lift manually. When this happened aboard *Vindex*, it took an hour for each cycle of raising and lowering a lift. Repairing such faults was usually beyond the resources aboard, although on *Vindex* the offending motor was swapped for that of one of the aft capstans – not an easy task on a ship at sea, but necessary.

Chapter 12

Over Desert and Sea

The great success at Taranto had been undermined to a great extent by the revenge taken by the Germans on *Illustrious*. Taranto had been abandoned as a naval base, with the heavy fleet units moved to greater safety further away. That was a major gain. Even the Luftwaffe and increased German naval presence can also be attributed to the plus side rather than as a debit. German forces drawn into the Mediterranean were forces lost elsewhere, easing the pressure on the Soviet Union, or perhaps on the UK.

Defending Malta was a priority, for without these islands, the Germans and Italians would have enjoyed virtually free access at all times to their forces in North Africa. While convoy lines to Malta were always fragile and costly, and often failed altogether, the same could be said of the Axis north-south convoy route, thanks mainly to Malta-based forces. Without Malta, the Suez Canal would probably have been lost. True, by 1941, Suez was being used to reinforce British forces in Egypt, rather than as a short cut to the Middle East and Oceania, but it was also the key to the Middle East.

A Formidable Arrival

Despite Pound's gloomy predictions over the fate of an aircraft carrier in the Mediterranean, *Illustrious* left and was replaced two months later by *Formidable*, another ship of the same class. The speed with which this was done showed a marked change of attitude at the Admiralty and growing recognition of the importance of air power in the war at sea. The need for a replacement aircraft carrier, and a modern one at that, was such that *Formidable* was ordered from the South Atlantic to join the Mediterranean Fleet within just two days of her predecessor being crippled. The new ship was joined by the Fulmars of 806 Squadron, whose pilots were doubtless glad to leave the almost constant air attacks and primitive conditions that war had brought to Malta, where the airfields received almost thirty times the weight of bombs that hit Coventry, a British industrial city that was almost obliterated in one night of the 'Blitz'. *Formidable* had arrived in the Mediterranean by the same route as *Illustrious* had left it, through the 'back door', the Suez Canal, having sailed around Africa rather than taking the direct route across the Mediterranean.

The arrival of the replacement carrier was delayed for several days by Axis air attacks on the Suez Canal, dropping mines which over the course of several days accounted for four merchantmen. Clearing the canal of mines proved a difficult task and at one stage, the defenders had to resort to the primitive but highly effective method of relying upon mine watchers ashore to spot where mines had entered the water, using frogmen to locate the exact position and then dropping depth charges. In the end, a crippled cargo ship had to be moved to the side of the canal and beached, leaving just enough room for *Formidable* to squeeze past on her way to the Mediterranean, and then for *Illustrious* to make her exit. It was also decided to send *Eagle* away, for apart from the problems with her fuelling system, she was desperately overdue for a refit. A crippled carrier was a liability, worse than no carrier at all. She would have had to be defended and maintained, but she could not be put to any good use.

It is interesting to note that Pound, despite his pessimism over carrier operations in the Mediterranean, had a good sense of the merits of the available ships. Early in 1941, when Cunningham challenged what he thought was the refusal of the Admiralty to allow him to use *Formidable* to transport Hurricanes towards Malta, he received a tart reply: 'The earliest date of getting Hurricanes to Malta by carrier is 28th March; delivery by this method has at no time been abandoned,' Pound signalled. 'Had *Ark Royal* been in *Illustrious*'s place, I am sure that you are in no doubt what her fate would have been, but the risk to the carrier is but one of many factors taken into account.'

The crux of the matter was, of course, that the single carrier available could never carry enough aircraft to maintain both an adequate defence and also, either transport aircraft to Malta, or maintain offensive operations. Even without the poor performance of the then naval fighters, the defences of a single carrier would always be likely to be overwhelmed. Putting the carriers at the disposal of the RAF to reinforce Malta was another difficult question. The carrier was at risk on such an exercise. On the other hand, a strong Malta-based fighter force helped to protect convoys and also backed up the carrier's air group. Again, the strategic position needs to be borne in mind. Fighter aircraft based on Malta had a short life, as many more were destroyed on the ground in the almost ceaseless air raids than were shot down by enemy fighters. To be sure of maintaining adequate fighter defences before a convoy arrived, aircraft had to be in position no more than a matter of days before the convoy's due date – it was not unknown for fighters to arrive, and be destroyed almost immediately they landed.

The carrier question, as the United States Navy demonstrated in the Pacific, could only be solved by operating a number of carriers together at the same time. *Formidable*'s own squadrons included the fighter squadron, 803, with Fulmars, the Albacores of 826 and Swordfish of 829.

Before this, on 9 February 1941, Force H had done its best to maintain the pressure on the Axis forces in the Mediterranean. Vice Admiral Somerville, Force H's flag officer, took the battleship *Malaya*, the battlecruiser *Renown* and the aircraft carrier *Ark Royal*, with a cruiser and ten destroyers as escorts, on a raid in the Gulf of Genoa. This was a risky venture, steaming into a relatively confined area close the enemy's mainland and close to that of Vichy France. Faced with the battleships bombarding Genoa itself, while the *Ark Royal*'s aircraft bombed the port of Leghorn and dropped mines off the naval base of La Spezia, the Italian Navy finally decided that it had to do something about it. The battleships *Vittorio Veneto*, *Guilio Cesare* and *Andrea Doria*, with three cruisers and ten destroyers, were sent to intercept Force H, which they heavily outgunned and outnumbered, but failed to make contact. This was the closest they came to the decisive naval engagement for which Cunningham had yearned – it would have been irony indeed had this event been handed to Somerville.

Impatient that the Royal Navy still survived to fight in the Mediterranean even though the Luftwaffe controlled the skies, the Germans managed to urge the Italian Navy to cut the supply lines between Alexandria, and Crete and Greece. At a stroke, the Germans wanted to ease the pressure on their campaign in Greece, and also make it easier to maintain their convoys running from Italy to North Africa. The Germans managed to convince the Italians that the Mediterranean Fleet had just a single battleship, rather than the three actually present. This is an interesting development, for the Royal Navy was convinced that Alexandria was crawling with Axis spies. It certainly also shows once again that Italian aerial reconnaissance was not very effective.

Formidable brought the new Fairey Albacore strike aircraft of her 826 and 829 squadrons to the Mediterranean for the first time. This aircraft, although still a biplane, had enclosed cockpits and was meant to be a replacement for the Swordfish. It wasn't. The Albacore was to prove to be unreliable, her Taurus engine being nowhere near as dependable as the Pegasus giving rise to the ditty in the *Fleet Air Arm Songbook* that:

The Swordfish relies on her Peggy,
The modified Taurus ain't sound,
So the Swordfish flies off on her missions
And the Albacore stays on the ground.
'Bring back, bring back,
Oh bring back my Stringbag to me.'

British reconnaissance was quick to spot the Italians at sea. This was the closest that Cunningham was to get to the decisive naval engagement for which he had longed since Italy's belated entry into the war. As it was, the Italian force was far less threatening than he had hoped, consisting of just one battleship, the *Vittorio Veneto*, but she did have an escort of no less than eight cruisers, several of them heavy and able to outgun their British opponents, while the Mediterranean Fleet had just four.

While British reconnaissance always seemed to be one step ahead of the Italians, the same could not be said of the respective intelligence services. This was because the Allied position was remarkably open to observation by enemy agents at both ends of the Mediterranean. In Gibraltar, ships could clearly be seen from Spain, and their progress through the Straits observed from Spain or the two Spanish enclaves in Morocco: Ceuta and Melilla.

Protecting the Convoys

On 18 April, another attempt was made to force oil and aviation fuel through to Malta from Alexandria, and as always, a sizeable and powerful escort was provided. Leaving 'Alex' at 07.00, the escort was headed by Cunningham's flagship, *Warspite*, accompanied by the Mediterranean Fleet's other two battleships, *Barham* and *Valiant*, and the carrier *Formidable*, as well as two cruisers, *Phoebe* and *Cairo*, with a large destroyer screen. All this was to provide cover for a single ship, the *Breconshire*. This demonstrates vividly just how serious the situation had become and how important Malta's survival was to the war effort. If the operation was successful, the escort would also be able to bring back four merchantmen from Malta. In order to put the ships to the best possible use, the convoy escort duty was being combined with a plan to bombard Tripoli, leaving the *Breconshire* on its own after dark on the evening of 20 April, with the bombardment being preceded by bombing of the port by RAF Wellingtons and Fleet Air Arm Swordfish from Malta.

Oddly, the aircraft from *Formidable* were to be limited to flare dropping and spotting for the guns of the fleet, rather than conducting a 'mini-Taranto' on the port, which would mainly be occupied by merchant ships and their escorts, usually nothing bigger than a destroyer. That this was seen as a substantial and complicated operation can also be judged by the positioning of the submarine *Truant* 4 miles off the harbour, showing a light to seaward as a navigation mark, so that the bombardment would be accurate, usually very difficult when attacking from the sea in the dark.

Steaming south through the night, the Mediterranean Fleet picked up another cruiser, *Gloucester*, steamed past the surfaced submarine *Truant* during the early morning of 21 April, just before daylight, and in what was literally the darkest hour before the dawn, at least for the Italian defenders, from 05.00 to 05.45, in Cunningham's own words, 'pumped 15-inch and 6-inch shell into the harbour and amongst the shipping. The *Gloucester*'s sixteen-gun salvoes must have been particularly effective.' In any such bombardment, those on the ships could see little of the damage being done, especially in this case as the air raids, which had only just ceased, had created clouds of dust and smoke from the fires started, but *Formidable*'s aircraft reported that five or six ships had been sunk, and it looked as if *Valiant*'s guns had set off an oil fire.

Despite the air raids, the Italians had once again been caught napping. It took twenty minutes before the shore batteries came into action and most of their shells flew over the attacking warships, which suffered no hits at all. On this occasion, the Mediterranean Fleet was in luck as the Luftwaffe also failed to put in an appearance, leaving Cunningham to surmise that perhaps the radio station at Tripoli had been put out of action. Before the operation, with the agonies of *Illustrious* in January still fresh in his mind, he had been expecting anything ranging from the loss of a major ship in an enemy minefield to the destruction of several ships, or heavy damage to all of them from a heavy Luftwaffe attack.

On the way back to Alexandria, three Junkers Ju88s attempted to attack, but Fulmars from *Formidable* shot down two of them and chased off the third.

During six days between 24 and 30 April, the Mediterranean Fleet took, or covered merchant ships taking a total of more than 50,000 men from Greece. Most of these were ferried to Crete, which now assumed prime importance.

By this time, the Axis had effectively cut the Mediterranean into two halves. Malta's plight was desperate, but without supplies and without the base that Malta provided, the fall of the islands to the Axis would consolidate their power and make the Mediterranean, and especially the central part of it, out of bounds to the British. Ships and men were by this time showing signs of strain – the ships needed refits and repairs, the men needed rest.

Despite this, it was decided to attempt to send a large convoy, Operation Tiger, with five large cargo ships through the Mediterranean, carrying tanks for the British Army in Egypt and Hawker Hurricane fighters for the RAF. The escort for the convoy would also include reinforcements for Cunningham, with the battleship *Queen Elizabeth* and the cruisers *Naiad* and *Fiji* sailing with Force H as far as the Sicilian Narrows, where they would pass with the convoy to the Mediterranean Fleet. Cunningham's outward voyage on this occasion was also to provide cover for two convoys from Alexandria to Malta, with one convoy consisting of four large merchant ships carrying supplies, the other two being tankers with fuel for the island. As usual, a side show was planned, and on this occasion Benghazi was to be attacked by a cruiser and three destroyers.

Both Force H and the Mediterranean Fleet were to sail from Gibraltar and Alexandria respectively on 6 May, but departure from the Egyptian port was slow and difficult as the larger ships had to be preceded by minesweepers as a result of mines being laid the previous day. Poor visibility due to a sandstorm also prevented operations by *Formidable*'s aircraft.

Unusually for the time of year, Cunningham's ships arrived off Malta to find very low cloud, 'almost down to our mast-heads', so while their radar showed enemy aircraft, they were not spotted. One of *Formidable*'s Fulmars found a Ju88 above the clouds and managed to shoot it down. Amongst the ships bound for Malta, one merchant ship was mined and another torpedoed, although she was able to continue, but the convoy on the whole suffered relatively lightly.

Returning with the reinforcements and the convoy for Egypt, the Mediterranean Fleet came under heavy aerial attack, but the heavy AA fire put up by the cruisers and the carrier drove them off. Despite the dangers of sailing directly across the Mediterranean, Operation Tiger was a great success and earned the Mediterranean Fleet the warm congratulations of the Admiralty. It could all have been for nothing, however, as Cunningham was astounded and infuriated to find that the tanks that had been carried across the Mediterranean at such cost and with so much good fortune and courage, had to spend fourteen days after being unloaded being fitted with sand filters for desert conditions, during which time they were vulnerable to enemy air attack. The same happened to the Hurricanes. This all-important item of equipment could have been fitted before despatch from the UK.

The extent of the convoy's near-miraculous good fortune can be judged from the loss in Malta of seven Hurricanes, most of them with their pilots, over the islands during a three-day period in mid-May. During the same period, air attacks damaged a further twenty-seven Hurricanes on the ground, as well as four Beaufighters and two Martin Marylands, with a Blenheim damaged so badly that it was written off.

The Battle for Crete

Then, on 20 May, after four days of bombing, the German airborne attack on Crete started; this was to be followed up by a seaborne invasion. Cunningham's forces attempted to intercept the Germans and engaged them, but they were running short of fuel and ammunition. Air cover was virtually non-existent, with just nine fighters in a mixed Fleet Air Arm and RAF contingent ashore, under naval command, while *Formidable* had been reduced to just four serviceable aircraft by the losses and damage of recent operations. There were no reserves of aircraft or flying personnel. HMS *Gloucester* was crippled and set on fire, with many of her crew killed as they were machine-gunned in the water. The cruiser *Fiji*, out of all but practice ammunition, was crippled by the small bomb dropped by a Messerschmitt Bf109, according to Cunningham, as it narrowly missed and blew in her hull in the area of the engine room, while half an hour later, another aircraft, presumably a bomber, hit the ship with three bombs which exploded in her boiler room, so that shortly afterwards she rolled over and sank.

Worse was to follow. Hastily returned to service on 25 May with a scratch complement of a dozen Fairey Fulmars, many of which were themselves not fully serviceable, *Formidable* was sent to attack Italian-held airfields in the Dodecanese, in a vain attempt to ward off Luftwaffe and Regia Aeronautica attacks, and stop the airlift of enemy troops into the captured airfields on the island. The Royal Navy had by this time lost two cruisers and four destroyers, with many other ships damaged, and all were running dangerously low on ammunition. The carrier also had some Fairey Albacores, hoping to be able to attack enemy shipping, including the invasion barges, or to bomb troop concentrations ashore.

Formidable arrived with the battleships *Queen Elizabeth* and *Barham*, at a point a hundred miles south-west of Scarpanto in the Dodecanese early on 26 May, and sent four Albacores and four Fulmars to attack, catching the enemy by surprise and destroying or damaging aircraft on the airfield. But despite the element of surprise and determined attacks, the carrier had too few aircraft to make any difference to the outcome. Worse, she was exposing herself to danger. As the morning passed, the carrier's radar caught successive waves of enemy aircraft looking for her, and with eight Fulmars operational, sent these on a total of twenty-four sorties during which they engaged Luftwaffe aircraft on twenty occasions, shooting some of them down. This was an unequal conflict and at 13.20, the flag officer, Vice Admiral Pridham-Whippell, decided to withdraw, just as twenty Luftwaffe aircraft approached, not from the direction of Greece, but from North Africa. The Germans pressed home their attack, led by Stuka dive-bombers, in a virtual repeat of the attack on *Illustrious*, seriously damaging the cruiser *Nubian* and hitting *Formidable* twice, badly damaging the carrier. Although not as badly damaged as *Illustrious*, the damage to *Formidable* was serious enough after being hit by two bombs, so she was forced to follow *Illustrious* to the United States for repairs.

The following day *Barham* was badly damaged, but by that time the decision had already been taken to evacuate Crete. The battle had cost the Mediterranean Fleet three cruisers and six destroyers, with two battleships and an aircraft carrier, and another three cruisers damaged so badly that they could not be repaired at Alexandria. *Formidable* had come close to sharing the fate of *Illustrious*. Having transported troops away from Greece, the Royal Navy now had to repeat the exercise at Crete, saving 17,000 men.

Much has been made of how tenuous was the hold of the German paratroops on Crete at first, even when reinforced by air-landed troops coming by glider and then in the ubiquitous Junkers Ju52/3M transports. Had not the British and Greek forces on the island lost much of their heavy equipment, and especially their communications equipment, in the retreat from Greece, the situation might have been better. On the other hand, the defenders had expected an attack by sea, not by air, despite the experiences of the German advance into the Low Countries. It is clear that the Mediterranean Fleet was successful in causing much damage to the clumsy barges of the seaborne invasion, but was short of fuel. Worse, at times the pressures forced the fleet to divide its forces, and this was when so many ships fell prey to determined Axis air attack. Had there still been two carriers in the Eastern Mediterranean, each with a full complement of aircraft and the right balance of aircraft, the outcome could have been very different.

A weakness of the Axis assault on Crete was that it was inspired and led by the Luftwaffe, with the German Army simply ordered to follow. A well-coordinated invasion, such as those mounted by the Allies, within a short period, and with airborne and seaborne troops complementing each other, would again have placed the rescue of British and Greek troops ashore in doubt.

The one benefit of the battle for Crete, although it was not realized at the time, was that German casualties had been so heavy that Hitler banned any future airborne assaults. This was one turning point in the defence of Malta. The history of the Second World War might well have been different had the Germans and Italians attempted to invade Malta first, and especially if Mussolini had managed to capture the Balkans without German support, since that would have left Germany free to launch Operation Barbarossa, the invasion of the Soviet Union, a good six weeks earlier, offering German forces a chance of seizing their key objectives before the onset of the Russian winter.

This good news was far from apparent at the time. Sending convoys to Malta from Gibraltar had become all but impossible. Sending convoys from Alexandria would also become more difficult, with German aircraft based on Crete able to attack the flanks of any convoy sailing west. The enemy was now closer to the convoy route, and to the Suez Canal.

It is easy when looking at the war in the Mediterranean to concentrate on the almost continuous encounters between opposing forces at sea and in the air, but a major part of the air and naval operations was in support of British forces fighting in North Africa. Running supply ships through to Tobruk was almost as difficult a task for Cunningham as running supplies to Malta. Shipping was the only realistic method of resupplying the British Army in the desert, since only ships could easily carry the vast volume of supplies needed. Overland movement was scarcely an option, given the few roads and the distances. Whilst fighting to defend Crete and then to evacuate the island's garrison, from May to July 1941 the Mediterranean Fleet lost four escort vessels and had two more seriously damaged in attempts to maintain supplies to Tobruk. Larger vessels were seldom used, drawing too much water to be safe so close to the coast. Cunningham wanted a chain of airfields along the coastline of Libya to provide protection for shipping and to maintain offensive operations against the Axis in the Eastern Mediterranean and the Aegean, but as always, the wish list of a commander in the field had to be weighed against those of other commanders elsewhere.

Taking the Offensive in Syria

The loss of Crete saw naval aircraft based ashore at Nicosia in Cyprus, within easy reach of Vichy French units in Syria, which was invaded by British and Free French forces on 7 June. It was from Cyprus that 815 Squadron attacked French warships on 16 June 1941, when five Swordfish attacked the flotilla leader, *Chevalier Paul*, and another destroyer, *Guepard*. The *Chevalier Paul* was promptly despatched, but Peter Winter and his pilot were shot down and rescued by the *Guepard*. Subsequent events can only be described as bizarre. Taken prisoners of war, the Vichy French contravened the rules of the Geneva Convention by handing over their PoWs to the Italians in Rhodes. Although Vichy forces managed to hang on until 14 July, prompt action by the British then saved the day for the PoWs, however, as the Vichy High Commissioner and Commander-in-Chief in Syria, General Dentz, was rounded up by the British, together with his staff, and held hostage. Three months later, Winter and another forty-nine British PoWs were repatriated in exchange for Dentz and his staff.

With the assistance of Free French forces ousting a pro-German Vichy administration, the invasion of Syria and Lebanon was a rare instance at this stage of the war of British forces going on to the offensive and actually gaining territory. It was possibly an operation too far, at a time when the situation in the Western Desert was far from safe, and despite this victory, it was clear that Cyprus could still not be regarded as safe.

Saving Malta

Further west, 1941 saw the fortunes of Malta at a low ebb. Two large minelaying submarines, *Cachalot* and *Rorqual*, were pressed into service to run fuel to Malta, plus any other essential supplies for which they might have room. Each submarine managed to carry enough aviation fuel to keep the RAF and Fleet Air Arm aircraft on Malta operational for about three days. Malta's agony was to be prolonged until almost breaking point was reached – truly the darkest hour before dawn – the following summer.

Meanwhile, there had been a number of smaller, but no less useful operations. Typical of these occurred after a Malta-based reconnaissance aircraft reported five Axis merchant ships near Cape Bon in Tunisia, escorted by three destroyers, at around noon on 15 April. Four destroyers, *Jervis*, *Nubian*, *Mohawk* and *Janus*, set sail from Malta at 18.00, using the Kerkenah Islands as cover. Sighting the convoy at 01.58 on the morning of 16 April, they discovered that there were indeed five merchant ships being escorted by a single large destroyer and two smaller destroyers. The British ships opened fire at 02.20 and in little more than five minutes a skirmish had developed. *Jervis* was showered with shrapnel and pieces of metal, some as heavy as 20 lb, as an ammunition ship blew up almost a mile away and the falling material made the sea around her appear as 'a boiling cauldron'. In due course, one destroyer was sunk and two others set on fire, while one merchantman was sunk and the other four set on fire, but the cost of this was the loss of *Mohawk*, although her CO, Commander J.W. Eaton and most of her crew were saved. The commander of the flotilla of destroyers, Captain M.J. Mack, later referred to the operation as the 'Skirmish off Sfax'.

By autumn 1941, the Axis was finding it almost impossible to keep ground and air forces in North Africa supplied.

The German involvement in the Mediterranean was not long in bearing results. On 13 November, *U-81* torpedoed Force H's aircraft carrier, *Ark Royal*, but the ship remained afloat until the next day, when she sank.

By this time Malta was approaching the nadir of her misfortunes. Heavy aerial attacks by Fliegerkorps II continued throughout April, so that three destroyers and three submarines were sunk, as well as a number of other ships; the Grand Harbour and the other harbour facilities between Valetta and Sliema, Marsamxett Harbour and the creeks off it at Sliema, Pieta and Msida were rendered virtually unusable. Submarines were forced to submerge in harbour during the day to avoid aerial attack, while a meagre dribble of supplies, and especially the all-important aviation fuel, were carried to the island on fast runs, known as 'club runs', by fast minelaying cruisers supplementing the work of the larger minelaying submarines.

Operation Pedestal

The terrible toll on merchant ships and naval vessels at this time can be attributed to the sheer absence of British naval air power – *Formidable* had not been replaced when she left the Mediterranean for repairs. But the lessons were not lost and the next attempt at a convoy had naval air power in abundance, and what is more, higher performance aircraft in the shape of the Sea Hurricane and the Martlet.

The Sea Hurricane was the first attempt to give the Fleet Air Arm the high-performance aircraft it needed. That the Hurricane prototype had made its first flight in 1935 shows the urgency that had been given to making good the deficiencies of the fleet, but even when it did first enter service with the Fleet Air Arm in July 1941, the aircraft were all basic conversions from RAF standard machines, fitted with arrestor hooks, and without folding wings so that not every carrier could operate these aircraft because of the limitations on wingspan imposed by some carrier lifts. The lack of folding wings also severely limited the number of aircraft that could be accommodated, whether when ranged on the flight deck or struck down inside the hangar. The early Sea Hurricanes had eight Browning 0.303 machine guns, but later aircraft had four 20mm cannon. On the early versions, the 1,030-hp Rolls-Royce Merlin III gave a maximum speed of 268 knots. The Hurricane had two advantages over the faster Spitfire, of which the Seafire variant had folding wings, namely that it had a tighter turning radius, always an important feature for a fighter, and it was easier to repair, again important with the limited number of aircraft that can be carried aboard ship.

The Seafire was well liked by some pilots, especially those who had good reason to be grateful for the armour protection afforded the pilot. Both the Seafire and the Sea Hurricane were short on range, which meant that their patrol periods were short. The Seafire was not strong enough for repeated deck landings, and had a tendency to bounce on to its nose.

Better still in many respects was the Grumman Martlet, as the Fleet Air Arm liked to call its Wildcats early in the war. The Martlet was a high-performance naval fighter, designed for the rough life of naval operations. First flown in 1937, it entered FAA service in September 1940. Its Pratt & Whitney Twin Wasp could provide 1,100 hp, but this could be boosted briefly to 1,200 hp for take-off. Maximum sped was 278 knots. The aircraft had been designed for the USN and had folding wings. Its retractable undercarriage was mounted under the fuselage, giving a narrow track, so that in rough seas the aircraft appeared to 'dance' from one undercarriage leg to the other!

The next convoy for Malta was code-named Operation Pedestal, although to the Maltese it became the *Santa Marija* Convoy, set to arrive on the feast day of the Virgin Mary. That this was a large convoy of fourteen merchant vessels immediately shows that heavy losses were expected, for Malta's small-scale port facilities could not cope with anything like fourteen merchantmen at one time. Vice Admiral Syfret led the escort with the powerful battleships *Nelson* and *Rodney*. There were no less than four aircraft carriers. The veteran *Furious*, by now the only survivor of the three converted battlecruisers, carried Supermarine Spitfire fighters to fly off to reinforce Malta's air defences. The most powerful escort force of any convoy also included the elderly carrier *Eagle* and the new *Victorious*, a true sister of *Illustrious*, and the even newer, *Indomitable*, a modified variant of *Illustrious* with a number of changes, including a second half-hangar extending aft halfway along the length of the upper hangar deck to allow a larger air group to be carried. In addition to this strong force, there were no less than seven cruisers and twenty-seven destroyers.

Victorious had embarked 809 and 884 Naval Air Squadrons with a total of sixteen Fulmars between them, while there were five Sea Hurricanes of 885 and, for anti-submarine and reconnaissance work, twelve Albacores of 832. *Indomitable* had nine Grumman Martlets of 806, as well as twenty-two Sea Hurricanes of 800 and 880. *Eagle* had sixteen Sea Hurricanes of 801 and another four of 813. Although working as an aircraft transport, there were four Albacores of 823 aboard *Furious* as spares.

By this time, the Italian Navy was confined to port as fuel shortages started to bite, but the Germans had E-boats and U-boats, and of course there was always the Luftwaffe.

Sailing from Gibraltar on 10 August, the convoy almost immediately ran up against Axis attack. First to go was *Eagle*, lost to four torpedoes from *U-73* at 13.15 on 11 August. She rapidly began to list to port and within four minutes she had gone. It seems almost miraculous that in sinking so rapidly, just 160 of her ship's company of 953 died. Many of the survivors had to spend hours in the water before a destroyer could risk stopping to pick them up. Considered too slow for fleet actions, after the appearance of the fast armoured carriers such as *Illustrious* and *Formidable*, after leaving the Mediterranean early in 1941, *Eagle* had been reduced to the more suitable and vital tasks of escorting convoys and acting as an aircraft transport, having flown off 183 fighters to Malta on several ventures into the Western Mediterranean.

Later that day, the first air attacks started, as thirty-six Luftwaffe aircraft sallied forth from their base in Sardinia to find the convoy at 20.45. The following morning started with an attack of twenty Luftwaffe aircraft at 09.15, before a combined force of seventy Luftwaffe and Regia Aeronautica aircraft attacked at noon. Around 16.00, one of the escort vessels found and sank a U-boat. Three hours later, another combined strike hit the convoy, this time of a hundred aircraft, sinking one of the merchant ships and so damaging *Indomitable* that she was put out of action. Her aircraft had to be recovered onto the crowded decks and hangars of *Victorious*. The Sea Hurricane could cope easily with the Ju87 Stuka, but was a poor match for the faster Ju88.

'The speed and the height of the Ju88s made the fleet fighters' task a hopeless one,' wrote Syfret. 'It will be a happy day when the fleet is equipped with modern fighter aircraft.'

That the lumbering Fairey Fulmar had managed to shoot down Ju88s the previous year seems to have been unknown to Syfret. In fighter operations as in all else, the contest was not just between aircraft of varying performance, but pilots of varying experience.

An hour later, twenty Luftwaffe aircraft attacked, sinking the cruiser *Cairo* and two merchant vessels, as well as damaging the cruiser *Nigeria* and three other ships, including the vital tanker *Ohio*. Darkness brought no relief when E-boats attacked, sinking five ships and so damaging the cruiser *Manchester* that she had to be sunk later.

Then, at 08.00 on 12 August, twelve Luftwaffe aircraft from Sicily struck at the convoy, sinking another ship and battering the *Ohio* still further. At 11.25, fifteen Regia Aeronautica aircraft found the convoy and, after further battering and on fire, *Ohio*'s master ordered the crew to abandon ship, but they reboarded her before they could be picked up as she remained afloat. By this time the main body of the convoy was entering

Grand Harbour, but the *Ohio* had to be taken alongside a warship and helped into Grand Harbour two days later, on 15 August. She was lucky, for another straggler was sunk by a U-boat.

All in all, nine merchantmen were sunk, with the loss of an aircraft carrier and two cruisers, as well as a destroyer, and with serious damage to two aircraft carriers and two cruisers. Oddly, the five merchant ships that reached Grand Harbour were spared any further attacks at a time when they would have been most vulnerable, despite the efforts of the defenders waiting to unload at Malta's very limited port facilities.

This was the turning point of the war in the Mediterranean. The defeat of the Italian and German armies at the Battle of El Alamein, which ended on 5 November, with Rommel retreating into Tunisia, marked a further step forward, removing German pressure on the Suez Canal, with at one point Rommel's forces reaching a point just 80 miles from Alexandria. Within days, on 8 November, victory at last appeared possible with the successful Allied landings in North Africa. These were followed by those in Sicily in July 1943, after which Malta was no longer in the front line. The substantial quantity of fuel aboard the *Ohio* meant that the RAF and Fleet Air Arm units on the island were no longer living a hand-to-mouth existence, and it fuelled an increasing level of offensive operations, once again putting Axis forces in North Africa under pressure.

Cunningham would not be with the Mediterranean Fleet for much longer. The following year he would become General Eisenhower's naval deputy, but in October 1943, still higher demands were placed on him, as he became First Sea Lord, taking over from the ailing Dudley Pound. By that time, Allied naval supremacy in the Mediterranean had been re-established.

Chapter 13

Protecting the Convoys

War broke out in Europe on 3 September 1939 after Germany had rejected an Anglo-French ultimatum to withdraw its forces from Poland. The period that followed has often been termed the 'Phoney War', which came to an end only with the German invasion of Denmark and Norway, followed by the push westwards through the Low Countries and into France. The German term for this period was the 'sitting war', meaning that the opposing armies merely sat and waited. There was no 'phoney war' at sea, however, for on the very first night of war at 21.00, the 13,500 ton liner *Athenia*, outward bound for the United States, was torpedoed with the loss of 112 lives, including twenty-eight US citizens. The Germans claimed that a bomb had been planted on the ship by the British to prejudice US-German relations. On 5 and 6 September, three more British merchantmen were sunk off the coast of Spain, with only the crew of one of them saved and the other two going down with all hands.

This was not the official start of the Battle of the Atlantic, however. That had to await the fall of France that enabled the Kriegsmarine to move its submarines to bases on the Atlantic coast of France, such as Brest and St Nazaire, cutting out the long and hazardous passage from the Baltic around the north of Scotland and the north of Ireland, that took the U-boats close to the British naval bases at Scapa Flow in Orkney and Londonderry in Northern Ireland, and then Devonport in the south-west of England. The Battle of the Atlantic is generally regarded as lasting from July 1940 to May 1945 and can be fairly said to have been the single longest running battle of the war.

In 1939, the British could still count their Merchant Marine as the largest in the world, at some 21 million tons of shipping. This was about the same figure as in 1914, due in part to the poor state of world trade between the wars, but the ships were larger and so there were fewer of them. Almost immediately, some 3 million tons were earmarked for use by the armed forces, mainly to supply the Royal Navy and support the British Army abroad, but also including a number converted to naval use, that could include anything from an armed merchant cruiser through minesweeping, anti-submarine trawlers and hospital ships down to motor fishing vessels on humble harbour duties. After taking into account the shipping needs of the British Empire, that left some 15.5 million tons to continue to carry Britain's foreign trade, a cut of more than a quarter over normal peacetime requirements.

Generally, the Battle of the Atlantic can be divided into four distinct phases, the first being from the fall of France to the Japanese attack on Pearl Harbor that bought the United States into the war. This was followed by a period to March 1943 when German U-boats reigned supreme, with numbers increasing more quickly than the Allied countermeasures could destroy them. In April and May 1943 came the arrival of escort carriers and MAC-ships combined to inflict heavy and unsustainable losses on the U-boats, which were temporarily withdrawn, many of them for re-equipping. Finally, there was the period from June 1943 to May 1945, with the closure of the 'Atlantic Gap' by escort carriers and ever longer-range maritime-reconnaissance aircraft, with growing losses by the U-boats.

At the outset of war in Europe in September 1939, Germany had just fifty-nine submarines, but the war years saw a total of 785 U-boats sunk, while in the North Atlantic alone, no less than 2,232 ships totalling 11,899,732 tons were lost.

German successes early in the battle could have been far higher but for the fact that the Kriegsmarine initially suffered problems with its torpedoes in combat conditions. Many commentators have wondered at this weakness given the German reputation for engineering excellence, but it could be that the problem was at least in part the result of the 'Führer system' in which intrigue played a part and any admission of weakness or underachievement was perceived as damning failure.

While the naval strength included a considerable number of surface raiders, for the most part the Battle of the Atlantic was a submarine war. The raiders were generally used in other theatres of war, including the South Atlantic, the Indian Ocean and the Pacific, far away from Germany and, more importantly, from British bases. The battleship *Bismarck* and her escort the cruiser *Prinz Eugen* were intended to mount such an offensive in Operation Rhine Exercise, but the early dispatch of the *Bismarck* by the Royal Navy put paid to this idea. Later, the two battlecruisers *Scharnhorst* and *Gneisenau*, with *Prinz Eugen*, posed a threat while they remained in harbour at Brest, and caused a considerable amount of British bombing effort to be devoted to these ships, with little real result. However, these too were removed from the scene during the so-called 'Channel Dash' of February 1942, that saw them return safely to Germany.

Sea power was not the only means available to the Germans. The fall of Norway and then France also freed air bases, and the long-range Junkers and Focke-Wulf maritime-reconnaissance aircraft operated from these bases over the Bay of Biscay, while others flew from France to Scandinavia via the west coast of Ireland, in almost a maritime-reconnaissance variant of British and American 'shuttle' bombing, posing a menace to convoys as they approached or departed the Irish coastline.

Land-based maritime-reconnaissance aircraft were amongst the most effective anti-submarine measures during the war years, but the aircraft of the day had limited endurance. Despite experiments by the British with air-to-air refuelling in the late 1930s, this had been for commercial flying boats and was not available for military operations during the war years. The result was that there was a significant stretch of the North Atlantic over which land-based air cover could not be provided – the celebrated 'Atlantic Gap', also sometimes referred to as the 'Black Gap'.

The Royal Navy was not left entirely on its own. While the United States was officially neutral from the outbreak of war in Europe until the Japanese attack on the US Pacific Fleet at Pearl Harbor just over twenty-seven months later, in September 1941, American warships began to escort convoys to a mid-ocean handover point, officially to ensure that neutral shipping was not engaged by German submarines. Inevitably, a U-boat eventually attacked an American warship, when the destroyer USS *Greer* found a German torpedo heading for it on 4 September 1941, while on passage from the United States to Iceland carrying mail and passengers. In response, the destroyer attacked with depth charges. Although a second torpedo was fired, neither the destroyer nor the U-boat was damaged.

After the United States entered the war, the Royal Navy made facilities available to the United States Navy at Londonderry in Northern Ireland. The new commander of US naval forces in the Atlantic, Admiral Ernest King, had remarked, on taking up his post, that it was like being given a big slice of bread with 'damn little butter', reflecting on the shortage of ships. After the battleships *Idaho, Mississippi* and *New Mexico* had been transferred with the aircraft carrier *Yorktown* from the Pacific to the Atlantic, the President of the United States, Franklin Roosevelt, asked King how he liked the butter he was getting. Came the reply: 'The butter's fine, but you keep giving me more bread.'

By the time the Battle of the Atlantic began in earnest, the Royal Navy had already lost two of its seven aircraft carriers, the sisters HMS *Courageous* and *Glorious*. While not the newest ships and of obsolescent design, these converted battlecruisers were nevertheless still amongst the best and most modern of the British carriers at the time, with only the new *Ark Royal* more modern. The loss of *Courageous* to torpedoes from *U-29* on 17 September 1939 while she was 'trailing her cloak' hunting for submarines, was especially wasteful. *Glorious* was sunk by gunfire from *Scharnhorst* and *Gneisenau* during the withdrawal from Norway. Both ships could have been better employed escorting convoys.

The First Phase

In 1940 from the end of August to the end of September, U-boats sank twenty-two ships from four convoys, a loss of 113,000 tons of shipping. At the outset of this period, between 29 August and 2 September, six U-boats sank ten ships totalling 40,000 tons from three convoys, HX66, OA204 and OB205. Later in September, five U-boats sank twelve ships totalling 73,000 tons from convoy HX72 that had set sail from Halifax, Nova Scotia. This was just a start.

There were two main areas for the U-boats. The first was the 'Atlantic Gap', that part of the mid-Atlantic out of reach of shore-based maritime-reconnaissance aircraft from either the British Isles or North America. Convoys from the United States and Canada, and from the Caribbean, some of which would have come through the Panama Canal to the Pacific, were the targets in this vast area of ocean. The other was the Bay of Biscay and the Atlantic off Portugal. On this route passed convoys to and from Gibraltar, which itself was the dividing point from where convoys would either proceed across the Mediterranean or south to the African territories of the British Empire. Often, a Mediterranean and a South Atlantic convoy would sail as one from the UK as far as Gibraltar. As the situation in the Mediterranean became increasingly desperate, convoys for the Middle East and Australia were forced out of necessity to route past the Cape of Good Hope, avoiding the Suez Canal. During 1941 and 1942, the chances of convoys successfully crossing the Mediterranean were so slight that British forces in Egypt were also supplied by way of the Cape route and the Suez Canal.

The situation worsened in October 1940. In the North Channel between Britain and Ireland, during the four days from 17 to 20 October, nine U-boats found the convoys SC7 and HX79 with a total of seventy-nine ships. Between them, the U-boats sank no less than thirty-two of the ships with a total tonnage of 155,000 tons, and would have continued but for the fact that they had exhausted their torpedoes. Just a few days later, on 23 October, just two U-boats accounted for no less than twelve ships, a total of 48,000 tons, from convoys SC11 and OB244. A further nine ships (53,000 tons) were sunk from convoy HX90 by U-boats in December. To put the losses into perspective, during 1940, the average number of U-boats at sea in the operational zones each day was around a dozen. The massive build-up to a hundred or so U-boats patrolling daily was some time away.

The U-boats were far from the sole predator. Armed and camouflaged merchantmen were deployed as auxiliary cruisers as early as April 1940, with *Atlantis*, *Orion*, *Pinguin*, *Thor* and *Widder* operating against Britain's trade routes, while in August the *Komet* managed to reach the Pacific by sailing north of Siberia. The term 'auxiliary cruiser' was hardly appropriate as these vessels were disguised as merchantmen, sometimes from neutral countries, and only displayed their true colours, and intent, at the last minute, making their operations more akin to piracy. During that second winter of war, the battlecruisers *Gneisenau* and *Scharnhorst* and the heavy cruiser *Hipper* operated in the Atlantic, and with the heavy cruiser *Scheer* in the Atlantic and Indian oceans, managed to account for forty-nine ships, or 271,000 tons of shipping, between October and March.

Overall, Allied shipping losses, which meant British and French, totalled 509,320 tons during the final four months of 1939, concentrated entirely in the Atlantic and North Sea. The following year, the total rose to 2,451,663 tons in the Atlantic and North Sea, with a further 13,170 tons in the Mediterranean and 12,223 tons in the Indian Ocean. Most of the North Sea was to be closed to convoys as a result with Germany holding the entire coastline of mainland Europe from the North Cape to the Bay of Biscay. The two worst months were June (with 356,937 tons lost in the Atlantic and a further 8,029 tons in the Mediterranean, with 8,215 tons in the Indian Ocean) and October (when 361,459 tons were lost in the Atlantic). To put this into perspective, the loss for the year was almost a sixth of the available tonnage of merchant shipping, although this would have been boosted by new construction and by vessels that had fled from the German occupied territories, with Norway and the Netherlands both maritime nations having considerable tonnages of merchant shipping, and continuing to operate with the British. Despite reaching a new monthly peak of 363,073 tons in May 1941, the overall total for the year fell to 2,214,408 tons in the Atlantic, but the figures for the Mediterranean rose to 54,200 tons, and while those for the Indian Ocean fell from 12,223 tons to 9,161 tons, no less than 40,666 tons were lost in the Pacific as Japan entered the war.

The escort carrier first became involved in convoy protection with Convoy HG76 which sailed from Gibraltar to Britain on 14 December 1941, with thirty-two ships, including the CAM-ship *Darwin*, escorted by the Royal Navy's first escort carrier, HMS *Audacity*, two destroyers, four sloops and nine corvettes, which together made up the 36th Escort Group. The 36th was commanded by the then Commander F.J. 'Johnny' Walker (later Captain Walker VC), the Royal Navy's leading anti-submarine commander in the sloop HMS *Stork*. Against this convoy were the seven U-boats of the *Seerauder* Group, which were guided to the convoy by the Focke-Wulf Fw200 Condors of 1KG40 based on Bordeaux. At dusk on 15 December, the most southerly of the U-boats discovered the convoy and was soon joined by a second boat. On the morning of 16 December, *U-131* was attacked by Wildcats flying from *Audacity*, before being attacked and sunk by destroyers. On 17 December, the destroyer *Stanley* was torpedoed by *U-434* and blew up, and in the frantic counter-attack led by Walker, *U-434* was depth-charged and forced to the surface, before being rammed and attacked by further depth charges. By this time the convoy escorts had also sunk *U-567*, commanded by Endrass, one of Germany's most experienced U-boat commanders. Nevertheless, the escorts themselves suffered a bitter blow on 20 December when *Audacity* was torpedoed and sunk by *U-751*. Despite the loss of the carrier, a destroyer and one of the merchantmen, four out of the seven U-boats were sunk.

It seems strange in retrospect that the ship carried Grumman Wildcats, known as Martlets to the Royal Navy at the time, rather than the Fairey Swordfish that was to prove the saviour of so many convoys when faced with U-boat attack, although passing through the Bay of Biscay, German maritime-reconnaissance aircraft were also a threat, and one against which the Swordfish was useless.

The Second Phase

Bringing the United States into the Second World War was the most dramatic move of the entire conflict, completely altering the strategic position. It formalized the unofficial alliance between the United States and the British Empire, and while the vital Lend-Lease supplies continued, it also opened the way for what some have described as 'reverse lend-lease', with a number of corvettes fitted with Asdic, or sonar, as it is now known, supplied to the United States Navy from the British and Canadian fleets.

Nevertheless, the Germans were anxious to strike while the United States Navy was still relatively weak, with its available resources divided between the Atlantic and the Pacific. On 13 January 1942, the Kriegsmarine launched Operation *Paukenschlag* (Operation Kettledrum Beat) against US shipping. Between January and March, they accounted for 1.2 million tons of Allied shipping in the Atlantic, with losses reaching a monthly total of 628, 074 tons in June. The figure for the year was to be 5,366,973 tons for the Atlantic alone. Added to this, however, were figures for the Barents Sea at 234,158 tons, while in the Mediterranean losses had almost quadrupled to 193, 644 tons as Malta began to starve to death, and 666,003 tons in the Indian Ocean, against which the Pacific losses of 85,494 tons faded into insignificance. The latter were undoubtedly a reflection of both the way in which the United States Navy bounced back so quickly, taking the war to the Japanese and putting them on the defensive within six months of Pearl Harbor, and also Japanese inability to take the war to American convoys and merchant shipping.

The losses were increased by the decision during the winter of 1941/2 that the Allies should send convoys to the Soviet Union. There were three routes to the USSR, of which the most famous was the Arctic route off the coast of Norway and round the North Cape to Archangel and Murmansk, mainly carrying supplies from the UK but also including materiel from the United States, so that many of these convoys were routed via Iceland. The other two routes included the main route from the United States via the South Atlantic and the Indian Ocean to the Gulf, with consignments offloaded in Iran for onward delivery to the USSR. A third route was from the West Coast of the USA and Canada to Vladivostok, but this was the least important in terms of equipment supplied, largely because the Trans-Siberian Railway was the only viable route to the battlefronts and this had severe limitations on its capacity.

This period saw the U-boats at their maximum strength in the North Atlantic when, from September 1943 to March 1943, there were more than a hundred craft in the area at any one time. Hitler had by this time decided that the Kriegsmarine's surface fleet was a waste of resources and the entire burden of pursuing the German naval offensive fell to the submarine, but despite the U-boats building up for what was to be the largest convoy battle of the Second World War, a decisive naval engagement did not take place.

This marked the peak of the U-boat campaign. It would never be as effective again and losses would begin to mount, bringing with them a loss of experienced personnel so that the life of a U-boat and its crew began to shorten dramatically. The arrival of the MAC-ships and the escort carriers was behind this complete change in the fortunes of the German submariner. Indeed, some would argue that the great convoy battle of 16–20 March 1943 had in itself marked the start of the decline of the U-boat as the massive fleet of a hundred submarines had been at sea for some time without finding and sinking a single merchantman. In fact, the entire U-boat campaign showed the same kind of missed opportunities that bedevilled the operations of the German surface fleet during the war years. Poor air-sea coordination was one feature, but poor strategy and bad tactics also played a part. One authority on the wartime German Navy, Jak Mallman Showell, maintains that two-thirds of the U-boat fleet, some 800 craft, never got within reach of the enemy, and that half of those that did only attacked four or fewer Allied ships. Most of the Allied losses were down to just 131 U-boats.

On 23 March, just a few days after the heavy losses suffered by the convoys SC122 and HX229, another convoy left Canada for the UK, but despite repeated attacks by U-boats, crossed safely to arrive on 8 April without a single ship being lost. This was despite the 'Atlantic Gap' still being some 500 miles wide.

The Birth of Canadian Naval Aviation

As the convoy war raged, the evidence was growing that air power at sea was vital. In Canada, plans for a Royal Canadian Naval Air Service dated from 1918, but had, in the words of one Canadian historian, 'been still-born'. Post-war, in 1920, Admiral Lord Jellicoe had drawn up plans for a Canadian fleet, including aircraft carriers, but the Royal Canadian Navy barely survived post-war, and even the Royal Canadian Air Force had a difficult and prolonged birth. By 1942, it had become clear that aviation had to be part of any navy that wished to or needed to engage the enemy on the high seas or in distant waters. Many Canadians had managed to make their way to the UK and join the Fleet Air Arm. Further pressure on the RCN to play a part in naval aviation came in December 1942, when the Admiralty in London asked for more Canadians to train as aircrew for the Fleet Air Arm while remaining in the Royal Canadian Navy. This could be viewed as a cheeky way for a hard-pressed Imperial power to ask the Canadian taxpayer to pay for those of their fellow countrymen assigned to the Fleet Air Arm, but it was also the case that none of the dominions took defence seriously between the two world wars, leaving much to the United Kingdom.

Captain Nelson Lay RCN, Director of Operations, and Captain Harry de Wolf, Director of Naval Plans, pressed Vice Admiral (later Admiral) P.W. Nelles, Chief of the Canadian Naval Staff, to send senior officers to obtain up-to-date information on naval air operations, in particular regarding escort carriers. They also proposed that Canada should have four escort carriers, one for each of the four escort groups provided by Canadian ships in the Atlantic.

De Wolf left to command a warship shortly afterwards and it was not until spring 1943 that Lay was able to visit both the United States and the United Kingdom, spending two weeks with the USN and two months with the RN. The greater amount of time spent with the Royal Navy was a reflection of attitudes at the time, when the 'British' model was usually taken rather than the American one. He made a report in August, proposing a Royal Canadian Naval Air Service modelled on the Fleet Air Arm. By this time, he recommended that two escort carriers be obtained to be manned and operated by RCN personnel, while shore-based, long-range, maritime-reconnaissance would remain the preserve of the Royal Canadian Air Force, again following United Kingdom practice rather than that of the United States. One difference between Canadian and British practice, however, was that the RCAF would also provide support for Canadian naval aviation at shore bases, something that was to have longer-term post-war implications for Canadian naval aviation.

The two escort carriers soon proved to be *Nabob* and *Puncher*, commissioned in September 1943 and February 1944 respectively. These were built at Seattle and moved to Vancouver in nearby British Columbia for the modifications, including installing additional watertight sub-divisions, that the British regarded as so necessary and so irritated the Americans. The RCN wanted the carriers for anti-submarine operations in support of convoy escort groups, but the Royal Navy had decided that these were to be strike carriers and won the argument, not least so that Canada did not appear to be receiving Lend-Lease aid from the United States. The ships remained on the Royal Navy's strength and were commissioned as 'HMS' rather than HMCS, being two of 'His Majesty's Ships' rather than two of his Canadian ships. Captain Lay took command of *Nabob*, while Captain Roger Bidwell took command of *Puncher*.

If the Canadians were unhappy that *Nabob* was to operate in the strike role rather than hunting submarines, at least she was involved in some of the more notable operations of the war, attacking the German battleship *Tirpitz* cowering in a Norwegian fjord. For *Puncher* the war at first was irksome and boring, for after she went to sea for the first time in April 1944, her initial role was that of an aircraft ferry and occasional troopship. It was not until February 1945 that an operational role was given to her, when fourteen Grumman Wildcats of the Fleet Air Arm's No. 881 Squadron were flown on with four Fairey Barracudas of No. 821. From thereon those aboard had plenty of action, again off the coast of Norway, but in *Puncher*'s case her first action was against German surface convoys. Then she joined HMS *Premier* and provided fighter escorts for that ship's Grumman Avengers on minelaying operations, something known earlier in the war to the RAF as 'gardening', no doubt because minefields are 'sown'. The next operation was to cover more minelaying, but also to protect British minesweepers. In early April, *Puncher* was to be part of a four-carrier group to attack a U-boat base at Kilbotn in Norway that had been menacing the Arctic convoys, but bad weather caused the operation to be cancelled. With five operations under her belt and the Royal Navy not needing her in the Pacific, Captain Bidwell's final task was to take the ship home to Norfolk, Virginia, where he handed her back to the United States Navy in January 1946.

The Third Phase

Naturally, the change in the fortunes of both the convoys and the U-boats did not happen overnight, although the change was spread over a fairly short period. The third phase of the Battle of the Atlantic started with two successes for the U-boats. Between 4 and 7 April 1943, fifteen U-boats sank six ships (41,000 tons) from convoy HX231, although this cost two U-boats. Then on 30 April and 1 May, *U-515* found a convoy off Freetown in Sierra Leone and sank seven ships totalling 43,000 tons, with nine torpedoes.

The success of *U-515*, while outstanding, was by this time the exception. In 1940, each U-boat on patrol sank an average of six merchantmen per month, but by 1942–3, it took more than two U-boats to sink a single merchantman.

Nevertheless, April and May 1943 are regarded as being a turning point in the Battle of the Atlantic. From this time on, the U-boats would be on the defensive. The successes of March and April became a disaster in May when more than forty U-boats were lost, many of them to aerial attack, while others were the result of collaboration between aircraft and surface escorts. Technical innovation would not be enough to ensure the survival of the U-boats. Schnorkels were progressively introduced from this time onwards to enable U-boats to recharge their batteries without surfacing, and indeed to run on diesel power under water. Heavier anti-aircraft armaments were also progressively introduced, although often at the cost of reducing speed while submerged still further. In fact, attacking a U-boat that had elected to remain surfaced in an aircraft such as a Fairey Swordfish, the obsolescent biplane operated from MAC-ships and the anti-submarine aircraft of choice for the British and Canadian escort carriers, took some nerve. On the other hand, a fast, well-armoured aircraft such as those operated by the Royal Air Force and United States Navy was a different matter altogether and for most U-boat commanders, the crucial factor was just how fast they could dive – known to them as the 'Battle of the Seconds'. Even so, there were a small number of instances of a U-boat inflicting fatal damage on a landplane, but the odds were against it, as the armament was too light and the firing platform unstable in the heavy Atlantic swell.

Between them, the MAC-ships and the escort carriers closed the 'Atlantic Gap', the 500 miles or so of mid-ocean that lay beyond the range of shore-based aircraft, forcing the U-boats to abandon their pack tactics. The impact on merchant shipping losses was dramatic, falling from fifty ships in August 1942 to just sixteen between September 1943 and May 1944, and only another five between then and VE-Day a year later.

Life aboard the escort carriers was hard and often uncomfortable, while aircrew were often waiting for hours in the ready room as the ship, with its single screw and hence more likely to roll, plodded at convoy speed across the Atlantic. Nevertheless, there were distractions, and one visitor, spotting aircrew squatting on the deck in the ready room playing dice or poker, thought that they looked 'like a lot of thugs out of *The Rake's Progress* gambling in a graveyard'.

The Fourth Phase

The fourth phase of the Battle of the Atlantic was marked by continual German technical innovation pitched against growing Allied aerial superiority.

Allied tactics started to change during this period, with a return to 'hunter-killer' operations as intelligence on U-boat operations improved. The early 'hunter-killer' groups were in the mid and South Atlantic, and were operated by the United States Navy, although later British and combined British-Canadian groups were formed. One reason for the creation of the 'hunter-killer' groups was that as the Atlantic Gap was closed by the escort carriers, U-boat tactics changed. The Kriegsmarine ordered the U-boats away from the North Atlantic shipping lanes and into the mid and South Atlantic.

On 11 June 1944, *U-490*, the last of the supply U-boats that had acted as *milch* (milk) cows for the fleet during extended operations, was sunk.

Too late, on 12 June 1944, *U-2321*, a class XXIII boat and the first of the much-needed electro-submarines, was commissioned, to be followed on 27 June by *U-2501*, the first large electro-submarine of class XXI. The pennant numbers give a false impression of the numbers of U-boats built – there were just under 1,200 commissioned altogether and the '2000' series pennant numbers indicate a step-change in capability.

Allied anti-submarine operations also underwent a radical change during the fourth phase. Convoys continued to be escorted and to enjoy the close protection of one or two escort carriers, but now anti-submarine sweeps by 'hunter-killer' forces of escorts with one or two escort carriers also reappeared, following American success with these techniques in the mid and South Atlantic. To say that anti-submarine sweeps 'reappeared' is simply to recognize that this was the technique that had fallen into disuse following the loss of the British fleet carrier HMS *Courageous* in September 1939, but this time the techniques were different. *Courageous* had just two escorts to protect her, and by this time between four and six per carrier was more usual. More important, *Courageous* had been hoping to find a submarine, but later in the war task groups knew where they would find U-boats refuelling and taking on supplies from the supply submarines, replacing hope with a high degree of certainty. Direction finding could detect the radio 'chatter' between U-boats, including their signals to base, while the breaking of the Germen Enigma codes also meant that the location of the ocean refuelling and resupply points became known. The submarines were now the hunted. Refuelling a U-boat at sea was difficult enough, transferring stores and ammunition between two low-lying craft rolling and pitching in a heavy mid-ocean swell was much more so, with the problems compounded by hatches that were too small for efficient stowage of supplies, but big enough for large waves to enter.

A significant feature of the fourth and final phase of the Battle of the Atlantic was that the Allies switched to completely different tactics. It was still wise to provide protection for convoys, but instead of waiting in effect for the U-boats to come and find Allied shipping, the emphasis switched to searching for enemy submarines. One reason for the change was that the location of the U-boats was known to the Allies thanks to Ultra intelligence – intercepts of the German Enigma codes. One weakness of the German submarine campaign was the regular reports sent from U-boat commanders, and the instructions from the centre, so necessary for the wolf packs to operate successfully. Even so, the chances of finding a U-boat were far from certain.

Hunter-killer Groups

Another escort carrier that saw service on a hunter-killer group was the British conversion, HMS *Vindex*. This ship had been laid down as the fast cargo liner, *Port Sydney*, but was commissioned in late 1943 as an auxiliary aircraft carrier intended for service on the Arctic convoys to Murmansk and Archangel. *Vindex* left the Clyde on 9 March 1944 to conduct operations against U-boats threatening transatlantic convoys. The intention was that she would operate with a second carrier, the Attacker-class US-conversion, HMS *Striker*, but escorts were still in short supply and *Striker* was needed for a convoy from West Africa to Gibraltar. Initially, *Vindex* was to be supported by a destroyer, two frigates and two corvettes of the 6th Escort Group, a Royal Canadian Navy flotilla.

While the USN operations had been daylight only, *Vindex* carried six Sea Hurricanes and twelve Swordfish, albeit with just eight complete Swordfish crews, and was able to operate by day and by night. While the risk of enemy air attack diminished as the task group steamed further west into the mid-Atlantic, the fighters were able to operate daylight patrols, looking for U-boats, while the Swordfish would handle the night patrols.

It is worth noting that despite more than four years of war, the routine aboard *Vindex* was not altered at first to cater for the needs of naval airmen engaged on operational flying round the clock. The wardroom (naval parlance for an officers' mess) served three meals a day, breakfast, lunch and dinner. Those flying patrols that took off after midnight were expected to fly on an empty stomach in the cold of the North Atlantic – so cold that on at least one occasion when flying was suspended, the enforced idleness saw many aircrew rolling a giant snowball on the flight deck. This was in addition to the constant threat of torpedo attack from a U-boat, or the risk of ditching once water was found in the aircraft fuel, when the time since the last meal could have a profound effect on the ability of the ditched airmen to survive. There was also the not unimportant fact that there were just eight crews to fly the Swordfish. It took a near mutiny on 17 March with a senior observer telling the ship's Commander (F) (Commander Flying, now known as Commander Air), Lieutenant Commander Percy Gick, that they would refuse to fly unless they were properly fed. The Commanding Officer, Captain Bayliss, defused the situation, quietly stressing the importance of their role in the war while, equally quietly, arrangements were made for more flexible mealtimes for aircrews.

It is also significant that it was not until comparatively late in the war, 1943, that the Royal Navy introduced an aviation medicine course at HMS *Daedalus*, the Royal Naval Air Station, Lee-on-Solent, on the Hampshire coast almost equidistant between Portsmouth and Southampton.

Other changes were in the air for the Swordfish. Getting the aircraft airborne when fully laden and in light wind conditions was difficult, given the slow speed of the escort carriers. One solution was the Robinson Patent Disengaging Gear that *Vindex* and many other British escort carriers had at the after end of the flight deck. An aircraft would be attached to this by a strop and the pilot would open up to maximum rpm, at which point the strop would be released and the aircraft would thunder along the flight deck. This was only sufficient for an extra knot or knot and a half.

Later, rocket-assisted take-off gear became available, known appropriately enough as RATOG. Between one and four of these rockets were placed under the lower wing on each side of the aircraft. The technique of using these safely was to have the aircraft start its take-off run normally, with the aircraft kept straight as once RATOG was fired, lateral control was difficult. The rockets were fired just before becoming airborne, otherwise premature firing could force the aircraft up into the air before full flying speed had been gained. If all rockets fired, and especially if they fired equally on each side, all was well and the rockets and their mountings could be ditched after the four-second burst of extra thrust. Using this technique, a full load of four depth charges could be carried safely.

Safety was another important consideration. Many of the relatively inexperienced pilots were seen to be dragging their aircraft into the air as soon as possible, which was not a difficulty in itself with the tolerant Swordfish. The problem arose if the ship was not facing directly into the wind, or if the wind suddenly veered, whereupon the aircraft would lack control speed. Pilots were ordered to use the full length of the flight deck and only pull the stick back at the last minute.

Fighting the Weather

It has often been said that on the Arctic convoys the weather was as much an enemy as the Germans, since the only route for those convoys lay around the northern tip of occupied Norway to the Soviet ports of Murmansk and Archangel. In summer, almost constant daylight left the ships open to attack from the air, as well as from U-boats and surface raiders. In winter, with almost constant darkness and just three hours of weak twilight in the middle of the day, the weather was worse, with extremely low temperatures and high seas with freezing snow. Ships could be overwhelmed as the build-up of ice made them unstable. One officer having difficulty eating a meal as his cruiser rolled to angles of 30 degrees consoled himself with the thought that life must have been even more difficult in the destroyers and corvettes, which rolled 50 degrees or more! The cold meant that airmen tried to wear as much as possible, limited only by the need to get into and out of the cockpit. Metal became so brittle that tail wheels could, and did, break off on landing.

The bad weather was a friend in one sense, since at the very height of the winter storms, not only were German aircraft grounded, but U-boat action also became difficult. The weather was such an important factor that, together with the long hours of daylight in the summer months, convoys had to be suspended at the height of summer, especially in 1943. Convoys were also suspended at the time of the Normandy landings in June 1944 as the number of escort vessels available was insufficient to cover the demands of the Allied armies in France and the convoys to north Russia. The shortage of escort vessels meant the destroyers and corvettes that were the staple of convoy protection as aircraft carriers were not involved in covering the Normandy beachheads, although many Fleet Air Arm squadrons were based ashore under the control of RAF Coastal Command for operations to protect the landings from submarines and motor gun and torpedo boats, the E-boats.

A total of 811 ships sailed in the Arctic convoys to Russia, of which 720 completed their voyages, another thirty-three turned back for one reason or another, and fifty-eight were sunk, giving a loss rate of 7.2 per cent. Of the ships that reached Russia, 717 sailed back (some were being delivered to the Soviet Union), and of these, twenty-nine were sunk, a loss rate of 4 per cent. This was the price of delivering to Russia some 4 million tons of war stores, including 5,000 tanks and more than 7,000 aircraft. It is worth reflecting that the sinking of a 10,000-ton freighter was the equivalent, in terms of lost equipment and ordnance, of a land battle.

Although much of the materiel from the United States to the Soviet Union went via the South Atlantic and Indian Ocean to what was then known as the Persian Gulf, and was offloaded at an Iranian port and taken overland, for aid from the United Kingdom, the main convoy route was from Scotland, often via Iceland, especially when some of the ships were also coming from the United States. This route involved sailing off the coast of enemy-occupied Norway and around the North Cape, calling for the larger aircraft capacity of the escort carriers, for both anti-submarine and fighter protection were needed. CAM-ships also appeared on the Arctic convoys. The convoys were looked after by RAF Coastal Command, operating from bases in Scotland, Iceland and the Soviet Union, and in British coastal waters often aided by Fleet Air Arm shore-based squadrons under RAF control.

Admiral Sir Andrew Cunningham, by this time First Sea Lord at the Admiralty in London, recalled:

> If the surface escorts and merchant ships suffered in the heavy gales and the bitter cold, the young men of the Fleet Air Arm operating from the frozen flight-decks of the carriers took their lives in their hands every time they took off. The conditions in which they worked were indescribable. The aircraft patrols might be flown off in clear weather, but when the time came to land on again with petrol nearly exhausted the carrier herself might be invisible in a lashing snowstorm. This happened many a time, and the number of close shaves in the recovery of these valiant young naval pilots is unbelievable. Many, numbed with cold, had to be lifted out of their cockpits. Their work was beyond all praise.

Convoy PQ18

After the terrible fate that had afflicted the ill-fated convoy PQ17, the last Arctic convoy to be without its own air cover, the first Arctic convoy to have an escort carrier was PQ18 in September 1942. This was an indication of the impact of the mauling given to PQ17 as escort carriers were an innovation, even a novelty, at this early stage of the war.

Convoy PQ18's escort carrier was the US-built HMS *Avenger*. She carried three radar-equipped Swordfish from 825 Squadron for anti-submarine duties as well as six Sea Hurricane fighters, with another six dismantled and stowed beneath the hangar deck in a hold, for fighter defence. The fighter aircraft were drawn from 802 and 883 Squadrons. The CAM-ship, *Empire Morn*, carried another Hurricane, one of the expendable standard aircraft operated by the RAF's Merchant Service Fighter Unit. Other ships protecting the convoy included the cruiser *Scylla*, two destroyers, two anti-aircraft ships converted from merchant vessels, four corvettes, four anti-submarine trawlers, three minesweepers and two submarines. There was also a rescue ship whose presence meant that the escorts would not be distracted from their work to rescue survivors, an urgent matter in such cold seas. Three minesweepers being delivered to the Soviet Union were also assigned to act as rescue ships.

Even getting to the convoy assembly point off Iceland was difficult. Rough seas swept a Sea Hurricane off *Avenger*'s deck, while steel ropes failed to stop aircraft breaking loose, or crashing into one another and into the sides of the hangar. Fused 500-lb bombs stored in the lift well broke loose and had to be captured by laying down duffle coats with rope ties, to be quickly tied up as soon as a bomb rolled on to the coats. On her way to the assembly point, *Avenger* suffered engine problems due to fuel contamination. Even Iceland was not completely safe, with the carrier bombed by a Focke-Wulf Fw200 Condor long-range maritime-reconnaissance aircraft, which dropped a stick of bombs close to the ship, but without inflicting any damage.

The engine problems meant that the convoy, already spotted by a U-boat whilst on passage to Iceland, left without the carrier. On 8 September, PQ18 was discovered by another Condor. By 12 September, *Avenger* had caught up with the convoy, only in time for a Blohm und Voss Bv138 flying boat to appear through the clouds. The carrier promptly launched a flight of four Sea Hurricanes, although not quickly enough to catch the flying boat before it disappeared.

The fighters' role was not limited to protecting the convoy from aerial attack. They also had to provide air cover for the Swordfish whilst they were on patrol and vulnerable to attack by German fighters. Typical of the work of the Swordfish were general reconnaissance patrols, which in at least one instance found Bv138s dropping mines ahead of the ships. Sometimes, U-boats were discovered on the surface, but attempts to attack them were foiled by heavy AA fire from the U-boats.

At 04.00 on 13 September, Sea Hurricanes were scrambled after Swordfish on anti-submarine patrol were discovered by another two Luftwaffe aircraft, a Blohm und Voss Bv138 and a Junkers Ju88 reconnaissance aircraft, but these disappeared into the low cloud before the fighters could reach them. Later that day a formation of Ju88 medium bombers made a high-level bombing attack on the convoy. Again, the convoy's fighters were unable to shoot down a German aircraft, largely because the early Sea Hurricane's machine guns could not concentrate enough fire on the bombers to have any effect. While the fighters refuelled and rearmed, the Luftwaffe attacked at 15.40. As twenty Ju88s flew over the convoy in a high-level attack, distracting the defences and causing the ships to take evasive action, twenty-eight Heinkel He111 and eighteen Ju88s made a low-level torpedo attack, following by a second wave of seventeen Ju88s. Sweeping in at around 20 feet above the waves, the attackers ignored the escorts and concentrated on the merchant vessels, the correct strategy. The Sea Hurricanes were still on the carrier's deck and could not take off.

A mass 45-degree turn was attempted, but the inexperience of many of those aboard the merchantmen and the large size of the convoy meant that not all of the ships managed this manoeuvre. Inexperience also showed in the wild anti-aircraft fire against the low-flying aircraft which exposed the anti-aircraft crews on other ships to fire from shells and bullets. Pressing home their attack with considerable courage, the Germans sank eight ships, the more fortunate crews being able to jump direct from their ships onto the ice-encrusted decks of the escort and rescue vessels. The less fortunate had minutes in which to be rescued or die in the cold sea. The temperature of the sea was academic for the unfortunate crew aboard the *Empire Stevenson*, loaded with explosives, as they disappeared with the ship in one huge explosion. During this attack, the convoy's combined AA fire accounted for five aircraft. The Sea Hurricanes drove off a later attack by Heinkel He115 floatplanes, but one was shot down.

A change of tactics saw the Sea Hurricanes rotated, each spending twenty-five minutes in the air before landing to refuel, keeping a constant CAP over the convoy.

On 14 September, the first Swordfish of the day found *U-589* on the surface, but she dived leaving the Swordfish to mark the spot with a smoke flare. Once the aircraft had gone, the submarine surfaced and continued charging her batteries. Alerted by the Swordfish, the destroyer *Onslow* raced to the scene. Once again, *U-589* dived, but she suffered for her impertinence when the destroyer attacked with depth charges and destroyed her.

The Germans also changed their tactics. Reconnaissance Bv138s and Ju88s were sent to intimidate the Swordfish, forcing them back onto the convoy, until the Germans were driven away by heavy AA fire. The Swordfish would then venture out, only to be found and driven back again.

A further attack by Ju88s later that day saw *Avenger* herself become the target, moving at her maximum 17 knots. The Sea Hurricanes broke up the attack and no ships were lost, but eleven Ju88s were shot down, again mainly by AA fire. Further attacks that day, including dive-bombing, saw another German aircraft shot down without any losses to the convoy. In a final attack, three of the four patrolling Hurricanes were shot down by friendly fire, although all three pilots were saved, after five Luftwaffe aircraft were shot down and another nine damaged beyond repair with five of these credited to the Sea Hurricanes. In this attack, *Avenger*'s commanding officer, Commander Copeland, successfully managed to comb the torpedoes dropped by the Germans, but the ammunition ship, *Mary Luckenbach*, blew up, again with the loss of all of her crew, taking her attacker with her as the aircraft had flown so low to ensure accuracy that it was caught in the explosion.

The following day, the remaining Sea Hurricanes and the Swordfish were again in the air, with the former breaking up further attacks. The day after, 16 September, the Swordfish were relieved of their patrolling by shore-based RAF Consolidated Catalina flying boats operating from Russia. The break was short-lived as later that day the convoy crossed the homeward convoy, QP14, with the survivors of the ill-fated PQ17, and *Avenger*, with her aircraft and some of the other escorts transferred to this convoy. The brief interval after shore-based aircraft had started to provide cover was used by the ship's air engineering team to assemble five Sea Hurricanes, more than replacing the four lost on the outward convoy. All in all, the Sea Hurricanes had accounted for a total of five enemy aircraft and damaged seventeen others.

Keeping the Convoy Route Open

Convoys were also suspended in mid-March 1943 as the battleship *Tirpitz*, battlecruiser *Scharnhorst* and heavy cruiser *Lutzow* were all based on northern Norway. The Allies were concerned that this powerful striking force would break out and the USN hastily assembled Task Force 22 at Portland, Maine, to reinforce the Royal Navy's Home Fleet and protect the Atlantic convoys in case of a breakout. Heavy losses in the North Atlantic, problems in cooperating with the Soviets and the longer hours of daylight, all meant that later, at the height of summer, convoys to the USSR had to be suspended until the darker days of winter.

Later, in summer 1944, the Normandy landings, Operation Overlord, took up the available escort and heavy units of the Royal and US Navies, which were needed not only to protect the invasion fleet but also to bring much-needed supplies from the United States and Canada. Once again, convoys to the Soviet Union had to be suspended. Operation DC saw three destroyers sail on 29 June with supplies for the escorts stranded in Soviet ports, starting their return on 4 July. Nevertheless, convoys were kept operational even up to and beyond the end of the war in Europe. There were two reasons for this. Hitler kept Norway well defended after its occupation believing, as the threat of invasion emerged, that this would be Churchill's preferred route back into Europe. The second reason was that the Admiralty feared that some rogue U-boats might continue to attack convoys even after the German surrender while Japan remained undefeated.

Despite Admiralty objections to the welded hulls of the American-built escort carriers, these ships did perform sterling service on the Arctic convoys whenever this was expected of them. Apart from *Avenger* mentioned earlier, other ships included HMS *Tracker*.

Before the Normandy landings, the assault on the U-boats continued at full pace. In March 1944, aircraft from HMS *Chaser* sank U-boats on three successive days. The following month, aircraft from *Activity* and *Tracker* worked with the surface escorts to sink three U-boats in as many days. On a homeward-bound convoy in May, aircraft from *Fencer* sank three U-boats in just two days. Later in the year, once the convoys resumed after the Normandy landings, there were successes by aircraft from *Campania* and *Vindex*. Cunningham noted that throughout 1944, at least twenty-three U-boats were sunk by convoy escorts on the Arctic route alone, with nine by carrier-borne aircraft and another three by carrier aircraft cooperating with surface vessels, and another six by surface vessels, plus one sunk by a British submarine and four by RAF Coastal Command.

On 1 April 1944, *Tracker* had been escorting the Arctic convoy JW58 when aircraft from her embarked composite squadron, No. 846 with Grumman Avenger bombers and Wildcat fighters, collaborated with the destroyer HMS *Beagle* to sink *U-288*. On 3 April, they had then joined aircraft from another US-built escort, HMS *Activity*, to sink *U-355*, and then went on to sink another U-boat, damaged three more and shot down six enemy aircraft during the convoy's passage.

The inclusion of escort carriers in the Russian convoys paid ample dividends, as they did also in the Atlantic, recalled Cunningham later. Allied losses in the Arctic convoys, which until VE Day remained one of the major and most difficult commitments in fulfilment of British and American pledges to their Russian allies, were greatly diminished.

After a spell 'poaching', attacking enemy convoys, it was time for *Nairana* to become gamekeeper again, providing air support for a convoy to Murmansk. Some might argue that these ships were better off on this work than attacking enemy shipping, especially taking considerable risks for such slender rewards as had occurred on the two-carrier mission at the end of January, but wars cannot be won, cannot be brought to a conclusion, by defensive measures alone.

Nairana sailed for Murmansk from Scapa Flow in Orkney after nightfall on 5 February 1945, joining the convoy code-named JW64 that had sailed from Greenock on the Clyde on 3 February. The convoy itself consisted of twenty-six merchantmen and the initial escort from the Clyde to a point

90 miles north-east of the Faeroes was three destroyers, four corvettes and three sloops, as well as a vessel from the Royal Fleet Auxiliary, the Royal Navy's fleet train manned by the Merchant Navy. *Nairana* was part of the First Cruiser Squadron, CS1, along with just one cruiser, HMS *Bellona*, and once again was paired with the escort carrier *Campania*, as well as eight destroyers. In contrast to PQ18, this meant that the convoy would have twenty-eight Swordfish and twelve Wildcats. The escort was commanded by Rear Admiral Rhoderick McGrigor, a Scot, who paid the carriers the compliment of flying his flag in *Nairana*, something for which no doubt the escort carrier was never designed.

The convoy's route was to keep it 200 miles off the coast of Norway until the last two or three days, when the need to avoid the southern edge of the Arctic ice pack would take it to within 100 miles. At first, the weather was good, very good for the time of year, and the convoy assembled and set off at 13 knots, which could have taken it the 1,300 miles to the Kola Inlet in just five days, if it could have been maintained. The burden of defending the convoy was to be shared between the two carriers, with one providing CAP while the other provided anti-submarine and surface vessel reconnaissance at any one time, and then switching roles. In addition, both ships had all their Swordfish ready to be scrambled in an emergency at any time, while the Wildcats not in the air would also be ready to be scrambled during the hours of daylight. There was an attempt to give this convoy some night-fighter protection with the addition of a Fairey Fulmar to *Campania*'s aircraft, although the Fulmar had never been able to compete with contemporary fighters even at the outset of the war, and was certainly obsolete by 1945.

The hope was always that the position of a convoy, indeed its very existence, would remain hidden from the enemy for as long as possible. Luck played a part in this, as discoveries were often made by accident, and JW64 was no exception, being discovered by a high-flying Luftwaffe aircraft on a routine weather flight early on 6 February. Later that day, as evening drew in, radar showed that the convoy was being shadowed by a Junkers Ju88, loitering at a distance of some 20 or 30 miles. The Wildcats were scrambled from *Campania* within seven minutes and directed to the Ju88 by radar, shooting it down, but one of the fighters failed to return to the carrier for reasons that were never established. As darkness fell, the convoy was without night-fighter cover as the Fulmar was unserviceable.

Inevitably, a fresh shadower arrived even before dawn on 7 January, and without a night fighter to contend with, was able to operate unmolested until first light. Daybreak found the weather worsening. The convoy had crossed the Arctic Circle during the night and was soon in a moderate gale with snow showers and the cloud base at less than 1,000 feet. As the weather continued to deteriorate throughout the day, the convoy's speed fell to 8 knots.

Attack by German bombers or submarines, or both, was expected, and the first air attack came at 07.40, with the aircraft flying so low that they were just 10 miles away when *Nairana*'s radar picked them up and her fighters were scrambled. This first attack was not pressed home in the face of heavy AA fire from the escorts, which shot one aircraft down while several 'probables' were also claimed. There was a similar result when Ju88 torpedo-bombers attempted to attack at 09.30, except that on this occasion the fighters were from *Campania*. Later, a shadower was shot down by Wildcats from *Nairana*. Expecting U-boat activity, round-the-clock Swordfish patrols were ordered. In the seventy-two hours between nightfall on 7 January and nightfall on 10 January, there were more than seventy such patrols by 813 and 835 Squadrons. Each patrol lasted between ninety minutes and three hours, with two Stringbags in the air at any one time.

The strain of such operations was compounded not only by the cold, but by the motion of the ship that made proper sleep impossible. John Godley, with the responsibility of running a squadron as well as flying, had a cabin at *Nairana*'s stern, in which sleep was almost impossible in bad weather due to the motion of the ship and, no doubt too whenever the stern lifted, the racing of the screws as they came out of the water.

The Swordfish sorties were meant to force U-boats to remain submerged, below periscope depth, at which they would have great difficulty getting into position to attack the convoy or mounting an attack even if the convoy steamed past them. On 9 January, shortly after 20.00, two U-boats were detected by their radio signals, one to the south and the other to the south-east of the convoy. It was essential that they should be forced down to prevent them reaching the convoy, and if possible destroyed. Six Swordfish from 835 Squadron were sent, two to fly a search pattern known as a 'Crocodile' and four to fly another known as a 'Lizard', two over the reported position of each U-boat. In such conditions, rocket projectiles could not be used and the aircraft were armed with depth charges. Squadron Commander, John Godley recalled:

> I flew a night Croc later and it was just about the most unpleasant flight I ever made. The temperature was far below zero Fahrenheit with a wind gusting to over fifty knots and in our open cockpits we were as exposed as ever to the elements. It was an absolutely pitch dark night and I was forced to fly almost the whole mission on instruments, just as George [his observer, Sub Lieutenant George Strong] had to keep his eyes glued to the radar screen. The ceiling was under 1,000 feet. I flew as high as I could without entering cloud, though there was little chance of locating the U-boat visually, to give George the best chance of finding her by radar. Just from time to time I'd catch a blurred glimpse of the whitecaps as we buffeted through the night ... *Nairana* was pitching like crazy when at last we approached to

land, but I've never seen anything more welcome than the heaving lights of her flight deck as we came in, guided as ever by Bob Mathe's inspired batsmanship. Our ground speed at touchdown must have been under ten knots and the landing was uneventful.

Not the least of the worries for the aircrew was that engine failure in such conditions would have been fatal. Even if they had managed to ditch successfully in the dark and such stormy conditions, getting out of the aircraft and into a dinghy, even if it had inflated properly, would have been very difficult, and it would have been unlikely that they could have survived very long in an open dinghy. Worse still, the storm would have swept them further out to sea towards Greenland. In such extreme conditions, watchful eyes continually swept over the instrument panel, checking the oil pressure and temperature gauges, while anxious ears listened out for any slight change in the engine rhythm, but the faithful Peggy droned on through the night.

The weather was so bad by this time that the convoy was making a mere 5 knots.

On the morning of 10 February, Godley and Strong were once again airborne, taking off before sunrise with a fresh gale blowing, although this was better weather than they had encountered on their previous sortie. On this occasion, the cloud was in two layers, with six- to seven-tenths nimbo-stratus at 500 to 800 feet, and eight-tenths cumulous and cumulonimbus above 4,000 feet. After taking off using RATOG into the strong headwind that saw their aircraft in the air with half of the deck left, they flew a Crocodile as no U-boat fixes had been made overnight. Another of 835's aircraft was in the air flying a half-Viper. Godley was to the south of the convoy, believing that any attack would come from that quarter, the direction of Norway.

Flying as high as possible, using breaks in the nimbus, he saw low cloud ahead and dived down to fly beneath it, only to find himself flying towards a formation of Ju88s heading northwards towards the convoy at just above wave height. He found himself wishing for some rockets, even though they were not intended for air-to-air combat, as Strong signalled the fleet: 'Beeswax from Topaz Able. Tally-Ho ten eighty-eights position 180ZZ30. Heading for convoy, Over.' Then came a brisk acknowledgement: 'Able from Beeswax. Roger. Out.'

By chance, with visibility of half a mile or less, they had been able to give the convoy an extra four minutes warning of a low-level attack, and identify the aircraft and the number which the radar operator would not have been able to do. This was just one of several attacks pressed home despite heavy AA fire that morning, but once again, no ships were hit as they successfully combed the torpedoes. *Nairana* herself shot down one of the Ju88s with her AA fire, while two aircraft were shot down by 835's

Wildcats and another were three claimed as 'probables' by 813. The escorts and the merchantmen shot down another five Ju88s and damaged eight.

Meanwhile, Godley was unable to land on during the attacks and had to remain on station. Still looking for U-boats, he suddenly spotted a lone enemy bomber heading for the convoy and, just for the 'hell of it', turned and dived towards the Ju88. A Stringbag threatening a Ju88 sounds most unlikely, but one of the enemy crewmen must have spotted a strange aircraft diving at them and, not recognizing it, but expecting a fighter, alerted the pilot, for the Ju88 suddenly went into a steep climbing turn and headed back towards Norway.

The excitement wasn't over. With the attacks ended, Godley descended through low cloud intending to land on and appeared above a 'box' of four destroyers, which managed to mistake his single-engine biplane for twin-engined monoplane bombers, and opened fire. He quickly climbed back into the cloud and sent an indignant signal to the Rear Admiral. When he did get back aboard the carrier, Godley found that 'friendly fire' from a merchantman had shot down one of 813's Wildcats, although the pilot had been rescued, while several other fighters had been damaged, including

Tired of being shot by AA gunners on ships in his own convoy who mistook his Swordfish biplane for a Junker Ju88s monoplane, Lieutenant Commander John Godley devised this 'Valentine Card'. (The late Lord Kilbracken)

two from 835. When the next attack developed just twenty minutes after the previous one had ended, there were just six or seven serviceable Wildcats between the two ships, but fortunately these were enough to fend off the attack.

By late on 10 February, there had been another fix on a U-boat. Although they did not know it at the time, no less than eight U-boats were waiting for the convoy and by this time the weather was improving, useful for friend and foe alike. Then, unexpectedly, an aircraft on patrol radioed that they had encountered fog, conditions in which neither aircraft nor U-boats could operate. Ahead of the convoy lay a fog bank and the decision was taken to order the four aircraft in the air to land straight away, while those ready for take-off would be delayed, leaving the convoy without air cover for the time being. A change such as this was no easy matter, with the aircraft ranged on the deck ready for take-off having to be manhandled forward of the barrier so that the returning aircraft could land on.

Emerging into clear weather at 01.30 on 12 February, the convoy changed course for the Kola Inlet, at 200 miles to the south less than a day's steaming. Shortly after dawn, the convoy rendezvoused with a small group of Soviet warships – the Soviet Navy played virtually no part in protecting the convoys – while occasional appearances of Soviet aircraft were meant to help chase off the U-boats, except that the aircraft were Bell Airacobra fighters, wholly unsuited to the task. Having got through repeated air attacks safely and kept the submarines at bay, at 00.29 on 13 February, the convoy suffered its only loss when the corvette HMS *Denbigh Castle* was struck by a torpedo fired from one of four U-boats lurking close to the shore. Her commanding officer managed to beach his ship, but she was a total loss. In fact, the crew were lucky, as a torpedo hit on such a small vessel could have resulted in massive loss of life.

Convoys back to the UK were almost as important as those to the Soviet Union. In running a convoy system, it was always important never to neglect the 'empties', and for the Germans, a ship sunk sailing homeward was a ship lost to the Allied cause, even if she was empty. The omens for the return voyage were not good. Having lost the *Denbigh Castle*, news now came in that two merchantmen under Soviet escort from Archangel to join the homeward convoy had been torpedoed and sunk, again by U-boats lurking close to the Soviet shore, an exercise that should have been extremely dangerous for the U-boats. In fact, a pack of a dozen U-boats had assembled at the entrance to the Kola Inlet and were eagerly awaiting the departure of the homeward convoy. Five escorts were sent to the mouth of the Inlet, and succeeded in sinking *U-425* at 01.07 on 17 February, the date for the convoy to sail. This was good news, but somewhat spoiled by the fact that the escort force was able to confirm the presence of a number of U-boats.

Meanwhile, in an attempt to improve aircraft recognition standards, John Godley and his comrades produced a 'Valentine' card for the escorts, although he later felt that this might not have been much appreciated.

Departing homeward on 17 February, with the same escorts as before, but with *Campania* down to nine Swordfish and two Wildcats, 813 and 835 were ordered to maintain continuous air cover for as long as the weather permitted. As usually happens in warfare, one defensive measure prompts a new countermeasure, and the presence of ASV radar was countered by growing use of the snorkel by German submarines at this time, allowing them to remain under the surface at periscope level almost indefinitely. The small 'snort' was too small to be picked up by the radar of the day and could only be seen with the naked eye at distances of up to 2 miles in good visibility, which did not exist with the four hours of daylight north of the Arctic Circle in February. Night patrols would have to be flown, but unless a U-boat obliged by coming to the surface, they would be useless and simply done to boost the morale of the crews aboard the thirty-seven merchantmen, making it seem that something was being done.

Leaving the Kola Inlet at 07.45, the first air patrols were by Swordfish, with three aircraft launched from *Nairana*, one flying a search pattern known as a 'Viper' and the other two flying 'Crocodiles'. The patrols between them believed that they had spotted a snorkel five or six times, but on closer inspection discovered these sightings to be scraps of wreckage or oil slicks. Continuous air patrols meant exactly that, and so as not to leave the skies clear, replacement patrols were flown off half an hour before the previous patrols were due to land on. Just nine minutes after these replacement aircraft had taken off and before they had reached their designated patrol areas, an acoustic torpedo from *U-968* blew the stern off the sloop *Lark*, causing a number of casualties, although the ship herself was saved and taken in tow by a Russian tug to Murmansk for repairs. It was clearly *U-968*'s day, for despite the convoy taking evasive action, with an emergency turn to north-north-east, and aircraft being sent to the location of the submarine, the merchantman *Thomas Scott* was next to be torpedoed. Her crew immediately abandoned ship, but reboarded her as there seemed to be no immediate danger of her sinking, but she went down before she could return to the Kola Inlet.

In an attempt to get away from the U-boat wolf pack, the convoy turned due north at 14.50, but instead this led them directly towards *U-711*, and at 15.23 one of her torpedoes struck the Flower-class corvette HMS *Bluebell*, setting off her magazine so that she simply disappeared. Just five of her crew were taken alive from the cold waters, but only one, a petty officer (the naval equivalent of a sergeant) survived. No aircraft were close enough to attack, but several escort vessels mounted a heavy, but completely unsuccessful, depth-charge attack. A considerable number of radio fixes were obtained after dark and a further emergency turn was made to avoid the position of a U-boat, but overall the wolf pack was being left behind as the presence of the Swordfish forced the submarines to remain submerged and unable to keep up with the convoy.

An idea of the many hazards facing the convoy came when a Stringbag crashed during take-off. The pilot had started his take-off run at 23.30 for a night patrol and failed to realize that he was not heading straight along the flight deck, so that when he fired his RATOG his aircraft struck *Nairana*'s island and then somersaulted over the side. Both the pilot and observer managed to escape, but this still left the danger of the depth charges blowing up, which could have severely damaged the carrier. By this time, depth charges were fitted with a device that stopped them exploding if they were still attached to the depth-charge rack on the aircraft, but it was known to be unreliable. A corvette on plane guard duty snatched the two men from the icy waters, unquestionably placing the small ship at considerable risk, but fortunately there was no explosion.

The weather worsened and by 15.30 on 18 February, the order was given for flying to cease. By midnight, the storm was so bad that the convoy began to scatter as winds hit Force 10. The inevitable Luftwaffe shadower appeared before dawn on 19 February, but nothing could be done to discourage this unwelcome guest as winds remained at over 60 knots, too high to launch a Wildcat. As the weather worsened, even the Luftwaffe had to suspend operations until almost midnight, after which the weather eased and an attempt was made to regroup the convoy, so that by 08.00 on 20 February there were only four stragglers.

Four Wildcats remained serviceable aboard *Nairana*, but with winds gusting at up to 55 mph, it was not clear whether these could be launched because of the difficulty of landing. At 10.00, radar picked up an attacking formation, which soon proved to be Ju88 torpedo-bombers, and the Wildcats were scrambled. Despite penetrating the defensive AA fire to launch their torpedoes, the attack was unsuccessful, with one Ju88 shared between two Wildcats and another rated as a 'probable', while the AA gunners claimed two confirmed hits, one probable and four aircraft damaged. The Germans had failed to find the four vulnerable stragglers. The first three Wildcats landed on safely, but the fourth bounced over the wires and into the barrier.

In fact, seven Luftwaffe aircraft failed to return from this attack and the pilots who did get back claimed to have sunk two cruisers, two destroyers and at least eight merchantmen, despite the convoy having had just one cruiser! Three German U-boats ordered to search for survivors or for signs of wreckage naturally enough found nothing.

While the weather remained bad, it was decided to keep the Swordfish on deck, although flying would not have been possible in the Force 8 gale. Nevertheless, the poor conditions meant that the convoy covered just 600 miles in its first four days at sea. By 16.00 on 21 February, another two stragglers had caught up with the convoy and it was decided to send four Stringbags to search for the two ships still missing. They located one of them 20 miles to the south-west and guided it back to the convoy, but there was no sign of the other ship. As the weather worsened again that night, radio fixes were made on two U-boats, but it was felt that the chances of finding them in the dark were so low that it did not justify the risk in sending off patrols. Nevertheless, aircraft were ranged on deck ready to be scrambled at first light, triple lashed, but eventually even these had to be struck down to the shelter of the hangar as the ship began rolling heavily, so much so that it was becoming difficult for the crew to maintain their footing on the flight deck – it took twenty men to move each aircraft and hold them in position in the lift while they were struck down into the hangar. At noon, the convoy was hit by a hurricane, with the anemometer stuck on its maximum registerable windspeed of 80 knots and kept there for twenty hours. Spray whipped up by the storm froze on the flight deck, which was now impossible for anyone to step onto. Below, in the hangar deck, work on the aircraft was impossible. Officers trying to sleep found the deck a better place than their bunks. The convoy started to scatter again and then, during the early hours of 23 February, the convoy broke in two, with most of the merchantmen and *Nairana* struggling on at 4 knots, while a number of others, including *Campania* and three or four destroyers, turned into the wind and simply maintained steerage way.

While it was still dark, Godley was awoken from an uneasy slumber, more of a state of half sleep, by a massive crash from a deck above. Still dressed, he made his way up the companionway to the hangar deck, hearing another massive crash as he went, to find a scene of devastation. The small tractor used to move the aircraft around the deck, bright yellow and weighing around a ton, had broken free from its triple lashings, supposed to keep it tight and secure against a bulkhead, and was now careering from one side of the deck to the other. The massive crash that had alerted Godley had occurred as it slammed against the starboard bulkhead for the first time, the second had been while it crashed into the port bulkhead. In between, as it slid across the deck, it demolished any aircraft that happened to be in the way.

Hangar decks were, and no doubt still are, notoriously difficult to keep truly dry and clean, quickly becoming covered in a thin film of oil. Godley was alone in the hangar at first, but he was soon joined by several others. He ordered them to get as many hands together as possible so that they could attempt to catch the wayward tractor which had already struck six aircraft, two of them possibly beyond repair. One man slipped on the deck, laughing at first as he slid along on his backside on the slippery surface, but his joy was short lived as he suddenly saw the tractor sliding towards him and only just managed to scramble out of the way in time, avoiding being crushed between it and a bulkhead.

Having assembled a team of twenty men with ropes, Godley led them in an attempt to catch the tractor, but each time they caught it, the ship rolled and the ropes parted, leaving the tractor to continue to ricochet between the bulkheads, damaging yet more aircraft. Leaving a junior officer in charge in the hangar to do the best he could, Godley raced up to the bridge in an attempt to get the commanding officer to turn into the wind, just for fifteen minutes, to give them a chance to catch the tractor. *Nairana*'s CO, Captain Villiers 'Strawberry' Surtees, refused, insisting on staying with the convoy, despite the desperate pleadings of 835's squadron commander. On returning to the hangar, he found sixty men with rope and steel cable, and organized them into teams, each under an officer or a chief petty officer (the naval equivalent of a staff sergeant), and they resumed their efforts to catch the tractor. After a further five minutes of struggling, the ship suddenly hit a patch of calmer water, lasting for just a few minutes but enough to enable them to catch the tractor, throwing ropes around it and every man grabbing at the machine, then as the ship rolled, they used the movement to edge the tractor to starboard and out of harm's way.

The cost of this episode was considerable. Out of thirteen Swordfish left, seven had been damaged, four of them beyond repair. One man suffered a broken leg, but there were no other injuries. Somehow, all six Wildcats parked at the forward end of the hangar, had escaped damage.

Reporting to the bridge, Godley was warned that he would have to be prepared to fly off at dawn if conditions permitted as the convoy had become badly scattered.

Dawn found conditions still too bad for operations, with the wind still at 70 knots. *Nairana* was in company with the cruiser *Bellona*, most of the escorts and a dozen merchantmen, while *Campania* was with her destroyers some 20 miles to the north. The escorts now had the additional task of finding the stragglers, rounding them up and getting them back to the convoy, without any help from the Swordfish. *Campania* caught up shortly after midday and at 14.00 was able to scramble two Swordfish, signalling *Nairana* to have Wildcats ready. At 14.20 came a distress call from the merchantman *Henry Bacon*, one of the stragglers some 50 miles east of the convoy, which had been caught by nine Ju88s. Fighters were immediately flown off, but by the time they reached the stricken ship the attackers had departed leaving her burning. A destroyer was guided to the ship by the Wildcats. The *Henry Bacon*'s gunners claimed two Ju88s as probables, but she had the unwanted distinction of being the last ship to be sunk by German aircraft in the Second World War.

Luckiest of all was the merchantman *Noyes*, the straggler from an earlier storm which had failed to be spotted on the searches and for which all hope had been given up, but which had in fact fallen no less than 300 miles behind the convoy yet still managed to reach Loch Ewe in the west of Scotland on 29 February.

On 28 February, *Nairana,* with *Campania, Bellona* and four destroyers, reached the safety of Scapa Flow. Flown ashore to Hatston in Orkney on 5 March, 835 found itself sent on another anti-shipping strike off Norway that had to be abandoned due to bad weather. It was a sad end to the career of the Fairey Swordfish as, after that, only 836 was left operating the aircraft off MAC-ships, while elsewhere they were replaced by the Barracuda and, in the Far East, by the Grumman Avenger.

Chapter 14

Back to the East

After the invasion of the South of France, the naval war in Europe began to run down. There was some mopping up of enemy forces in the Adriatic, especially to hinder the retreat of German forces, plus mine countermeasures as ports in the Low Countries became available as Allied forces pressed on towards Germany, and, of course, continued operations against German convoys off Norway. Nevertheless, the main body of the Royal Navy was now free for operations against Japan.

The return of the Royal Navy to eastern waters was met with considerable reservations by many senior officers in the United States Navy, many of whom saw the British role at best as being centred on the reconquest of Burma. Many senior USN officers felt that they could finish the job without any British help. On the other hand, the British had strong political reasons for wishing to play an active part. They did not want to be seen to be leaving an ally on its own, or abandoning Australia and New Zealand. They also needed to put pressure on the Japanese to relieve that on British forces, fighting to protect India from Japanese attack in Burma. Finally, much of the territory overrun by Japan was British, including Hong Kong, Singapore and Malaya, as well as Burma.

There were practical difficulties to be resolved, such as coordination and liaison, and this could be difficult with any large force, even within a single navy – in the Battle of Leyte Gulf, parts of the United States Navy were not been where they were expected to be. A condition laid down by the United States Navy was that the Royal Navy could not expect any use of American facilities in the Pacific theatre. Two of the senior American commanders, Chester Nimitz and Ernest King, felt that the British lacked the experience of mounting mass air attacks from carriers and the means of supporting a fleet so far from its bases. The British had little experience of putting together a modern fleet that was both balanced and adequate in strength, which was why they lost so many important ships early in the war. British ships also tended to be short on range, and some eyewitnesses could attest to the Royal Navy's slow progress when refuelling at sea compared to the Americans. The distances over which the war in the East was fought have to be taken into account – from Japan to Singapore was about the same distance as Southampton to New York.

The British started to resolve these problems. They were able to use Simonstown in South Africa as a base, with South African Air Force airfields available for carrier aircraft disembarking as the carriers went into port. Ceylon provided a forward base with many naval air stations ashore, and others in southern India. Australia became yet another base and, especially important for the British Pacific Fleet, with Sydney and Brisbane having air stations ashore. Nevertheless, the prospect of having additional ships and aircraft appealed to many other senior American officers. The problems of cooperation were resolved, partly by ensuring that at first the British Eastern Fleet operated in one area, while the US Fifth Fleet operated elsewhere. This did not mean that there was no cooperation, and British, Australian and New Zealand ships did sometimes operate with the Americans, under their command. Liaison officers were exchanged.

Cooperation on a small scale was attempted at first, so that the two navies could get used to each other. During the spring of 1944, the USS *Saratoga* was attached to the British Eastern Fleet, joining *Illustrious* for the early raids on Sabang in Task Force 70. This was to prove to be the ideal target for the Fleet Air Arm to hone its techniques in massed aerial attack. It was well away from the Americans and posed no threat to them, but it was also a useful target, on a small island off the northern end of Sumatra, with a harbour and airfields vital to the Japanese war effort in Burma. This was also to prove to be the baptism of fire for a new high-performance fighter for the Fleet Air Arm: the American Vought Corsair, sometimes described as the 'best American fighter of World War II'.

This was not the first example of RN/USN cooperation in the East. The shortage of flight decks felt by the three carrier-operating navies during the Second World War resulted in some unusual compromises. One of these was that the British fast armoured carrier, HMS *Victorious*, second ship of the successful Illustrious-class, spent much of the winter of 1942/3 being refitted at the Norfolk Navy Yard before going 'on loan' to the United States Navy, being given the temporary name of USS *Robin*, until later relieved by the American interpretation of the fast carrier, the USS *Essex*, lead ship of the class of the same name with no less than twenty-five large carriers in all. The *Robin*, alias *Victorious*, operated with the US Pacific Fleet, and no doubt helped to improve inter-operability between the two navies.

The first attack on Sabang was made on 19 April 1944, with Corsairs escorting Barracudas, an aircraft that had seen action in Europe, notably against the *Tirpitz*, but which was to prove ill-suited to tropical conditions. Operating under the command of Admiral Sir James Somerville, the British Eastern Fleet was to be a thorn in the Japanese flesh. The initial raid was unexpected by the Japanese, and devastating, despite the poor performance of the Barracuda. These aircraft were quickly exchanged for the more capable and reliable Grumman Avenger, and both ships were able to launch a second successful attack in May, against an oil refinery outside Surabaya on the island of Java, with the loss of just one aircraft.

Operating together quickly exposed weaknesses in British organization. The British carrier air group was smaller than that of the Americans, but even more important, the Fleet Air Arm had to learn the importance of a fast turnaround of aircraft on the flight deck and in the hangar. Fortunately, these lessons were learnt very quickly.

Completely integrated carrier operations by the two navies took time, but coordination became increasingly important and as the war progressed was much in evidence. The Americans also came to appreciate the strength of the Illustrious-class carriers, especially under Kamikaze attacks. As one American officer aboard a British carrier put it succinctly: 'When a Kamikaze hits an American carrier, it's six months repair at Pearl. In a Limey carrier, it's a case of "sweepers, man your brooms!"'

Stopping Japan's Oil

Several targets fell, particularly to the Fleet Air Arm. One of these was Palembang, with oil refineries and port facilities on the island of Sumatra. The most important of these was on 24 January 1945, in Operation Meridian I, and involved aircraft from 820, 849, 854, 857, 887, 894, 1770, 1830, 1833, 1834, 1836, 1839 and 1844 NAS, operating from *Illustrious, Indefatigable, Indomitable* and *Victorious*. The Japanese were subjected to heavy attacks throughout December 1944 and January,1945.

The attention which the Royal Navy gave to Palembang was partly the result of a decision by the Commander-in-Chief, British Pacific Fleet, Admiral Sir Bruce Fraser. He believed that, in the light of prevailing American attitudes, the Royal Navy should produce some successes in the Far East to prove its worth to the Americans. The output of the oil refineries near Palembang, at Pladjoe and Soengei Gerong, provided 38 per cent of Japan's aviation fuel. Recognizing their importance, the Japanese, by this time increasingly defensive-minded, had surrounded the area with no less than four fighter air stations and many anti-aircraft batteries. Fraser's confidence in the Fleet Air Arm was not shared by the Admiralty, who had to be convinced that the FAA was up to it. Fraser won, and so it was that the heaviest attacks were mounted by the British Pacific Fleet as it was *en passage* from the Indian Ocean to the Pacific. As already mentioned, *Illustrious* had gained invaluable experiences of these operations earlier, although this also had the unintended effect of alerting the Japanese to what they could expect from the Allies in future.

Before leaving Trincomalee on 16 January, the British Pacific Fleet conducted an exercise with the Royal Air Force, simulating an attack by a carrier fleet on Ceylon's airfields and harbours. Most of the carrier aircrews carried out as many as three sorties a day from before dawn until dusk, so that the skies over Ceylon were filled with aircraft. One pilot involved in the exercise, Henry 'Hank' Adlam recalled that it was exhausting, but it was right that they were made to do it as it was typical of many days to come in the Pacific. Even so, the exercise was not without cost, as two Corsair pilots were killed in accidents during their last deck landing of the day aboard *Illustrious*.

Naturally, such an exercise would have been invaluable in early 1942 before the Japanese carriers had approached Ceylon for their attacks. On the other hand, not the least of the problems that the Royal Air Force in Ceylon, and indeed in Malaya, had faced as the Japanese had raced westwards was the lack of suitable aircraft that could have a chance of meeting the aggressor on equal terms.

As it progressed ever eastwards, the British Pacific Fleet had four large, fast, armoured carriers with more than 200 aircraft between them: *Illustrious, Indefatigable, Indomitable* and *Victorious*. As a sign of changing times, there was just one battleship, *King George V*, but the four cruisers and nine destroyers that also accompanied the carriers were probably just the minimum escort for such valuable ships. The fleet refuelled at sea before it reached the flying-off position near Enggano Island off the west coast of Sumatra on 23 January in the worst of the monsoon weather.

The 200 plus aircraft included the new Grumman Avenger, probably the most effective bomber and torpedo-bomber to operate with any navy during the Second World War, and the Grumman Hellcat, successor to the Wildcat – it was debatable whether this or the Vought Corsair was the best carrier fighter. The Corsair had one nasty habit for a carrier fighter in that it tended to bounce on landing, and being nose heavy, many ended up nose down on a carrier flight deck. There was also the new British fighter-bomber, the Fairey Firefly. In contrast to the early aerial strikes by the Fleet Air Arm, there were fighter escorts on each operation, with the Hellcats providing medium cover and the Corsairs top cover. The role of the Fireflies was to race ahead of the Avengers and make a rocket attack to suppress the anti-aircraft defences. Each Avenger carried four 500-lb bombs. The strike force comprised around 150 aircraft, while Seafires, too short on range to accompany the main force, remained behind flying combat air patrols over the carriers.

The skies started to clear before dawn on 24 January 1945, when the aircraft began to take off and formate in skies that were not yet clear, and which one pilot described as 'hectic', but the pilots had been trained for this and it paid off. A take-off accident and problems with serviceability meant that the Fireflies were amongst the last to join the formation before it set off, although an accident had also involved two Avengers. At least one pilot questioned the need for a pre-dawn take-off, believing that an extra half hour would have made no difference as he was sure that the Japanese had already manned their radar stations.

1. Looking suitably piratical at Lemnos during the Dardanelles campaign, Squadron Commander Charles Rumney Samson was indeed one of the pioneering naval airmen of the period before and during the First World War. In addition to combat sorties, he and his men would take up submarine commanders on orientation flights. *(IWM Q 13542)*

2. A North Sea class :ship, one of the first to ave a cabin as opposed to a modified aircraft ıselage. The distinctive hape of this semi-rigid airship is due to the three internal air bags. As can be seen, ground handling was very labour intensive. *(IWM Q 27433)*

3. The First World War battleship HMS *King George V* with a tethered observation balloon in the background. *(IWM SP 365)*

4. An early VC for the RNAS was that for Flying Sub Lieutenant Reginald Warneford, who shot down a Zeppelin over Belgium. He is seen here with fellow officers: note the eagle above the curl on his jacket sleeve. (*IWM Q 69479*)

5. Flying boats could cope with worse weather than airships and were much more manoeuvrable, but they lacked endurance. This is an FBA flying boat. (*IWM Q 33761*)

6. The seaplane carrier HMS *Engadine* with a Fairey seaplane aft of the hangar. (*IWM SP 413*)

7. An RNAS observer prepares to drop a bomb from an airship. Note the modified aircraft fuselage. Clearly both bomb design and bomb aiming were primitive at this time. (*IWM Q 67695*)

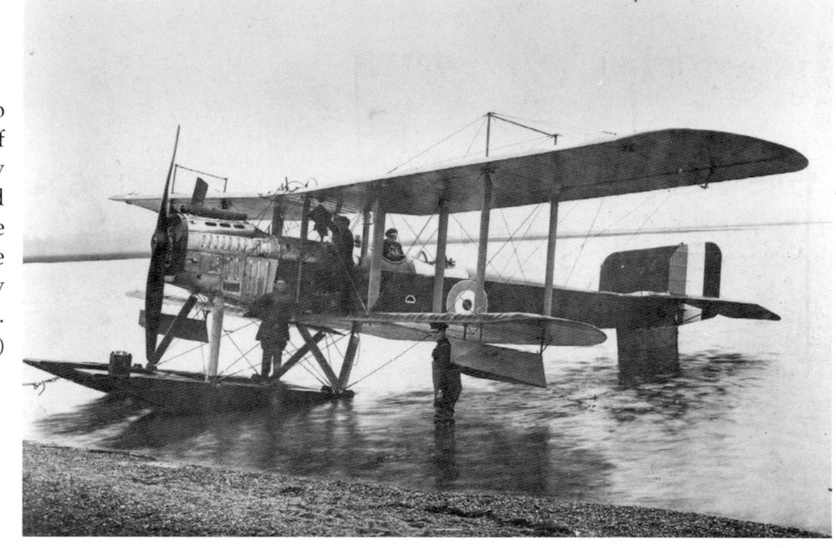

Despite being able to e a trolley for take-off om a wooden runway built on the converted r, HMS *Campania*, the ey Campania biplane was still penalized by the drag of its floats. (*IWM Q 69382*)

9. In desperation to get fighter landplanes into the air, one solution tried was that of towing lighters at high speed behind destroyers: it worked, but the aircraft could only be used for a single sortie. The shapes on the deck of the lighter are naval ratings lying prone after earlier helping to weigh down the bows of the lighter. (*IWM Q 27511*)

10. Shore-based naval aviation provided increasingly capable maritime-reconnaissance as the war progressed. This is a Curtis Large America flying boat on the slipway, probably at Felixstowe. (*IWM Q 67581*)

11. There was only one solution to the problem providing air cover for t fleet: the aircraft carrier, or, as they were known first, 'aerodrome ships'. This is the first, HMS *Furious*, after the second stage of her conversion which provided a 'landing-on' deck at the stern. Unfortunately, th superstructure remainec problem. (*IWM Q 195557*)

12. *Furious* was not the only battlecruiser to be converted to an aircraft carrier, as her two sisters, *Courageous* and *Glorious*, were converted between the two world wars, albeit with starboard islands and arrester wires across rather than along the deck. Both were lost early in the war; this is a photograph from an unknown source showing *Courageous* sinking after being torpedoed by a U-boat on 17 September 1939.

. *Glorious*, the day before she was sunk by the German battlecruisers Scharnhorst and *Gneisenau* ɪring the withdrawal from Norway. The RAF Hurricanes flown aboard her by airmen who didn't ant their aircraft to be lost can be seen clearly.

The most up-to-date aircraft carrier with the Royal Navy in 1939 was *Ark Royal*, with the novelty :hree lifts, which can be seen clearly here, and the first British aircraft carrier to have two hangar :ks. The extensions of the flight deck over the bows and the stern in particular can also be seen e. (*The late S.H. Wragg*)

THE TIMES

CRIPPLING BLOW TO ITALIAN NAVY

LATE LONDON EDITION — LONDON THURSDAY NOVEMBER 14 1940 — PRICE 2d

ITALIAN BATTLE FLEET CRIPPLED

TARANTO BASE ATTACKED BY NAVAL AIRCRAFT

USE OF TORPEDOES AT TARANTO

DROPPED FROM A LOW ALTITUDE

FROM OUR NAVAL CORRESPONDENT

It is now known that the Fleet Air Arm's attack at Taranto was made with torpedoes, and its success illustrates how effective those weapons are, against even the heaviest ships, when skilfully and resolutely handled. Some bombs may have been dropped, too, but the use of protective nets by the enemy, mentioned in the last communiqué, shows that it is torpedoes that he fears most.

The dropping of torpedoes from aircraft has often been illustrated in published photographs, which show that the aeroplane comes down to less than mast height for the drop, much closer even than for dive-bombing. The attackers had thus to brave both a protective balloon barrage and short-range A.A. guns, and the fact that they only lost two aircraft is evidence of the high standard of skill achieved.

The "four shapes" seen under water in the inner harbour are presumably the

FAIREY SWORDFISH AIRCRAFT The attack on Taranto was made by aircraft of the Fleet Air Arm from aircraft carriers

F.A.A. Attack on Taranto; Aircraft, H.M.S. Illustrious

EFFECT ON ITALIAN COMMUNICATION

15. An early victory for the Royal Navy at a time when most of the news about the war was bad w at Taranto, on the night of 11/12 November 1940, when aircraft flown off HMS *Illustrious* put three Italian battleships out of action, damaged other warships and destroyed harbour installations. This is how *The Times* reported it.

16. The 'Ark' was a happy ship, and here naval tradition is being followed with her commanding officer, Captain Holland, giving the Christmas pudding a stir with an oar in the galley. *(The late S.H. Wragg)*

17. Morale was also maintained by civilian entertainers who came aboard to give concerts wh British warships were in p and were sure of an appreciative audience at a time when major warships did not have their own pip television channels. *(The late S.H. Wragg)*

The last word in aircraft-carrier design when she joined the fleet in 1940, *Illustrious* was still hout high-performance aircraft, as this picture shows. Notice the heavy 4.5-in AA armament in ht turrets on either side, and fore and aft on the flight deck. *(The late S.H. Wragg)*

19. The 'Ark' may have been the latest in aircraft carrier design, but the same couldn't be said for the Fairey Swordfish, ranged here ready for take-off. Starting the Pegasus radial engines was a demanding task for the maintainers. (*The late S.H. Wragg*)

20. More modern in appearanc but burdened by having a two man crew, was the Blackburn Skua; these belonged to 800 NAS and are seen aboard *Ark Royal*. (*The late S.H. Wragg*)

21. So desperate was the Royal Navy for flight decks during the Battle of the Atlantic that merchant aircraft carriers, or MAC-ships, were devised, with flight decks built over the cargo spaces of grain carriers and tankers, but even so, delays meant that they did not appear until 1943. Here is *Adula* with a Swordfish taking off on an anti-submarine patrol.
(*The late Lord Kilbracken*)

22. The small size of the deck on the MAC-ships is clear to here as a Swordfish lands.
(*The late Lord Kilbracken*)

23. Known to the Royal Navy as auxiliary carriers, the escort carriers were a big improvement on the MAC-ships, and did more than provide convoy escorts, as later in the war they were used to support the Allied landings in Italy and the South of France, and then in the Pacific. Here is HMS *Empress*. *(C.S. 'Bill' Drake)*

4. The escort carriers could lso replenish other convoy escorts, largely because most escort carriers came from the United States and thus had the longer ranges to which the USN was accustomed. Here *Ameer* refuels a destroyer. *(C.S. 'Bill' Drake)*

25. Accommodation aboard the escort carriers brought things such as bunks, instead of hammocks, to the lower deck. This is the wardroom aboard *Atheling*, almost certainly in port as there are ladies aboard. The officer on the right without the executive curl could be a constructor sub lieutenant. *(The late Mrs M.J. Schupke)*

26. Not all convoys were escorted by MAC-ships or even escort carriers, as those to Malta required the large fleet carriers. This is the famous Malta convoy of August 1942, Operation Pedestal, or 'The Santa Marija Convoy' to the Maltese. This photograph was taken from the flight deck of HMS *Victorious* with *Indomitable* following and astern of her, *Eagle*, shortly before she was torpedoed and sunk. Foreground is a Sea Hurricane of 885 NAS while an Albacore of 827 takes off from *Indomitabl*
(IWM A 15961)

27. A Barracuda 'lands on' a carrier, showing just what strong nerves the 'batsman' had to possess. *(IWM A 22693)*

28. While another batsman runs for his life as a Fairey Fulmar fighter misses the arrester wire.
(The late S.H. Wragg)

29. Wartime aircrew training would have been a major obstacle to the expansion of the Fleet Air Arm to meet the Royal Navy's pressing needs but for the Towers Scheme, which enabled aspiring naval airmen to be trained by the USN at Pensacola in Florida. One of the training aircraft used was the North American T-6 Harvard. (*The late Mrs M.J. Schupke*)

30. Nevertheless, ground crew training remained with the RAF for some time longer as the Royal Navy struggled to establish its own training and support infrastructure for the Fleet Air Arm. These young recruits are to become air mechanics (E). (*FAAM*)

31. A Supermarine Walrus amphibian, an aircraft type that would normally be flown off battleships and cruisers as a fleet spotter, being manhandled aboard an aircraft carrier. The single red dot on the Standard of St George painted on the nose shows that this is an 'admiral's barge' and that the officer is a vice admiral. (*The late S.H. Wragg*)

32. Far more modern was the Vought Corsair supplied from the United States after the USN initially believed that it was too large and heavy to be flown from aircraft carriers. The Royal Navy proved that it wasn't! Some described it as the 'best carrier fighter' of the war.

33. Not that fighters were always a sure defence against Japane Kamikaze suicide bombers, which hit the British Pacific Fleet, creating much damage to aircraft ranged on deck, but carriers, such as *Formidable* shown here, survived thanks t their heavily armoured flight decks. (*FAAM CAR F-36*)

34. Five days later, they were back, and this is the flight deck of *Formidable* again. (*FAAM CARS F-39*)

35. Post-war, peace was short lived. When war broke out in Korea, the RAF's heavy commitments and the scarcity of secure airfields ashore at one stage of the war, meant that British airpower had to be carrier-based. Good targets were few and far between as North Korea had relatively little heavy industry, so the obvious targets were bridges to disrupt communications. This bridge was attacked by aircraft from the British light carrier *Theseus*. (*FAAM Camp/23*)

36. Perhaps one of the outstanding achievements was that of Peter 'Hoagy' Carmichael (who later rose to the rank of commander) who led a formation of four Hawker Sea Furies which encountered a formation of MiG-15 jet fighters, one of which he shot down. (*IWM A 32268*)

37. The 1960s saw the Royal Navy with five aircraft carriers and two commando carriers, while new frigates and destroyers were being built with helicopter platforms and hangars as standard. Nevertheless, even within one warship class, there could be significant differences, as this photograph of *Centaur* at Gibraltar with the then new *Hermes* berthing astern shows. *Hermes* has the 3-D radar and fully-angled flight deck, making her look like a scaled-down refitted *Victorious*. (*The late S.H. Wragg*)

38. While the general-purpose frigate replaced destroyers in many roles, the County-class of guided-missile destroyers were the largest destroyers for the Royal Navy at the time, and also had a helicopter platform and hangar, somewhat overdesigned as it was tailored for the Westland Wessex! This is *Devonshire* during the late 1960s when she made a goodwill visit to Helsinki and Leningrad (now St Petersburg). (*The late S.H. Wragg*)

39. Delays in completion of the first aircraft carrier designed to operate vertical and short take-off and landing aircraft, *Invincible*, meant that *Hermes*, which had been converted for the commando carrier role, was modified yet again to become a 'Harrier carrier', and during the Falklands Campaign, her superior aircraft capacity was much needed. (*FAAM FALK/104*)

40. Differing in many respects from the Harrier, the Sea Harrier proved to be an effective fighter with a good air-to-surface capability. This is one of 800 NAS's aircraft about to land. (*IWM FKD475*)

41. The Falklands campaign was sometimes described as the 'Winter War', and here is *Invincible* in the mist of the South Atlantic. (*IWM FKD 477*)

42. Keeping an aircraft carrier fully operational and safe for personnel and aircraft involves many routine tasks, and one of the most important is keeping flight and hangar decks clean and free from oil deposits. Aboard *Hermes* during the Falklands Campaign, they did things the hard way. Sea Harriers are in the background with a Lynx helicopter, possibly from a frigate, closest to the camera.

. *Invincible*'s 801 NAS was commanded by
ɛutenant Commander (later Commander)
gel 'Sharkey' Ward, who shot down three
gentine aircraft. (*IWM FKD 541*)

44. Lieutenant Dave Morgan of 800 NAS with his Sea Harrier, complete with the hole shot in his tail during a sortie over Port Stanley.

The future for the Fleet Air Arm involves the Lockheed Martin F-35, or 'Joint Strike Fighter', in
STOVL variant, and the Westland Merlin multi-role helicopter with ASW and Anti-Surface vessel
ability, which is now well-established in service. (*Agusta-Westland*)

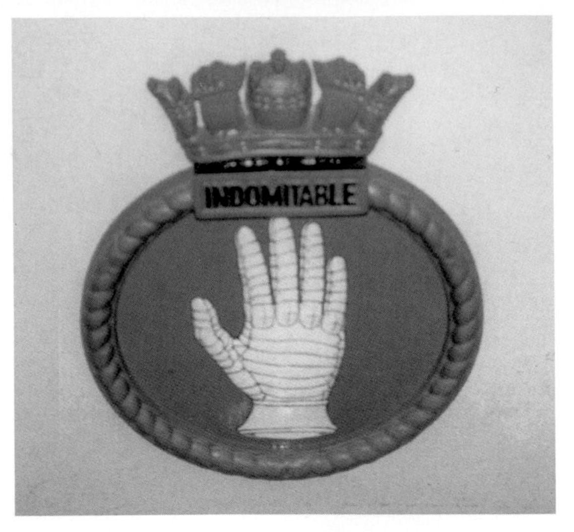

46. Crests: Ship's crest of *Indomitable* (*top left*); Ship's crest of *Ark Royal* (*top right*); Ship's crest of *Glorious* (*middle left*); Squadron crest of 890 NAS (*middle right*); Squadron crest of 1844 NAS (*bottom*
As the number of squadrons increased, numbers had to be introduced in the 17XX and 18XX serie

One problem for the fighter escorts was that they had to keep pace with the slowest aircraft, the Avengers, which in itself was difficult, but it also gave the fighter pilots the problem that if they encountered enemy aircraft, they would be flying too slow for combat. The situation improved after they crossed a mountain range and the Avengers gained speed as they raced down towards the target area.

It was also at this time that Japanese Army Air Force Tojo fighters were spotted racing downwards towards the fighters. The cry of 'Bandits! Three o'clock up' came over the radio and the fighter leader then ordered the Hellcats to 'Break right – Go!' The Hellcat pilots pushed their throttles wide open.

'Hank' Adlam recalled:

> I turned hard and fired almost immediately ahead of one of the Tojos as it hurtled on its way past me towards the Avengers. I didn't see the actual hits but my bullets must have deflected him off his course. I turned the Hellcat half on its back and pulled it hard round to follow the Japanese down. He kept on straight past the Avengers and, although by this time he was well ahead of me, I longed to follow because my Hellcat eventually would have caught him in the dive. But I remembered my strict orders that, this time, the fighter escort must not desert the Avengers.

This was good training and discipline. Late in the war, the lesson had been learnt that fighters must remain with the bombers. Even the Luftwaffe, with its experience of the Spanish Civil War, found that during the Battle of Britain, the fighter pilots deserted the bombers to look for dogfights, seeking to increase their score at the cost of leaving the bombers unprotected.

While this was going on the Avengers had closed the target, the pilots could see how vast the oil refinery was and that it was protected by a ring of fat barrage balloons whose cables could tear off the wing of an aircraft. Intense anti-aircraft fire of all types was also coming up, and those in the fighter escort admired the persistence of the Firefly pilots as they raced downwards regardless of the balloon cables and the heavy AA fire. Having lost the rest of his formation, Adlam headed for the rendezvous point and found many of the Avengers already there as well as six Hellcats from his formation. There was a lot of excited radio chatter which made it difficult to know what was going on – something that was soon discouraged – but eventually the aircraft reformed and started the flight back to the aircraft carriers, which proved to be uneventful. It was just 09.30 when they hooked on aboard *Indomitable*.

It was only afterwards that many pilots discovered that a force of twenty-four Corsairs had been sent ahead of the main group to 'ramrod' the fighter airfields – that is, make a fast strafing attack – to suppress the fighter defences, but had arrived too late with the Japanese fighters already in the air. The Corsairs from *Illustrious* and *Victorious* persisted with their attack, shooting up the airfield installations, but five of the aircraft were shot down in an intense Japanese crossfire. Some of those involved feel that the Corsairs should have called off their attack as it was pointless.

At least the Corsairs had suffered from enemy action – when the Seafires landed back on *Indefatigable,* they suffered so many of the usual Seafire landing accidents that other carriers had to find aircraft to maintain the CAP.

The Avengers had caused significant damage to the refinery, but the problem was that they had been badly mauled by Japanese fighters after making their bombing runs as they flew towards the rendezvous. Adlam realized that he should have followed the Avengers instead of heading straight for the rendezvous and it appears that this would have been a good use of the Corsairs as well. The aircrew were also told off in no uncertain terms for their unnecessary radio chatter.

It was a sad reflection on the role of the British aircraft industry and procurement policies that, even this late in the war, there was no British fighter or fighter-bomber capable of operating reliably from an aircraft carrier, and landing reasonably safely back on it again afterwards. Nor were all the problems in the skies. After withdrawing from the flying-off positions, the British carriers started to refuel but, through lack of experience, this took two whole days, and that was even with the tankers not carrying all of the fuel needed, so that instead of making a total of three strikes against Palembang's refineries, just one more could be mounted.

BPF aka Task Force 57

The British Pacific Fleet was under overall American direction, with the BPF becoming Task Force (TF) 57, part of the US Fifth Fleet, or Task Force 37, depending on which US admiral, Spruance or Halsey, was in command at sea at the time, with the other admiral ashore planning the next campaign. Rear Admiral Sir Philip Vian commanded the British carriers and, once again, these were *Illustrious, Indefatigable, Indomitable* and *Victorious,* although *Illustrious* had to be replaced by *Formidable* after suffering heavy damage from aerial attack. The squadrons included those already mentioned, with the addition of aircraft from 848, 885, 1840, 1841, 1842 and 1845 Squadrons. The British also had the battleships *King George V* and *Howe,* five cruisers and escorting destroyers.

Changes continued to take place so that organizationally the British could match the Americans. The concept of the naval air wing had evolved in 1943, but in 1945, the Royal Navy formed the squadrons embarked in both the fast fleet carriers and the new light fleet carriers into carrier air groups. On a more practical level, changes to make interoperability between the two navies easier included changes to the batsmen's signals so that the two navies were in accord. Before this, some directions had precisely the opposite meaning!

The BPF, or TF57 when part of the integrated Allied force, operated against the Sakashima Gunto group of islands, through which the Japanese ferried aircraft to Okinawa and did much to cut Japanese reinforcements. On and off, the carriers sent their aircraft to targets in the Sakashima Gunto from 26 March to 25 May 1945, as the BPF took part in Operation Iceberg, the attack on Okinawa.

Operations in the Pacific, as the Allies closed in on the Japanese, had more than the usual hazards for the naval aviator, or even those additional hazards of flying over inhospitable terrain. The Japanese never felt bound to observe the rules of the Geneva Convention and the fate of pilots shot down could be grim. Many squadron commanders wore uniforms of a lower rank as some means of protection against interrogation and torture, and to avoid providing a propaganda coup for the Japanese.

The role of the aircraft carriers in the US Navy's TF58 was to provide air support for the assault on Okinawa. The Royal Navy's TF57 had the role of protecting the left flank of the US Fifth Fleet, and especially TF51, the escort carriers providing close air support for the ground forces. The initial landings on Okinawa were on Sunday, 1 April 1945, when the US Tenth Army landed with four divisions on the west coast of the island. A breakdown in the Japanese chain of command proved helpful, with initial resistance being light, but on 6 April, British and American forces started to suffer from the attentions of the Japanese Kamikaze suicide aircraft. In all, between 6 April and 29 May, 1,465 aircraft from one of the Japanese home islands, Kyushu, were used in ten massed Kamikaze attacks, with another 250 aircraft from Formosa. On top of this, there were almost 5,000 conventional sorties. The main target for the Japanese aerial attacks were the ships of the combined British and American fleet, and in six weeks, twenty-six ships of destroyer size and below were sunk, and another 164 damaged, including *Illustrious*, *Formidable*, *Indefatigable* and *Victorious*.

Within days of the attacks starting, on 9 April, TF57 was ordered to attack airfields in northern Okinawa, while its role in attacking the airfields of the Sakashima Gunto was taken over by TF51. A pattern then developed, with the carriers striking hard at their targets and then being rotated out of battle every few days to replenish their rapidly exhausted fuel and munitions. The demands on the ships of TF57 varied according to the overall strategic situation, so that by 4 May, TF57 found itself off Miyako in the Sakishima Gunto again. This was when *Formidable* was struck by her first Kamikaze, which found the ship relatively lightly protected since the battleships, which could do so much to provide a dense curtain of AA fire around the fleet, were away shelling coastal targets. Unfortunately the attack, at 11.31, came while the flight deck was crowded as aircraft were ranged for launching, and so while the ship merely suffered a 2-foot dent in the flight deck near the base of the island, eight men were killed and forty-seven wounded. It might have been worse. The Medical Officer had moved the flight deck sick bay from the Air Intelligence Office at the base of the island, and the AIO was the scene of many casualties.

Worse was to come. On 9 May, *Formidable* was struck yet again. On this occasion, the Kamikaze hit the after end of the flight deck and ploughed into aircraft ranged there. A rivet was blown out of the deck and burning petrol poured into the hangar, where the fire could only be extinguished by spraying, with adverse effects even on those aircraft not on fire. Seven aircraft were lost on deck, with another twelve lost in the hangar. The ship refuelled and obtained replacement aircraft. Nine days later, on 18 May, an armourer working on a Corsair in the hangar failed to notice that the aircraft's guns were still armed. He accidentally fired the guns into a parked Avenger, which blew up and started another fierce fire. This time, thirty aircraft were destroyed. Even so, the ship was fully operational by the end of the day.

The BPF continued to operate alongside the US Fifth Fleet as the war was taken to the Japanese home islands. In the closing days of the war in the Pacific, the Fleet Air Arm was striking at targets in the Tokyo area, and it was then that it earned its second Victoria Cross of the war, but again, posthumously. On 9 August, Lieutenant Robert Hampton Gray RCNVR was leading a strike of Corsairs from *Formidable*'s 1841 and 1842 Squadrons to attack a destroyer in the Onagawa Wan, when he came under heavy AA fire from five warships. He pressed ahead with his attack, even though his aircraft was damaged, and succeeded in sinking the destroyer before his aircraft crashed into the harbour.

Earlier, a small number of the Royal Navy's escort carriers had found their way to the Pacific, predominantly acting as aircraft transports, and as maintenance and repair ships, but first, a number were also deployed to the Indian Ocean to provide trade protection. One of these was HMS *Ameer*, maintaining anti-submarine patrols in the Indian Ocean, through which convoys from the United States passed on their way to the Gulf, then usually known as the Persian Gulf. The bulk of supplies for the Soviet Union were shipped via the Gulf, with transhipment to land transport at an Iranian port.

Ameer was also present when Ramtree Island off the coast of Burma was attacked by the Royal Navy and Royal Indian Navy in January 1945, a few months before combined amphibious and overland assaults saw the fall of Rangoon. The landing beaches were within the field of fire of Japanese artillery hidden in caves, but these were silenced by the guns of the battleship *Queen Elizabeth* and cruiser *Phoebe*, supported by *Ameer*'s twenty-four Grumman Hellcat fighters of No. 815 Squadron, allowing the island to be taken as a springboard for the capture of Rangoon in May.

Another operation was in the Netherlands East Indies in April 1945. Operation Sunfish, on 11 April 1945, saw Force 63 – led by the battleships *Queen Elizabeth* and the French *Richelieu*, with the cruisers *London* and *Cumberland*, the latter leading the 26th Destroyer Flotilla, and including the escort carriers *Emperor* and *Khedive* – attack Sabang and Oleheh. On 16 April, the same force turned their attentions to Emmahaven and Padang, the two escort carriers sharing No. 808 Squadron with its twenty-four Grumman Hellcats. The Squadron was officially embarked in *Khedive*, but six of its aircraft were detached to *Empress* for some of the operations.

VE Day in Europe, 8 May 1945, found HMS *Ameer* arrive at Colombo in Ceylon, now Sri Lanka, with No. 896 Naval Air Squadron. There was little cause for celebration in the Far East, where American, Australian, British and New Zealand forces were gradually easing closer to Japan in the face of heavy resistance, with fiercer resistance still expected if, as everyone believed likely at the time, the Japanese home islands would have to be invaded.

Neither the Squadron nor the carrier was new to warfare. No. 896 had operated from *Victorious* and from the escort carrier *Pursuer* against the German battleship *Tirpitz*, which had spent almost its entire career tucked away safely in Norwegian fjords, menacing Allied convoys to the Soviet Union. *Ameer* had been engaged in trade protection duties in the Indian Ocean, with 845 Squadron embarked with its Grumman Wildcat fighters and Avenger bombers, before moving to a more combative role with No. 804 Squadron, whose Grumman Hellcats had covered landings on both Ramree Island in Operation Matador and Cheduba Island in Operation Sankey. Then 804's Hellcats had provided fighter cover for 888 Squadron on Operation Stacey as it conducted photographic reconnaissance over the Kra Isthmus, Penang and northern Sumatra. At the time, this was seen as steady progress towards the eventual liberation of Singapore, with no one in South East Asia Command aware that the Japanese surrender would be forced by the use of nuclear weapons.

Later, 804 Squadron was to have its aircraft assigned to other escort carriers, including *Empress* and *Shah*, for raids on the Andaman Islands and the coast of Burma, before returning to *Ameer* in June for attacks on Sumatra and Phuket in Thailand. No. 896, meanwhile, transferred to *Empress* to cover minesweeping off Phuket.

When Rangoon was eventually liberated in May, No. 807 Squadron embarked in *Hunter* to provide fighter cover throughout much of April and May, and then air cover for anti-shipping strikes. No. 809 Squadron aboard *Stalker* undertook similar duties.

Sink the *Haguro*

By spring 1945, the British were re-establishing themselves in Burma, eventually retaking Rangoon from the Japanese, who were anxious to keep hold of the oilfields in Burma, supported by the British Eastern Fleet. The landings near Rangoon, Operation Dukedom, were covered by escort carriers including *Emperor*, although *Shah* would also have been involved had not a fault appeared with her catapult. The fleet was in Trincomalee on 9 May when Ultra intelligence discovered that a Japanese Nachi-class cruiser was to leave Singapore the following day to evacuate the garrison in the Andaman Islands. Almost immediately, the fleet sailed hoping to intercept the Japanese. Japanese reconnaissance, not always reliable, on this occasion did succeed in warning the cruiser, *Haguro*, and her destroyer escort, *Kamikaze*, that the Royal Navy was at sea, and the two ships returned to Singapore.

Ultra was able to warn that the two ships had sailed again on 14 May, and also confirmed that the Japanese supply vessel *Kurishoyo Maru*, escorted by a submarine chaser, had successfully carried out an evacuation of the Nicobar Islands and was on her way to Singapore. The following day, the escort carrier HMS *Emperor* launched a strike of four Grumman Avengers from 851 Naval Air Squadron, commanded by Lieutenant Commander (A) Michael Fuller RNVR. The four aircraft were armed with bombs and attacked the two ships, but one aircraft was shot down by heavy AA fire, although its crew were able to take to their dinghy. A second strike, again of four aircraft, was then launched from *Emperor*, again led by Fuller, but one aircraft was forced to return with engine trouble. Two of the remaining aircraft then sighted five destroyers and spent thirty-five minutes trying to identify them, eventually deciding who they were, which was fortunate since it was the 26th Destroyer Flotilla at sea in an attempt to intercept the *Haguro*. By this time, the two aircraft were short of fuel and had to return. This left Fuller on his own, with orders to search for the dinghy carrying the aircrew downed on the first strike. He jettisoned his bombs to increase range, but failed to find the dinghy as he had been given the wrong search coordinates; instead he found *Kurishoyo* and the submarine chaser, and started to fly around them while fixing their position. At this point, Fuller noticed two more ships some 15 miles to the south of his position, heading north, and keeping out of AA range, succeeded in identifying them as a Nachi-class cruiser and a Minikaze-class destroyer before they changed course to the south-west having spotted his aircraft.

'She was very large and very black against a very dark monsoon cloud,' Fuller recalled later. 'An enormously impressive sight, just as a warship ought to look.'

He was convinced that the Japanese were trying to remain unobtrusive, wanting to keep out of sight. Not being inclined to oblige them, he signalled the rest of the British fleet at 11.50: 'One cruiser, one destroyer sighted. Course 240. Speed 10 knots.' He maintained this flow of information for an hour before climbing directly over the *Haguro* at 12.50 to make a final signal, giving the direction finders with the fleet the chance of making an exact fix, before returning to the carrier to land with just ten minutes' fuel left.

Haguro was still some considerable distance from the *Emperor*, but the carrier launched three more Avengers which found the cruiser and dive-bombed her. They achieved one direct hit and another near miss. Their return flight of 530 miles was the longest attacking flight from any British carrier during the war, and the one and only occasion that a major enemy warship at sea was dive-bombed by British naval aircraft. The attack left *Haguro* only slightly damaged and heading for Singapore, but after dark she was finally cornered by the 26th Destroyer Flotilla and sunk by gunfire and torpedoes in the entrance to the Malacca Straits early on 16 May.

Chapter 15

An Uneasy Peace

The end of the Second World War was greeted with rejoicing in the victorious nations, except that most of the rejoicing occurred with the return of peace in Europe, and even though there were further celebrations when the war with Japan ended, by the time the ships, squadrons and men came home, all this was in the past. Not for nothing did the great naval historian, John Winton, describe the British Pacific Fleet as 'The Forgotten Fleet'. There was a sense of anti-climax with the return of the ships to their home ports. These units were far away and the war in the East had not impinged on the consciousness of the man in the street as the war in Europe had done; a cynic would say that the war in the East had not impinged on the average citizen's security and well-being in the way that the European war, with the 'Blitz' and the flying bombs, had managed to do.

The new Colossus-class light fleet carriers that had hastened to the Pacific ready to play their part in the closing stages of the Pacific War, as it reached its grand finale with the invasion of Japan, found that they had arrived too late for action. While the Japanese were prepared to defend their home islands to the death, with a fleet of 2,000 Kamikaze aircraft filled with much of the little fuel left to the Japanese, and with the majority of Japanese starving, sanity finally emerged with the dropping of an atomic bomb on Hiroshima on 6 August 1945, followed by a second bomb on Nagasaki on 9 August. Two bombs were only just enough to force the Japanese to surrender, and an anti-surrender faction still clung to the idea of a glorious last battle.

The new light fleet carriers found themselves in a new, but unexciting role, being present at the surrender of Japanese forces in Hong Kong, Singapore and Malaya, and then bringing home the prisoners of war. Hangar decks, intended to be filled with aircraft, were instead filled with camp beds. This was not what the ships were intended for, but no one wanted to delay their homecoming after four years or so of unbelievable brutality. No doubt the accommodation aboard these ships was limited and uncomfortable for all concerned, with heads and messes under pressure, despite the absence of aircraft and in some cases the aircrew and maintainers. By 'some cases', many of these men also came home aboard the ships with their Lend-Lease aircraft left behind in Australia for the United States to collect. Troopships were also used, but what survived of the world's ocean liner fleet was much diminished and in need of refitting, so the carriers had to be used.

Yet the peace was uneasy and unreal. There was nothing to celebrate in much of Eastern Europe. Life was hard in the former occupied countries of Western Europe, with rationing, scarcely habitable housing and concerns about those members of families who had gone away to work in Germany and were out of touch until they suddenly returned. The Easterners, however, had simply exchanged one occupation for another. Warning bells were sounding in the chanceries of Western Europe, and in North America and further afield, as first one country and then another succumbed to Communism. The biggest to go was, of course, mainland China, but this was not unexpected. The battle between the Nationalists and the Communists had been prolonged and difficult, not least for those in the West who found the Nationalist leader, Chiang Kai-Chek, an unpalatable ally, and what is more, one who was incompetent.

While the armed forces were scaled down in the United States, the United Kingdom, Canada, Australia, New Zealand and South Africa, the Indians went home to independence and division, and rebuilding started in the former occupied countries, anti-Communist defensive alliances were formed and the Soviet Union once again became a pariah state. This was the start of the Cold War. The most successful of the defensive alliances, and the only one to survive to the present, was the North Atlantic Treaty Organisation (NATO), but there was also a South East Asia Treaty Organisation, which united Australia and New Zealand with the United States and United Kingdom, and both these countries were also members of the Baghdad Pact, with their Arab allies, which included Iraq at that time, and which became the Central Treaty Organisation, or CENTO, after Iraq became a dictatorship and left. Of these alliances, only NATO had a formal command structure.

The French and the Dutch had some difficulty in reasserting colonial rule, but the Royal Navy was not at first involved as Britain regained her colonies from Japan. Malaya had Communist bandits which the Army and the Royal Air Force had to counter, and did so successfully, but after 'liberation' from colonial rule by the Japanese, many were no doubt glad to see Britain back. In any case, India had shown that independence was a distinct possibility. The 'emergency' in Malaya nevertheless did see the Fleet Air Arm make its first heli-lift of troops into a combat zone on 20 March 1953, using Westland Whirlwind helicopters.

So it was that the first of the Cold War hotspots came, not in a former European colony, but in a former Japanese one, Korea.

The Korean War

The unusual feature of the Korean War was that it was not fought by proxy, with one side or even both using 'client' or satellite states and terrorist groups, as happened in Vietnam, for example. At the time North Korea invaded South Korea, the Soviet Union was boycotting the United Nations and so could not use its veto against action.

A Japanese colony since the early years of the twentieth century, it was agreed in 1945 that the Soviet Union, which did not declare war on Japan until August of that year, would take the Japanese surrender in Korea north of the 38th parallel, and the United States would take the surrender in the south. The inevitable result was that the south became a pro-Western democracy and the north became a 'People's' republic backed by the USSR and Communist China, which were still close allies at the time.

The United States had in fact dropped its guard over Korea, with the Republic of Korea Air Force, the RoKAF, being little more than a training organization. As with Pearl Harbor, war broke out early on a Sunday morning, 25 June 1950, but in this case it was also just before the rainy season when no one expected an attack. North Korea claimed that South Korea had invaded and had been repelled, but this was a clumsy lie as no army has ever managed to mount an immediate counter-attack. At this early stage of the Cold War, the concept of mutual defence had still to be recognized, and the North Koreans doubtless thought that they could occupy the South unchallenged.

The outbreak of war, which required all United Nations members to assist South Korea, also caught the British in a weak position. While troops were sent quickly from Hong Kong, the Royal Air Force was so overstretched that it could play little part in combat operations. This, and the shortage of secure bases ashore, meant that conduct of the British air campaign fell to the Fleet Air Arm and the Royal Navy was at last able to put its light fleet carriers to use, with HMS *Triumph* being present for the Inchon landings on 15 September, which marked the start of the UN campaign. At this time, HMS *Illustrious* was the Royal Navy's trials and training carrier and mainly based in home waters, while her sister ship, *Victorious*, was starting a long and very extensive refit, virtually being rebuilt. Four Colossus-class ships were rotated on operations off the coast of Korea, and in addition to *Triumph*, these included *Ocean*, *Glory* and *Theseus*, augmented by their sister ship, HMAS *Sydney*, and supported by the maintenance carrier, HMS *Unicorn*.

The United States Navy had several ships of the much larger Essex-class present throughout the Korean War, and for the most part these operated off Korea's east coast in the Sea of Japan, while the British and Australian ships operated off the west coast in the Yellow Sea.

Post-war modernization had not yet taken full effect at this time. The Fleet Air Arm still had many Supermarine Seafires as well as the Hawker

Sea Fury, a potent naval development of the Tempest fighter capable of speeds of up to 450 mph. There were also Fairey Firefly fighter-bombers, another piston-engined type. Although the first operational helicopters were available in the form of the Sikorsky S-51, which was being built under licence in Britain by Westland as the Dragonfly, there were no helicopters embarked in *Triumph*, so she was loaned a USN S-51 and pilot for plane guard duties, with the helicopter being far quicker and cheaper than an escort vessel in picking up downed pilots from the sea. Ranged against them were various versions of the Russian Yakovlev 'Yak' piston-engined fighters and – an unexpected shock as no one was sure that the USSR had jet fighters at the time – the Mikoyan MiG-15.

Triumph had been visiting Japan with two cruisers and eight destroyers, and was in position off the coast of Korea on 12 July; on 29 July, she was joined by *Sydney* which was supported by two destroyers and a frigate. They found the USN already had a balanced force in the area with an attack carrier group which had been blockading Korea since 3 July.

The British carrier's arrival was delayed because she was already on her way home at the time and had to return to Kure in Japan to collect her aircraft. She was operating Seafires and Fireflies at the time.

For the Fleet Air Arm, which still had a substantial number of Second World War veterans on its strength, the Korean War was, in the words of some, 'curiously unreal'. In contrast to the war years, the enemy lacked the means to attack the carriers. The rest of the surface fleet was kept busy either countering North Korean mines in coastal waters and ports, or bombarding North Korean forces ashore and, from time to time, being shelled back by shore batteries. By contrast, the carriers maintained regular steaming patterns to launch and recover their aircraft unharassed by enemy action. For the aircrew, there were the usual dangers of technical failure, anti-aircraft fire and enemy fighters, with the risk of death or injury, or of being taken prisoner, interspersed with convivial evenings in the wardroom.

'You could fly four sorties in a day,' recalled one Fleet Air Arm pilot. 'Then come below, change into mess dress, and sit down for an evening of sherry, bridge and brandy.' Nevertheless, the weather could also be a problem. The winters were harsh and cold, while the summers were hot, some even maintaining this was worse than winter.

'Operating in summer was the worst,' recalled one pilot. 'Temperatures in the glasshouse cockpit soaring to 140 degrees, the crews flying in underpants and overalls, soaked in sweat from take-off to landing.'

The ever-present risk of fire meant that, despite the heat, scarves and chamois-leather gloves were still worn and every inch of flesh was protected.

No matter how relaxed the evenings might have been, the days were ones of intense pressure, as a signal from HMS *Ocean* on 17 May 1952 makes clear:

> Our pilots today have broken all existing records for British light fleet carriers in flying 123 sorties over our operating area. From dawn to dusk, the area has been pounded by rocket and bomb attacks. The destruction included three bridges downed, four coastal gun emplacements shattered, fifteen ammunition-laden oxcarts exploded, an oil dump fired, smoke and flames have been coming from this for most of the day ... Serviceability has remained excellent and we continue with sixty-eight sorties tomorrow.

Better still was the warm recognition by the commander of the USN forces when the carrier was rotated out of the operational area:

> The unprecedented record set by the *Ocean* evokes pride and admiration in us all. This is the kind of warfare by the UN which the Commies do not mention in the Truce negotiations.
>
> Aggressiveness and top drawer training of pilots, ground crew and ship's company reflected in your operations are noted with profound pleasure. To the commanding officer and each man of the *Ocean* and her squadrons, Rear Admiral George C. Dyer sends 'Well Done'.

The routine that was quickly established was that the British carriers followed a nine-day operational cycle, with four days' flying broken by a day's replenishment at sea, and then another four days' flying before a brief visit to Japan. The target was to fly 544 sorties in nine days, sixty-eight a day. A sortie involved an aircraft flying 120 miles from the ship to the target area and remaining airborne for up to two hours. Throughout the day, aircraft took off in waves every two hours in flights of between four and six aircraft. Briefing for a day's operations took place the previous evening. The aircrew were awakened soon after 04.00 ready to start flying at 05.00 during the long summer days.

Strikes against ground targets apart, the fighter pilots were also making their mark on North Korean forces. At 06.00 on 9 August 1952, four Sea Furies were flying north of Chinimpo, returning from a raid on railway lines and trains. They were attacked by eight MiG-15s at 3,500 feet, and in the dogfight that ensued, one MiG-15 was shot down and another two damaged. The aircraft shot down was by Lieutenant (later Commander) Peter 'Hoagy' Carmichael, the flight leader.

'The MiG is a beautiful aircraft,' he told a journalist. 'Though the piston-engined Sea Fury is about 200 mph slower, it can cope so long as the MiG can be seen. If the MiG comes in and fights, we are confident of the result.'

Most, if not all, of the MiGs were flown by Russian pilots, despite the aircraft having North Korean markings.

By the time of the Korean War, the Fairey Firefly was obsolescent, even though it had been warmly welcomed late in the Second World War as an improvement on earlier British naval fighters. It was slow and like many other piston-engined carrier fighters and fighter-bombers, was nose heavy and prone to bounce when landing on a carrier flight deck. The advice over Korea to the pilots was that if they met a MiG jet fighter, they had to cut their speed to 125 knots, lower their flaps and make a tight turn as the MiG-15 pilots would not be able to fly slowly enough to catch them. The saving grace of this aircraft was that it could carry sixteen rockets and was fitted with four 20mm cannon. Even so, the Sea Fury was a more dashing steed. The Colossus-class could barely manage 24 knots and a Firefly needed 30 knots of wind over the flight deck to get airborne when fully armed and fuelled. On a still day, the aircraft would sink alarmingly as it left the catapult, disappearing out of sight before reappearing and beginning a slow and laborious climb to 10,000 feet.

Accidents were a continual danger. When making a rocket attack, the tail fins sometimes broke off the rocket and could hole the aircraft's radiator, with disastrous consequences. Someone changed the position of the switch for a Firefly's rocket-assisted take-off gear, or RATOG, one day without telling the pilot, and he accidentally ignited it, blowing a man on the flight deck overboard; he was never recovered.

Not taking any chances, an aircraft was always kept ahead of the carrier on anti-submarine patrol, while a CAP of Sea Furies was also maintained. Neither of these measures was needed, but again, with Second World War experience still fresh, it would have been a foolish and overconfident commanding officer to have ignored these precautions. In any event, having given covert support to the North Koreans in the air, no one could be sure that the Russians would not do the same under the waves.

Morale amongst the airmen was high.

'I strafed an ox-cart and I think I hit it while I missed another,' recalled Lieutenant William Jacob, a Firefly pilot embarked in HMS *Ocean* during the spring of 1952. 'Each of the two runs I did ... left the cart surrounded in dust and smoke from which emerged an ox-cart going like a train. The man, however, was killed ... My landing was good for a change.'

Success and Failure – Suez

While Britain had maintained an armed presence in the Suez Canal Zone from 1882, and virtually ran Egypt as a colony until 1922, British forces were not finally withdrawn until 1956, by which time the Egyptian monarchy had been overthrown in 1952 by a nationalist army officer, Gamel Abdel Nasser. Nasser's nationalization of the Suez Canal Company, jointly owned by the United Kingdom and France, caused alarm in many countries. For the British, the fear was that this vital route might be closed to their shipping operating to Australia, India, East Africa and the Middle East. At first, international outrage was such that armed intervention had widespread support, but, despite Britain having bases conveniently close in Cyprus, neither Britain nor France was actually capable of mounting an operation at short notice. The delay in getting ready saw international support on the wane. Had both countries been able to act decisively in July, all might have been well. Many countries, including the United States, were far more concerned about establishing good relations with the new regime than supporting the British and French. The Americans at the time had relatively little use for the canal, but couldn't really afford to take a high moral tone given that they had run Panama for many years to protect their investment and strategic interest in the Panama Canal!

The British Prime Minister, Sir Anthony Eden, in deciding on military action, had failed to ensure that he had the forces available. The British armed forces, still overstretched in the twilight of the colonial era, and with a massive new post-war commitment in the occupation of part of what was then West Germany, did not have the manpower. Worse, they did not have sufficient landing craft, and many of those that were nominally available in reserve were found to be unseaworthy. This was just part of a list of deficiencies, which included an absence of tank transporters. The tanks had to be moved to Southampton, where the British Army had a major facility of its own at Marchwood, close to the main port area, by Pickfords, a commercial haulier better known for its household removals but which, fortunately, also included a fleet of low loaders. Many of the weapons equipping the British armed forces were found to be unsuitable for desert conditions.

The plan which the British and French developed centred round an Israeli pre-emptive offensive against Egypt in Sinai, which would be followed by Anglo-French intervention in the Canal Zone. Successive British governments have denied British complicity in the Israeli attack. The French started to re-equip Israel's armed forces while a joint British and French command was established, and both countries deployed naval and air forces to the central and eastern Mediterranean. Reservists were mobilized and a fleet assembled.

International opinion started to move in favour of Egypt and swung against any military operation by Britain and France. Yet preparations continued, slowly but steadily. There could be no element of surprise as the intentions were increasingly obvious and could be seen at many naval British bases, including Portsmouth.

On 29 October, Israel launched her attack against Egypt and two days later, British and French shore and carrier-borne aircraft launched an attack in the opening of what had been code-named Operation Musketeer, bombing Egyptian military targets. The landings did not start until 5 November, by which time world opinion was strongly opposed to the action.

Seven aircraft carriers were used for the Suez Campaign, five of them British and two French, with the latter including *Arromanches*, a Colossus-class light fleet carrier, and *La Fayette*, a loaned United States

Independence-class light carrier. The British carriers included HMS *Albion* and her sister ship, *Bulwark*, which were heavier and faster developments of the British light fleet carriers, displacing 23,300 tons and with a maximum speed of 28 knots. A third British carrier was *Eagle*, one of the two largest aircraft carriers operated by the Royal Navy. At 43,000 tons and able to steam at more than 30 knots, she had an aircraft capacity of more than sixty at the time, although this was reduced in later years by the growth in aircraft sizes. She had entered service with a straight flight deck, but by the time of Suez she had a half-angled deck. These three ships were to act as attack carriers, carrying fourteen squadrons of aircraft between them, including: the jet Armstrong-Whitworth Sea Hawk, based on a Hawker design and essentially a straight-wing naval development of the Hunter jet fighter; the de Havilland Sea Venom; and the turboprop Westland Wyvern; as well as Fairey Gannet turboprop anti-submarine aircraft and the piston-engined Douglas AD-4W Skyraider airborne-early-warning aircraft.

Amongst the naval air squadrons involved were Nos 800 with Sea Hawk FGA6s, 802 with Sea Hawk FB3s and 809 with Sea Venom FAW21s aboard *Albion*, while aboard *Bulwark* were Sea Hawk FGA6s of No. 804 and 810, while *Eagle*'s aircraft included the Wyvern S4s of 830. The ship had earlier had Gannet AS1s of 812, but for the operation these were sent ashore to RNAS Hal Far in Malta.

The other two British carriers were HMS *Ocean* and *Theseus*, two Colossus-class carriers which accommodated 600 men of No. 45 Commando, Royal Marines, and helicopters. The mainstay of the helicopter force were licence-built versions of the Sikorsky S-55, the Westland Whirlwind, but these were augmented by small Bristol Sycamore helicopters which were, nevertheless, expected to play a part in the assault phase of the operation.

The first attacks were at night. One British instructor on secondment to the Egyptian Air Force later recalled that the 'Egyptians had thought it thoroughly unsporting of the British to attack at night since they didn't like night flying!' Priority was accorded attacking Dekheila airfield, followed by attacks on Egyptian army units, then Port Said and Gamil Bridge, during which one of No. 830 NAS's Wyverns was hit by AA fire, but the pilot, Lieutenant McCarthy, managed to glide his aircraft 3 miles out to sea where he was rescued by *Eagle*'s search and rescue helicopter. Within forty-eight hours, the Anglo-French coalition had complete control of the air. Even so, a second Wyvern was lost on 5 November while bombing and making rocket attacks, but its pilot, Lieutenant Commander W.H. Cowling ejected and again was rescued by a SAR helicopter.

The commando operation, the first airborne assault from a carrier – although the United States Marine Corps had been transported off carriers during the Korean War – had an improvised feel to it. Aboard *Ocean* were the Joint Experimental Helicopter Unit and 600 men of 215 Wing, RAF Regiment, who were to protect air bases ashore, and half of the men of No. 45 Commando. The remaining marines were aboard *Theseus*, with No. 845 Helicopter Squadron.

Lieutenant Jack Smith, commander of 45's Z Troop, recalled:

> The sea passage from Malta to Port Said took three days, an intense period of briefing, rehearsal and preparation. In HMS *Ocean* these were complicated because there were two types of helicopter, the Army version of the Whirlwind with a load of only five fully-equipped armed men, and the Sycamore, capable of carrying three. Each man, as well as carrying his own ammunition, rations, water, respirator and spare clothing, had to carry some support weapon ammunition ...
>
> A loaded Sycamore presented an extraordinary sight. The back seats, side panels and inessential fittings had been stripped to increase the lift. The three passengers sat on the floor, one hunched in the middle with six mortar bombs on his lap, and the other two with their legs dangling over the side, each holding a 106mm anti-tank shell about three feet long. The man in the middle was responsible for the two outboard members not falling out. The Whirlwind was a little more orthodox, but there were no seats. The five passengers hung on to any handhold available. On approaching the landing zone, the Bren gunner was ordered to put down suppressive fire out of the window if necessary, while the rifleman covered the area of the door. Communications between troops and pilots in both aircraft was either by shouting or tugging at the pilots' legs.

The heli-borne assault began at 05.45 on 6 November. The helicopters took off in waves and flew slowly towards the landing ground before breaking away to land their marines. Inevitably, it took more than one lift to get the entire force of 45 Commando ashore. On jumping out of his helicopter, one marine was hit by a bullet, was pulled back on board and was in *Ocean*'s sick bay being treated in just twenty minutes. A helicopter from *Theseus* had to ditch, but there were no casualties.

No doubt the success of this operation, using such primitive and inadequate equipment compared to that available today, was largely due to the limited opposition. Meanwhile, British troops were being landed in an amphibious assault while paratroops descended from the skies.

Yet no sooner had the land war started than it was all over with a ceasefire on 6 November. The operation had been condemned by the United States and by a number of countries in the British Commonwealth. American refusal to continue to support the pound sterling and the French franc led to an almost immediate ceasefire. Some 15 per cent of Britain's gold and currency reserves had been withdrawn during the operation, so that she had to seek a loan of US $1.5 billion (£530 million, at the rate of exchange then prevailing) from the International Monetary Fund to maintain the value of the pound. The loan could not be obtained without American support.

Sadly, despite the innovation involved, the Suez Campaign does not have an official battle honour for any of the warships or squadrons involved – no doubt an early manifestation of political correctness! The Fleet Air Arm had done its bit and all that was expected of it, as had the Royal Marines, and indeed the other two services. Nevertheless, the politicians had miscalculated. They sought an interventionist role without having made the resources available to the armed forces. However, Suez was to have other consequences. Equipment was to be updated, which was good, and the armed forces were to be comprised entirely of volunteers plus reserve forces, which in itself was probably a step in the right direction as equipment became more complex – after training it became difficult to utilize conscripts effectively in the short time left before demobilization. In any case, conscription had been a wartime emergency measure extended into peacetime because of the scope of Britain's commitments post-war. The casualties in all of this, however, were the reservist aircrew in both the Fleet Air Arm and the Royal Air Force, who rapidly became a distant memory.

Africa and the Middle East

The Korean War and the Suez Campaign were the two most significant events to involve the Fleet Air Arm during the 1950s. After all, peace had returned, even if it was not complete, with so many hot spots throughout the Cold War years. The Royal Navy had its share of duty as the world's policeman, and with the varied capabilities of the aircraft aboard the carriers, as well as the facilities of the ships themselves, the Fleet Air Arm was in the thick of it. Despite the obvious need for a strong outside force that could help to protect vulnerable states, many of them former British colonies, successive British governments began to retrench. 'Withdrawal' became the watchword and as between the wars, when Singapore had been neglected, what became known as 'East of Suez' became the obvious place. Much of this was driven by politicians who compared British defence expenditure as a percentage of GNP with that of the European members of NATO, overlooking the fact that most of these had lower-cost conscript forces and were usually focussed on just one aspect of defence, such as facing Warsaw Pact forces across the Iron Curtain. GNP in any case also ignored the poor performance of the British economy throughout much of the post-war period.

The United Kingdom had granted independence to Malaya in 1958, and in 1963 created the Federation of Malaysia, incorporating the city state of

Singapore, Malaya and a number of small but prosperous territories in Borneo, including Sarawak and Sabah, in the belief that the smaller states could only maintain independence if grouped together. Another consideration was that it would allow British forces in the area to be substantially reduced. Singapore later left the Federation after differences between the Malay and Chinese communities, but as international disagreements go, this was very minor and both countries remained members of the British Commonwealth, democratic and essentially pro-Western.

The real threat came from opposition to the creation of Malaysia from Indonesia, which enjoyed Soviet support for the dictator Achmed Soekarno, who wanted not only to destroy the Federation but also to absorb some of its territory. The threat was mainly based on infiltration by Indonesian forces rather than outright warfare. British, Australian, Malaysian and New Zealand forces in the area were reinforced, which for the Royal Navy included the aircraft carriers *Ark Royal* and *Victorious*, and by *Albion* and *Bulwark*, converted in the light of the Suez experience into commando carriers, but significantly larger and faster than the Colossus-class ships. Instead of attacking Indonesian territory, the policy of confrontation was contained by countering the infiltrators in the jungle, and by using helicopters and small naval craft to search for intruders attempting to reach the Malaysian coastline, in which the Fleet Air Arm was supported by Avro Shackleton maritime-reconnaissance aircraft of RAF Far East. A measure of Soviet support for Indonesia was that the country was equipped with the Tupolev Tu-16 long-range jet bomber, giving it the only strategic bomber force outside of the USA, UK and USSR. Confrontation ended with the downfall of the Soekarno regime in the mid-1960s.

The Royal Navy was not only involved in the Far East. The Fleet Air Arm was called upon for assistance in three other unconnected incidents at this time. Growing tension between Iraq and its small but oil-rich neighbour Kuwait in 1961 was defused by the rapid deployment of Royal Marine commandos from HMS *Bulwark*, followed soon after by the arrival of the extensively refitted and rebuilt *Victorious*, which initially provided fighter cover for Kuwait and the forces ashore, and when the Royal Air Force took over, *Victorious* remained providing air-defence radar cover and fighter control for both FAA and RAF aircraft. Just three years later, a local crisis in East Africa with a mutiny in the army of newly independent Kenya was ended by the arrival of HMS *Albion* and *Centaur*, while *Victorious* stood by.

If this wasn't enough, in 1965, after prolonged negotiations over the manner in which independence would be granted to the last significant British colony in Africa, Rhodesia (formerly Southern Rhodesia), the country's government declared a unilateral declaration of independence.

Even though Rhodesia was landlocked, it was heavily dependent on supplies, especially of oil, coming via the port of Beira in Mozambique. Thus started what was variously known as the 'Beira blockade' or the 'Beira patrol', as the Royal Navy attempted to stop supplies intended for onward shipment to Rhodesia from reaching Beira. This required the presence of an aircraft carrier, with HMS *Eagle* and *Ark Royal* rotated onto the patrol. The tedium of the routine was enlivened by beauty parades staged by the female passengers aboard the Union Castle liners that at this time still continued up the coast of East Africa to Mombasa.

Despite the constant demand for the Royal Navy and for the aircraft carriers in particular, the government of the day was still anxious to cut the size of the defence budget, even though it was never short of tasks for the Royal Navy. In 1965, it was announced that aircraft carriers would be phased out and HMS *Centaur* was withdrawn almost immediately. She was followed in 1969 by *Victorious,* the last of the famous and successful Illustrious-class – the excuse was given that she had been badly damaged by a fire while in dockyard hands. Linked to this decision was the one to withdraw all British forces from east of Suez, which was widely condemned everywhere except in Aden, where the Army had been engaged in counter-insurgency operations against guerrillas infiltrated from neighbouring Yemen. The sole exception to the withdrawal was Hong Kong. In vain did the supporters of naval aviation point out that without bases established ashore, the carriers would be more important than ever.

The announcement was all the more shocking because the Royal Navy had been promised two 'super carriers', known to the planners as CVA01 and CVA02, which would have been far larger than even *Ark Royal,* at 54,000 tons deep-load displacement against 45,000 tons.

The government brazenly played off the RAF and the Fleet Air Arm against one another. What was effectively an ultimatum indicated that the Fleet Air Arm would become just a helicopter force, or a substantial proportion of the Royal Air Force would be cut to pay for anything more substantial. Even though many RAF officers realized that they needed the Fleet Air Arm to maintain aerial superiority until bases could be established ashore, this set the two services at each other's throats. It was also the case that only the Fleet Air Arm could guarantee producing senior naval officers who knew how to use air power in a crisis. What showed that the decision had no basis in reason was that the aircraft carriers were to be withdrawn at the 'end of their active lives', which was nonsense. Either carriers were worth having and should have their lives extended or be replaced, or they were a costly anachronism and should be withdrawn as soon as possible – but of course they weren't.

Meanwhile, the two largest carriers ever operated by the Royal Navy underwent modernization, although this was done in a miserly fashion.

While both were given fully angled flight decks with waist catapults, *Eagle* was given the three-dimensional radar salvaged from *Victorious* while *Ark Royal* received an extended deck area. The two sister ships no longer looked the same and *Eagle* was to have greater difficulty operating the new McDonnell Douglas F-4K Phantom fighters than the 'Ark'. Later, *Hermes* was to lose her catapults and be converted to a commando carrier – the one ship to replace both *Albion* and *Bulwark*.

Chapter 16

Into the Jet and Helicopter Age

The closing years of the Second World War had seen significant developments in aviation. The first jet fighters entered service with the Luftwaffe having the Messerschmitt Me262, while the Royal Air Force received the similar-looking Gloster Meteor. The Germans also had the rocket-powered Me163 Komet, a high-altitude interceptor intended to counter the menace of the high-flying Boeing B-17 Fortress heavy bombers. Work on the first practical helicopters was also well advanced.

The theory of jet propulsion dated back to experiments made by Hero of Alexandria around AD 100, but helicopters had been of much more recent interest, with Leonardo da Vinci credited with some of the early designs during the period of the Renaissance, around 1500. Interest grew during the early twentieth century, but the materials and the propulsive units of the day were not up to the demands of rotary wing flight, which in itself was also not completely understood. An interim measure was the autogyro or gyroplane, of which the most prominent pioneer was the Spaniard, naturalized Briton, de la Cierva, but his machines were not true helicopters and his aim was not that of hovering flight but of preventing aircraft from stalling during take-off and landing.

There were other developments as the First World War drew to a close. The Allies had enjoyed the advantage of radar on most of their surface vessels, but radar waves could not 'bend' to look over the horizon, so a low-flying attacker could escape detection until the aircraft crossed the horizon and could be picked up by radar. The solution to this was airborne radar, which made its first operational appearance in the Douglas AD Skyraider, a single-engined piston aircraft that was later to become an effective attack and counter-insurgency aircraft over Vietnam. Post-war, this aircraft also passed into the Fleet Air Arm's inventory, seeing action at Suez, and later was replaced by an AEW variant of the Fairey Gannet.

Early Helicopter Trials

The Fleet Air Arm was to the fore in experiments with the early helicopters as it was agreed between the UK and the USA that trials would be conducted by the United States Coast Guard and the Royal Navy. Nevertheless, the first helicopters, the Sikorsky R-4, had been allocated to the United States Army Air Force first and it was on 7 May 1943 that Colonel Frank Gregory of the USAAF landed a prototype XR-4 helicopter on the tanker *Bunker Hill*. The USN itself had also greeted the helicopter with considerable enthusiasm, reporting to its Bureau of Aeronautics, or BuAer, that the new machine possessed many of the advantages of the airship within a much smaller airframe, was more easily handled on the ground, or on deck, and had far greater manoeuvrability in the air. Even at this early stage, it seemed that the helicopter could cover a much wider area than an escort vessel, and do so more quickly and with much lower fuel consumption. Trials focussed on the suitability of the helicopter as an anti-submarine aircraft and two ships were fitted with landing platforms, the USCG cutter *Governor Cobb* and the British SS *Dagheston*. The first sea-going trials were on the latter, starting on 28 November 1943. Flying a specially modified machine fitted with floats, the USN and USCG combined made 166 landings on the ship while the Royal Navy made 162. A Helicopter Service Trials Unit was established by the Fleet Air Arm and two Sikorsky YR-48 helicopters were embarked aboard the *Dagheston* with five HSTU pilots, one from the USCG and four from the USN.

Post-war, trials continued separately. On 29 November 1945, one of the RN's first R-4 helicopters made its first air-sea rescue. In September 1946, Lieutenant Alan Bristow landed a Sikorsky Hoverfly on a British destroyer, followed by a landing by Lieutenant K. Reed on the new battleship HMS *Vanguard* in February 1947. It was clear from the start that the helicopter was the means of providing an air element for warships other than aircraft carriers.

Helicopters were needed by the aircraft carriers, however, initially for plane-guard duties picking up downed aircrew, especially during carrier landings and take-offs. Developments in carrier design were to ensure that the chances of survival in an accident improved and the helicopter became more worthwhile – not just an up-to-date gimmick. By the time of Suez, a heli-borne assault was realistic, although aided by the poor defence put up by Egyptian troops, and later helicopters relieved fixed-wing aircraft of anti-submarine duties, even aboard the aircraft carriers, aided by the invention of 'dunking' sonar buoys, so that the helicopter could actively seek a submarine. It was a short step to ensuring that all new frigates and destroyers were fitted with a helicopter platform and hangar as standard, starting with the Rothesay-class frigates built between 1956 and 1961, which were converted to carry helicopters. These were soon augmented by no less than twenty-six of a development, the Leander-class, which proved to be a successful design that was also taken up by the Netherlands, New Zealand, India and Australia. Even so, while the Leander suited the helicopter well, some other designs, such as the Tribal-class frigates and the

County-class guided-missile destroyers, had the landing platform relatively high up, making landing during rough weather more difficult. While the County-class could accommodate a Westland Wessex anti-submarine helicopter, its hangar was shaped for this machine and nothing else, so as the Wessex began to be retired and replaced by the much more capable Sea King, the County-class had to make do with the small ship helicopter, the Westland Lynx. Essentially, the County-class ships were a triumph of design over practicality.

The application of the helicopter to small ships was helped by the development of small helicopters such as the Bristol Sycamore and the Westland Wasp, the naval version of the Scout anti-tank helicopter. The Wasp had its limitations, but it could carry and drop an anti-submarine torpedo, guided by the sonar of its mother ship. In the naval version of the Westland Lynx, developed jointly with Aerospatiale of France, although Westland had design leadership, the Royal Navy finally obtained a world-class, small-ship helicopter with high speed and the ability to engage fast-moving surface targets such as high-speed patrol boats with its BAe Sea Skua missiles. The Lynx was bought by many navies apart from the Royal Navy and the *Marine Nationale*, including Norway, Denmark, Germany, the Netherlands, Portugal, Brazil and New Zealand.

In short, few escort vessels today are built without the ability to carry and support a helicopter.

The Jet Age Comes to Sea

The first generation of jet aircraft was not without its drawbacks. Range was short and initial acceleration on the ground low with unreheated engines. In an echo of the past, when many senior British naval officers believed that high-performance aircraft could not be operated from aircraft carriers, many believed this of the jet aircraft. Early jet aircraft were indeed faster than their piston contemporaries, although some, notably the Meteor, were less manoeuvrable.

The Royal Navy had also been slow to adopt twin-engined aircraft aboard its carriers, although on 25 March 1944, Lieutenant Commander Eric 'Winkle' Brown put a de Havilland Mosquito BIV fighter-bomber safely onto the deck of HMS *Indefatigable*, the first time this had been done aboard a British carrier. A development of the Mosquito, the single-seat Sea Hornet F20, was planned to join the fleet but the end of the war in the Pacific meant that the aircraft only entered service in small numbers. Nevertheless, after joining No. 801 NAS in June 1947, Sea Hornets did eventually go to sea, with 801's aircraft moving from Ford to Arbroath and then joining HMS *Implacable* in 1949. Another development, the Fleet Air Arm's first carrier-borne night fighter, was the Sea Hornet NF21, a twin-seat, radar-equipped aircraft, which entered operational service with No. 809 NAS at RNAS Culdrose on 20 January 1949, and later went aboard

HMS *Vengeance* in May 1950. Nevertheless, these aircraft saw service in small numbers and were later replaced by Sea Furies in the case of 801 and Sea Venoms for 809.

Putting a large twin-engined aircraft aboard a light fleet carrier such as *Vengeance* seems odd, but the first landing of a jet aircraft on a carrier was again aboard a light fleet carrier, HMS *Ocean*.* On 3 December 1945, Lieutenant-Commander Eric 'Winkle' Brown landed a de Havilland Sea Vampire aboard the ship while she was steaming in the English Channel.

The rapid improvement in aircraft design and performance was accompanied by a series of improvements to the design of aircraft carriers intended to make operations easier and much safer. There were three inventions in total, all of them British: the angled flight deck, the steam catapult and the mirror deck-landing system.

Undoubtedly the most important of these inventions was the angled deck. This allowed aircraft to land and take off at the same time without interference between the two operations, even on the smaller aircraft carriers. It also enabled the forward part of the flight deck to be used as an aircraft park if the catapults were not in use, without any danger of landing aircraft overshooting into the aircraft park. Not the least of the advantages was that an aircraft overshooting could go round and make a second attempt to land providing the pilot was quick enough to change throttle and flap settings. If he wasn't, then at least he could pancake in the sea without fear of being run down by the ship.

The angled flight deck was the brainchild of a British naval officer, Captain D.R.F. Cambell, but ironically the first ship to incorporate the interim half-angled flight deck, which could be installed with minimal changes to the ship's structure, was the USS *Antietam* in 1952. The following year, HMS *Centaur* joined the Royal Navy with a line painted on her flight deck, not quite a half-angled flight deck. It was not until the ship had completed her trials that the first landing was made on her by Captain H.P. Sears in May 1954. The fully angled deck was, of course, a far superior option and made much better use of a ship's existing deck space, and made the installation of a waist catapult easier.

One of the most gruelling and dangerous tasks aboard an aircraft carrier was that of the deck landing officer (DCLO), more usually known as a 'batsman'. These were pilots who knew all about the dangers of landing on a carrier, but lost their flying pay when they took up this unenviable role. At around the time that the angled flight deck was being introduced, the mirror deck-landing system was invented by Commander H.C.N.

*In fact, a Ryan FR-1 Fireball did land on the USS *Wake Island* on 6 November 1945. The Fireball was a 'compound' aircraft, which had a piston engine with a small jet engine to boost performance. The failure of the piston forced the pilot to make an emergency landing as the jet alone could not sustain flight.

Goodhard, another Royal Navy officer, and first appeared in 1954. The mirror deck-landing system replaced the batsman and, by reflecting the landing light of an approaching aircraft, showed whether the aircraft was too high or too low, thereby playing its part in the introduction of faster and heavier aircraft to the carrier fleet.

Preceding all of these ideas was the steam catapult, introduced to bridge the growing gap between ever higher aircraft take-off speeds and the relatively static maximum speed of aircraft carriers. The existing catapults aboard carriers had been known to the Royal Navy between the wars as accelerators and were pneumo-hydraulic, but while they did assist take-offs, the performance was inadequate for larger and faster aircraft which needed a heftier push forward. Based on an idea by Commander C.C. Mitchell, a Royal Naval Volunteer Reserve Officer, the steam catapult was developed by Brown Brothers of Edinburgh, and underwent fourteen months of trials aboard the light fleet carrier HMS *Perseus* before the first live take-off by Lieutenant Commander J.M. Glaser in July 1951. The steam catapult became operational in 1953. Even before the steam catapult appeared, British practice had been modified so that catapults used a strop rather than launching trolleys, which originally had been favoured by the Royal Navy for both seaplanes and landplanes.

Steam catapults replaced the older type on the foredeck, with smaller carriers such as the light fleets having just one, while larger ships had two, but later an additional catapult was placed on the angled flight deck on even the largest British carriers; the even larger United States ships had two, making four catapults altogether. Initially, it was claimed that steam catapults could propel an aircraft into the air even when the ship was at anchor in nil wind conditions – this was true and a Supermarine Sea Hawk was sent off HMS *Eagle* in this way while the ship was moored in Malta's Grand Harbour, but as aircraft weights and speeds rose, this became an impractical proposition. One practical result was that navies continued, whenever possible, to fly their aircraft to a shore station before entering harbour.

Eagle and the slightly larger, by inches, *Ark Royal*, were originally intended to have been part of a class of four ships, with the other two being *Malta* and *Gibraltar*, but the two latter ships had been cancelled. Many believe that the money spent on these two ships would have provided better value than the heavy cost of rebuilding *Victorious*, whose design was changed as ideas on aircraft carriers developed. The high cost of conversion or rebuilding also reflected the difference between British and US practice at the time. On British carriers, the flight deck and hangar deck were part of the hull, while US carriers had these as part of the superstructure, even when hulls were plated up to flight-deck level. This meant that conversion, or even repair, of the British carriers was more expensive and took more time. On the other hand, it also meant that British carriers had heavily armoured flight and hangar decks.

Eagle had originally been laid down as HMS *Irresistible*, and *Ark Royal* as *Audacious* – names which reflected their development from the original British fast armoured carrier, *Illustrious*. Both ships had two hangar decks.

The Centaur-class was originally ordered during the Second World War as a class of eight ships intended to be faster, larger and more robust than the Colossus- and Majestic-classes. When peace came, four were cancelled and cancellation and scrapping of the four ships already building was considered, but it was clear that not only had most of the fast armoured carriers suffered badly during the war, they also suffered from having a lack of height in the hangars and could not accommodate the larger aircraft entering service. The fourth ship of the Centaur-class, HMS *Hermes*, did not join the fleet until 1959, by which time *Albion* and *Bulwark* were serving as commando carriers. *Hermes* had a fully angled flight deck and all of the modern aids, including a three-dimensional radar, and it seems a shame that her sisters were not refitted to the same standard in the light of the decision to cancel *Malta* and *Gibraltar*. The commando requirement could have been met by converting *Theseus*, *Glory*, *Ocean* and *Perseus*, which were sent to the breakers. If this seems extravagant, it is worth bearing in mind that with just two commando carriers, one was always likely to be unavailable due to routine refitting or even simple maintenance.

The Aircraft

Post-war, the Fleet Air Arm was intended to account for a third of the Royal Navy's strength, but to dispel any notions that it was a service within a service, the title 'Naval Aviation' was adopted in 1946, even though informally it was still the Fleet Air Arm, and the old title was readopted during the late 1950s. Meanwhile, in 1947, four Royal Naval Volunteer Reserve squadrons were formed, one each with Supermarine Spitfire 4s and 17s, one with Fairey Fireflies and one with North American Harvard advanced trainers.

Nevertheless, the peacetime Royal Navy was considerably slimmed down and this was especially noticeable with the Fleet Air Arm as so many of its carriers were US-built escort, or in RN terms 'auxiliary', carriers provided under Lend-Lease, and so had to be returned to the USN. In fact, a number were so badly damaged that they were hulked in British waters. The only two pre-war survivors, *Furious* and *Argus* were withdrawn and fit only for the breakers. Many of the Colossus-class and the uprated version capable of handling heavier and faster aircraft, the Majestic-class, went straight into reserve, but by and large not for too long as they were soon seeing service with other navies, as the *Marine Nationale* took *Colossus* herself, while others went to Australia, Canada, India and the Netherlands, as well as to the Argentine and Brazil.

There were other changes. The most important of these was that the pilots and observers who had transferred from the RAF in 1939, and the wartime intake of pilots and observers, all belonged to the Air Branch and were essentially still airmen who went to sea, as with the days of RAF control, rather than sailors who could fly. This changed, with pilots and observers regarded as part of the executive branch and expected, when aboard a ship not under combat conditions, to take their share of watch-keeping and navigation. This meant that command of warships was open to them and so too was the way to flag rank.

The Fleet Air Arm did not remain in ignorance of jet aircraft for long, for with the coming of peace, a number of Gloster Meteors were provided for evaluation. This was not an aircraft suitable for carrier operation, but a number were obtained for second-line duties including target towing.

While the de Havilland Sea Vampire had been first to make a carrier-deck landing, it did not become an operational aircraft, but instead the RN used Vampires for training, as did the RAF. The first British carrier-borne jet aircraft was the Supermarine Attacker, which first flew on 27 July 1946, but did not enter service until 1949. This was an unusual jet aircraft as it had a tail wheel rather than a tricycle undercarriage. Despite Saunders-Roe developing a flying-boat jet fighter, the SR-A/1, it was clear that in the post-war Fleet Air Arm, landplanes were the way forward. Armstrong-Whitworth supplied the Sea Hawk, a close relation to the RAF's highly successful Hawker Hunter, and which proved popular with naval pilots, but while this first flew on 2 September 1947, it did not enter service until 1949, when it was joined by a development of the Sea Vampire, the Sea Venom; both aircraft had straight wings reflecting the dominance of conservative attitudes in the Royal Navy. The Sea Vampire and Sea Venom were both twin-boom aircraft, a feature of the de Havilland jet fighters.

A distraction was the Westland Wyvern, a turboprop strike aircraft, which was favoured because it was felt that a turboprop would have a better take-off performance, and at low altitudes. The aircraft, which was also ordered by the RAF, failed to perform adequately, partly because of development problems with its engine, so that early RAF models were delivered with piston engines. In the end, both services opted for an all-jet combat aircraft force as soon as practical.

The interest in turboprops at the time is understandable. The turboprop offered better acceleration than unreheated jet engines and lower fuel consumption, while the world's first operational turboprop airliner, the Vickers Viscount, was not only operationally successful and attracting passengers, it was also taking the British aircraft industry into markets that it had never served before, such as the United States, France, the Netherlands and Italy.

Far more successful was another turboprop type, the Fairey Gannet, with its Armstrong-Whitworth Double Mamba turboprop, for anti-submarine duties. The first of a significant number of these entered service in 1954 after another anti-submarine type, the Short Seamew, intended for operations from light fleet carriers, was abandoned. In fact, the Gannet could be operated from the light fleets and did so with the Royal Australian Navy. The Gannet was soon displaced when it was realized that helicopters with dunking sonar were far more successful. The Fleet Air Arm's first helicopters so fitted were Sikorsky HO4S-3s delivered to No. 845 NAS under the US Mutual Defence Aid Programme, which had also supplied Sikorsky HRS-2 helicopters in January 1953 for use as transports against Communist bandits in Malaya. In addition, the MDAP provided twenty Hiller HTO-1s for helicopter pilot training.

Nevertheless, most Sikorsky helicopters for the British armed forces were built under licence by Westland with British engines and, in the case of the S-58, known in British service as the Wessex, Westland fitted a turboshaft engine in place of the original piston. Westland was also allowed to build helicopters under licence for naval use in Europe and the Commonwealth.

It was a matter of considerable pride for the Fleet Air Arm that it provided 300 aircraft for the Coronation Flypast for Britain's new sovereign, Queen Elizabeth II, in June 1953.

Meanwhile, new variants of the Gannet were supplied for airborne-early-warning, displacing the Douglas Skyraiders, while the ASW Gannets were converted to carrier onboard delivery aircraft, or COD aircraft, to deliver supplies to carriers at sea.

By the late 1950s, the Westland Whirlwind, the licence-built Sikorsky S-55, which had served at Suez, was being replaced by the new Westland Wessex as both a troop transport and an anti-submarine helicopter, while both the Fleet Air Arm and the Royal Air Force received search-and-rescue versions as well.

The same period saw the Fleet Air Arm receive its first swept-wing jet fighter, the transonic Supermarine Scimitar, which also had a nuclear-strike capability. Fitted with two Rolls-Royce Avon unreheated turbojets, one can only speculate on what could have been the result if the aircraft had been further developed with reheated Avons, as used by the RAF's Mach 2.0 English Electric Lightning interceptors. Some believe a further development of the Scimitar was planned, but cancelled. One complaint about the Scimitar was that hangar decks, and ashore floors, tended to be covered in leaking oil. This was a reflection on the engine rather than the aircraft as one heard the same comment about the Lightning, with RAF hangar floors covered in drip trays! To some extent, this aircraft was rivalled by the de Havilland Sea Vixen, the production model of the DH110 that had broken up so tragically at a Farnborough Air Show. The twin-seat Sea Vixen was also transonic, but a night fighter, as opposed to the single-seat Scimitar, which eventually found itself downgraded to support duties, including the important role of a flying tanker using 'buddy-buddy' refuelling techniques, which essentially meant carrying fuel in underwing tanks rather than inboard.

The Scimitar lost its nuclear role to another aircraft, possibly the most iconic Fleet Air Arm strike aircraft since the Swordfish, the Blackburn NA39 Buccaneer, although most aircraft were produced under the Hawker Siddeley name as consolidation of the British aircraft industry into two big groups, the British Aircraft Corporation and Hawker Siddeley, had been forced through by the British government. It was the Buccaneer S2 that was the really effective aircraft, a carrier-borne, twin-seat, twin-engined bomber capable of carrying a nuclear weapon or up to sixteen 1,000-lb bombs, powered by two Rolls-Royce Spey turbojets. The earlier version of the aircraft was sold to the South African Air Force, but further deliveries were banned because of a UN arms embargo on that country. There were also reports that it might have been bought by the USN or, perhaps and also, the United States Air Force, but left-wing pressure meant that a Labour government would not do so because of the US involvement in the Vietnam War. The Buccaneer used airbrakes as well as an arrester hook for landing, and to strike down into the hangar deck, its nose cone had to swing out of the way. This was not the exclusive preserve of the two large aircraft carriers as Buccaneers also fitted onto *Hermes*. One test observer, when asked by a mess mate how he liked the aircraft, maintained that it had everything an observer might wish for in the back seat, but one had to be quick to turn everything on otherwise it wouldn't have warmed up before the test flight ended.

When the British Aircraft Corporation's TSR-2 strike aircraft was scrapped during the 1960s, the RAF was provided with Buccaneers instead, which replaced the English Electric Canberra jet bomber over which the Buccaneer was an incredible advance.

This was the first time in naval aviation history that aircraft designed for operations from aircraft carriers matched the performance of those designed for shore-based operation. The Buccaneer was not alone – it was a generational step change in the quality of naval aviation with outstanding aircraft matched to outstanding ships. The Americans had the McDonnell (later McDonnell Douglas) F-4 Phantom, an interceptor that could also become an effective fighter-bomber and the Ling-Temco-Vought A-7 Corsair II. Both were designed for the USN and USMC; both saw service with the USAF and in the case of the Phantom, other air forces as well.

By the time the decision to abandon Britain's aircraft carriers had been taken, the McDonnell Douglas F-4 Phantom had been selected for both the Fleet Air Arm and the Royal Air Force. To offset both the foreign exchange costs and criticism of buying American, it was decided that these aircraft, known as the F-4K for the Fleet Air Arm and F-4M for the RAF, should have Rolls-Royce Spey engines. This political decision had some benefits both in the performance of the aircraft and in that the Americans were so impressed with the aircraft that they took out a licence for Allison to build the engines in unreheated form for versions of the LTV A-7 Corsair. In any case, the Spey saw widespread use in the United States in service in BAC One-Eleven airliners and Grumman Gulfstream II business jets.

The controversy over the Phantom purchase had been fuelled by the fact that the purchase was necessary at all because of the cancellation of yet another British combat aircraft, the Hawker Siddeley HS1184, intended to be a supersonic vertical take-off jet fighter and a development of the Hawker P1127 Kestrel prototype. The Fleet Air Arm, by now accustomed to twin-engined aircraft, didn't like the idea of a single-engined fighter.

Nevertheless, with the days of the big carriers in RN service numbered, it was important to find a means of maintaining fighter protection for the fleet. Hawker Siddeley had meanwhile developed the P1127 into the Harrier, and received an order from the RAF for this as a tactical attack aircraft, followed by an order from the United States Marine Corps. When the Harrier entered RAF service in 1969, it marked fresh hope for the Fleet Air Arm. A new class of ship, termed a 'through-deck cruiser' was developed to operate a mixture of Harriers and Sea King helicopters. Work commenced on the concept, which lacked catapults or arrester wires, despite no sign of an order. The Harrier, meanwhile, was demonstrated on trials from the helicopter landing platforms of warships, including the British Tiger-class cruisers, two of which, *Tiger* and *Blake*, were modified to operate and support up to four Sea Kings, and the amphibious transport dock vessels, HMS *Fearless* and *Intrepid*, and the French aircraft carrier *Foch*.

It was intended that the Harrier should be built under licence in the United States for the USMC as the AV-8A, but the small initial order did not justify this and it was not until the uprated AV-8B that production started at McDonnell Douglas. The USMC soon found that the aircraft had exceptional manoeuvrability, and the Marines experimented with using this in flight, developing a technique known as 'viffing' which enabled an experienced Harrier pilot to outperform a Phantom in a low-level dogfight, despite the Harrier being barely transonic and the Phantom capable of Mach 2.2. It was also found that giving the Harrier a short take-off into the wind, using STOL rather than VTOL, its weapon load or range could be substantially increased. This concept was taken further by the brainchild of Lieutenant Commander R.D. Taylor RN, which was taken over by the manufacturer, by this time British Aerospace, and proved that a low-angled ramp, inevitably known as the 'ski-jump' at the end of the take-off run also improved warload and the initial rate of climb.

By this time, shipbuilders on both sides of the Atlantic were inspired by the potential of the Harrier. Vosper-Thorneycroft in the UK developed the

'Harrier Carrier', displacing just 6,000 tons and capable of carrying four Harriers and four Sea Kings, while rival Vickers produced the MAC-ship, meaning 'maritime-area command ship'. The US saw the design appear for the 'Sea Control Ship', also designed to operate Harriers and Sea Kings. Later, both Italy and Spain designed and built ships capable of operating Harriers, and Spain eventually sold a smaller vessel to Thailand.

When finally ready for service with the Royal Navy, the Harrier had developed into the Sea Harrier, with radar and a redesigned fuselage that gave a canopy with an all-round view, a feature adopted for later versions of the Harrier. The new through-deck cruisers had become the Invincible-class, fitted with a 'ski-jump'. The Sea Harrier FRS1 was to prove to be the saviour of the Fleet Air Arm.

Chapter 17

The Falklands Saves the Carriers

The commissioning in 1981 of the first of the through-deck cruisers, HMS *Invincible,* seemed to forecast a period of renewal for the Fleet Air Arm. With her design dating from a 1966 plan to replace the helicopter cruisers, or command cruisers, *Tiger* and *Blake,* with anti-submarine escorts for the planned super-carriers CVA01 and CVA02, but much modified to accommodate additional helicopters and, if necessary, Sea Harriers, *Invincible* had been modified so that she was in all respects an aircraft carrier. The new class looked odd, as the first British carrier since the original *Eagle* of 1922, converted from a battleship that had originally been ordered by Chile, to have twin funnels. She was the largest gas turbine-powered ship in the world at the time, displacing almost 20,000 tons full load and powered by four marine versions of the Rolls-Royce Olympus turbojet, the same engines used to power the Concorde supersonic airliner. Drawbacks included having an oversized superstructure that impinged on both flight deck and hangar deck space, and lifts that were positioned so that they overlapped with the take-off run on the flight deck. Nevertheless, she was a carrier and could take fixed-wing and rotary-wing aircraft to sea.

At the outset, she was not alone. With *Ark Royal* withdrawn, the sole surviving Centaur-class aircraft carrier, *Hermes,* was also converted from commando carrier to operate Sea Harriers, and she also gained a 'ski slope' ramp forward, one which, if anything, was rather sleeker than that on *Invincible.*

With the Amazon-class Type 21 frigates, the Broadsword-class Type 22 frigates, intended to be *the* replacements for the successful Leander-class, and the Sheffield-class Type 42 anti-aircraft destroyers, all having helicopter hangars and platforms, the Fleet Air Arm had a substantial presence throughout the fleet. New Royal Fleet Auxiliaries were arriving complete with helicopter platforms and hangars, while the RFA also manned *Engadine,* a helicopter support and training ship which many felt showed a low-cost but highly effective option for the future deployment of ASW forces. The Wasp was being replaced by the naval version of the Lynx, a fast helicopter somewhat similar in appearance to the Bell UH-1 Iroquois, but with four-bladed rotors and a much higher speed, as well as a retractable undercarriage. Other ships that could handle helicopters, but by some oversight were built without hangars, were *Fearless* and *Intrepid*, originally known as transport-dock vessels, but were more usually known as assault ships.

The Wessex helicopters were on their way into retirement, except for those retained aboard the surviving County-class destroyers. Their successor was the Westland Sea King, a powerful, twin-engined, single-rotor, licence-built version of the Sikorsky S-61. This too had a dunking sonar, but the Sea King was also available as a transport for Royal Marine commandos. With endurance of up to four hours, a maximum speed of 150 knots and an anti-submarine capability equivalent to that of a small frigate, the Sea King was a potent addition to the Fleet Air Arm.

Comparing the combination of the Sea Harrier and the Sea King aboard a ship, especially one on convoy escort duty, seemed as far away from the situation on the Atlantic and Arctic convoys of the Second World War as from the Stone Age.

There were reasons to be optimistic, and certainly the Sea Harrier pilots soon had a great regard for their aircraft and were confident of its capabilities which, as it turned out, was to be just as well.

Tied up by John's Knots

In the midst of this revival, so welcome after the doubts and uncertainties of the 1960s and 1970s, came a bombshell. The new Conservative government, elected in spring 1979, had conducted a defence review. Such reviews are clearly necessary from time to time, but this was a root-and-branch review with far-reaching conclusions. The review had come to the conclusion that the effort expended on providing air cover for the fleet was excessive, especially since 'out-of-area' operations, which really meant operations outside the area of the North Atlantic Treaty Organisation, were extremely unlikely. Not for the last time, ministers spoke of ships and aircraft simply as 'platforms', which many regarded as a soulless attitude.

The new Secretary of State for Defence, Sir John Nott, spared no one in condemning the status quo. The Royal Navy could make do with just two carriers, and since a third Invincible-class was planned, the nameship was to be sold to the Royal Australian Navy, while *Hermes*, once retired, was to go to the Indian Navy. The assault ships, *Fearless* and *Intrepid*, could go into reserve. The Antarctic patrol ship, HMS *Endurance*, was also amongst those ships to be withdrawn.

Even while this news was being digested, Nott's opposite number at the Foreign Office was discussing the future of the Falkland Islands – far outside the NATO area in the South Atlantic – with Argentina.

The Falklands Campaign

The Argentine had long laid claim to sovereignty over the Falkland Islands, known to them as Las Malvinas. The islands had never been colonized by the Argentine, although Spanish and Argentine explorers had reached the islands before the British, who were the first to maintain a permanent presence in both the Falklands and South Georgia. While the settlers on the Falklands mainly farmed sheep, the attractions of the islands to the Argentine have generally been regarded as fishing rights and, still more important, the strong possibility of valuable oil and natural gas resources.

The Argentines made much of the Falklands being part of the South American continental shelf, although this was something of an irrelevance given that they were still 400 miles off the coast! They also claimed sovereignty over South Georgia, 1,500 miles away. Instead of resisting the claim and refusing to negotiate, Britain had been looking for a compromise for some years – to the dismay of the population of the Falkland Islands. In fact, it was Argentina that remained committed to its insistence that the islands be handed over, and which refused to negotiate.

Argentina at the time was governed by a military dictatorship, untrammelled by the many considerations and checks inherent in a democracy. Diplomatic pressure having failed, Argentine forces eventually invaded the Falklands on Friday, 2 April 1982. Even for a dictatorship, this was a gamble. They knew that all that stood in their way was a small detachment of seventy Royal Marines, protecting the population of almost 2,000 spread over an area about the size of Wales. The arrival of Argentine scrap metal merchants on South Georgia had gone unchallenged by the British, who had a small detachment of twenty-two Royal Marines on the island.

There seemed to be every chance that the British would do little more than mount diplomatic protests. Recovery of the islands once occupied seemed, to the Argentine military, almost impossible. The Falklands were some 8,000 miles from Britain, they were small, insignificant, with a very small population, and meant little to the British. To some extent they were right in these assumptions. A substantial number of British people had no idea where the Falklands where. There were even some who thought that they were somewhere off the coast of Scotland.

One reason for Argentine optimism about the British reaction was that the armed forces had suffered repeated reductions in their strength and capability over the years. American assistance could be ruled out, for despite a close alliance between the United Kingdom and the United States, American interests also involved friendly relations with as many Latin American countries as possible. Furthermore, the Americans were also against anything that smacked of colonialism and many Americans refused to accept the United Kingdom's continued claim to Northern Ireland.

Another reason was that, without intending to do so, the British had been sending out the wrong kind of signals, ones that were likely to encourage rather than discourage or deter Argentine adventures.

A third reason was that, despite the Argentine claim on the Falklands, the British had been active in pursuing the sale of military equipment to Argentina. In recent years this had included two modern destroyers of the Sheffield-class. Argentina had been sold aircraft, and even an ex-Dutch aircraft carrier, the *Veinticinco de Mayo*, which needed, and got, British support to keep her operational.

Meanwhile, the commanding officer of the ice patrol ship, HMS *Endurance*, had reported his suspicions about Argentine intentions, including the landings in South Georgia, and these had been ignored.

In many ways, Nott's defence review was simply an extension of the policies followed by earlier British governments in their haste to retreat from the wider world. Successive governments had more or less followed a policy that dictated that the armed forces would only be involved when shore bases were available. There were no shore bases within easy reach of the Falklands. Tristan da Cunha had no facilities at all and the terrain was unsuitable. There were no alliances in place with any Latin American state and although Chile was friendly, it was on the other side of South America. British dislike of South African domestic policies had put the Simonstown Agreement in abeyance, denying the use of airfields and ports in South Africa, although these were, in reality, also some distance away.

Initial landings on the Falklands by Argentine troops were from landing craft and smaller warships, including corvettes. Fierce resistance was met from the Royal Marines, who eventually had no option but to surrender as several thousand troops came ashore. The landing force was followed by reinforcements flown in aboard the Fuerza Aerea Argentina's Lockheed C-130 transports, augmented by chartered civilian Fokker F-27 Friendship airliners.

Rather more difficult was the landing on South Georgia. Here the ice patrol vessel *Bahia Paraiso*, 9,600 tons, was used, with an Aerospatiale Puma and two Alouette III helicopters operated from the vessel. Failing to shoot down the Puma with a 66-mm anti-tank rocket launcher, the Royal Marines machine-gunned it until it retreated across a bay and then crash-landed. They then shot down one of the Alouettes, before damaging a corvette with another rocket launcher. When the marines finally surrendered, the Argentine forces found it hard to believe that they had come close to defeat at the hands of such a small group of men.

Argentina did not use her aircraft carrier during the Falklands campaign. At first, British observers had suspected that the ship was kept offshore and out of harm's way, but later it was discovered that she was kept in port. Boiler trouble was suspected, but the truth was even more incredible: her steam catapult had been dismantled and was in Britain for overhaul.

The news was greeted in London with anger and disbelief. Parliament, in recess for Easter, was recalled. It took just seventy-two hours for a Task Force to be hastily assembled and its first units put to sea. The Royal Navy centred this around its two remaining aircraft carriers. The flagship was the larger of these, the elderly HMS *Hermes*, while the other ship was the new purpose-designed 'Harrier-carrier', HMS *Invincible*. Between them, these two ships managed to take just twenty Sea Harriers. Yet less than twenty years earlier, the Royal Navy could have put five aircraft carriers to sea, with two of them almost twice the size of *Hermes*, and added two commando carriers as well. Later, this impressive force was augmented by two landing dock assault ships, *Fearless* and *Intrepid*, with stern docks that could flood so that landing craft could be floated off, and helicopter landing platforms. Fortunately, while both ships were due for disposal under the defence review, and one had been placed in reserve already, they were still available to join the Task Force. Dockyard workers and naval personnel laboured to ensure that the ships were ready to go to the South Atlantic.

There were the inevitable frigates and destroyers, but even here there were signs of future problems and weaknesses. It had been decided to end naval gunnery, closing the gunnery school at Whale Island, just off Portsmouth, and a new generation of frigates, the Broadsword-class, was entering service without a main-gun armament, just 20-mm cannon and guided missiles. The crisis was such that it was essential to requisition merchant ships, including the Cunard liner *Queen Elizabeth II*, and the P&O cruise ships *Canberra* and *Uganda*, the latter becoming the Task Force's hospital ship. A container ship, *Atlantic Conveyor*, was modified to carry helicopters. Royal Navy survey ships were pressed into service as hospital ships, later becoming 'ambulance' ships, taking the wounded to the *Uganda*.

Surprise was impossible. The departure of the Task Force, the core of which sailed from Portsmouth, but which included ships from other ports, was shown across the world on television. The United States attempted to broker a deal between the United Kingdom and Argentina, but without success, while many American newspapers had started to draw comparisons between the Argentine dictatorship and a democratic ally. Eventually, American support and collaboration was given. New Zealand offered to take over some of Britain's commitments in the Pacific area to release units for the operation. Chile, secretly, was to provide support, including a refuge for a British secret mission against an Argentine air base.

As the task force sailed south, technical problems emerged with the still new *Invincible*, with the press reporting that she was unable to go astern due to problems with her gearbox – the largest on any ship at the time. 'The Royal Navy is not going anywhere backwards,' retorted one senior officer.

The Empire Strikes Back

Many in the United Kingdom were pessimistic over the chances of regaining the Falklands. One of the most extreme examples was that of a senior officer at the Fleet Air Arm's only remaining fixed-wing Royal Naval Air Station, at Yeovilton, who told the wives of the pilots that they were to expect heavy casualties, probably as high as 80 per cent! A Labour Party candidate in a by-election, one Tony Blair, opposed sending a Task Force. Truly, the odds were against the British, but they had a number of factors on their side.

Commander Nigel 'Sharkey' Ward was in command of No. 801 NAS aboard *Invincible* and was senior air adviser to Rear Admiral Sandy Woodward (later Admiral Sir Sandy), in command of the Task Force. Ward was to fly over sixty sorties, and managed three air-to-air kills, witnessing many more.

'On the way down it was very clear we were short of air defence,' he recalled. 'The Air Force couldn't provide it, and we had twenty aircraft against what we were told were 200 Argentinian aircraft.'

In contrast to the Argentine forces, whose army was overwhelmingly composed of conscripts, the British fielded a completely professional force. To the Argentine conscript, the cold, bleak Falklands landscape posed great difficulties. To the British Royal Marine Commandos and the Parachute Brigade, it was hard going, but remarkably similar to much that had been encountered during training. There was no question of the 'paras' being able to parachute anywhere, since the Falklands were far beyond the range of their Hercules transports. Membership of NATO had also had its benefits – the British were well exercised.

Even so, there were moments of intense stupidity, in one case even after hostilities had started. Reports in newspapers that members of the British Army's elite Special Air Service Regiment, the SAS, and their Royal Marine equivalent, the Special Boat Service, SBS, had landed in the Falklands were premature, and warned the Argentine forces of exactly where to expect a landing. This appeared just before the landings at San Carlos Water. Claims in the British media that Argentine bombs had failed to explode, largely because the Argentine pilots had flown so low that the fuses could not arm themselves, were a warning to the Argentines to either modify their fuses or fly higher. The information came from an official press release from the British Ministry of Defence. As many as three quarters of all bombs dropped by the Argentine Air Force and Navy failed to explode, with sometimes as many as four bombs hitting a warship without sinking it. This announcement on 23 May could have marked the start of considerable bloodshed amongst the Task Force's ships, with loss of equipment and life which could have made this risky operation fail.

Air operations began on 30 April 1982, with combat being encountered on 1 May, and attacks against Port Stanley.

Dave Stanley, who was flying with No. 800 NAS, recalled:

> I came round the side of the airfield. At that stage I saw tracer start to come towards me, and realised that someone was trying to shoot down my mum's little boy, and there was a bloody great bang and the whole aircraft started vibrating and I realised that I had been hit. I discovered ... that a 20mm high explosive shell had gone through my tail. It left a very neat small entry hole on the left hand side of the tail ... had the aircraft patched up and flying again the next morning.

Given modern communications, the progress not just of the war but of actual operations was broadcast to the world. Brian Hanrahan was the British Broadcasting Corporation's war correspondent and was sailing aboard *Hermes*. He was not allowed to tell his audience how many aircraft were sent on the first operation against Argentine forces, but gave great reassurance to many at home with relatives and friends amongst the pilots by saying: 'I am not allowed to tell you how many went, but I counted them all out and counted them all back.'

The problem was, of course, that the transonic Sea Harrier was facing the highly effective supersonic Dassault Mirage III and Mirage V, as well as Israeli-built 'Dagger' developments of the latter.

Ward recalled:

> For our tactics of fighting against the enemy, we used a manoeuvre called the 'hook manoeuvre', which was quite simply sending one aircraft in ahead and one behind ... putting the enemy in a problem, they're in a sandwich, somewhat like the army pincer movement. It's commonsense, good strategy, good tactics, and it worked. On day one we shot down two aircraft using this method.

The way it worked is illustrated by an encounter between two Sea Harriers of No. 801 NAS with two Mirages on 1 May. Lieutenant Steve Thomas was flying a Sea Harrier and attempted to lock on a Sidewinder air-to-air missile without success. As he flew between the two Mirages, two missiles from one of the aircraft shot past him. The pilot of the other Sea Harrier, Lieutenant Paul Barton, succeeded in locking a Sidewinder on to a Mirage, fired and saw the aircraft blow up. Not to be outdone, Thomas tried again and fired a Sidewinder at the second Mirage, but the aircraft raced into cloud before the missile could strike, leaving Thomas unable to claim a kill. His missile had a proximity fuse and, unbeknown to him, damaged the aircraft. It remained flyable and so the pilot decided to nurse his aircraft back to base, having lightened his warload by dumping it –

unfortunately, it fell amongst Argentine troops who, convinced they were being attacked, shot down his aircraft.

Thomas was to have more success the next day, as the Sea Harriers battled to protect the troops making their initial landings on the Falklands, when he shot down two Daggers on one sortie. Before long, the Sea Harrier was known to the Argentine pilots as *La Muerte Negra*, the 'Black Death'.

Both sides suffered serious losses. The British nuclear-powered submarine, HMS *Courageous*, sank the Argentine cruiser, *General Belgrano*. This remains controversial to this day as the ship was supposed to be steaming away from the Falklands. The Royal Navy suspected, wrongly, that she had been modified to carry Exocet guided missiles, which posed a real threat to the ships of the Task Force. In fact, whether or not she was steaming away, or carried Exocet missiles (which can be fitted relatively easily to a warship), was irrelevant. In the open ocean, a large ship can make better progress than a smaller vessel, and she could outgun the British frigates and destroyers. She was a threat and the two countries were at war.

The British lost two destroyers, including the class leadship of the Type 42 destroyers, HMS *Sheffield*, which sank after being hit by an air-launched Exocet missile, her sister ship, *Coventry*, and two Amazon-class frigates, *Ardent* and *Antelope*. In terms of the success of the operation, the worst loss was that of the converted container ship, *Atlantic Conveyor*, which took most of the Task Force's troop-carrying helicopters with her. The lost ships were in no small part due to the fact that the Fleet Air Arm had lost its Fairey Gannet AEW aircraft, and neither *Hermes* nor *Invincible* could operate such an aircraft if it still had them.

Nevertheless, on 21 April, a small force was landed on South Georgia. After initial difficulties due to the severe weather, which necessitated further landings, a force of 120 men took on an Argentine force of 200, before moving on against other Argentine forces on the island. An Argentine submarine, *Sante Fe*, was so badly damaged by missiles fired by a helicopter as South Georgia was retaken, that she had to be beached.

At no time could the Task Force bomb Argentine bases on the mainland. The attempts by the RAF to mount long-distance strategic bombing raids using Hawker Siddeley Vulcan bombers were costly, needing twelve refuelling aircraft for each one aircraft sortie, and did relatively little damage to the runway at Port Stanley, although a radar station was destroyed on one attack. Nevertheless, Argentine use of the base was limited to Pucara light-attack aircraft, leaving the Air Force and naval pilots operating from the mainland, 400 miles away, at a disadvantage.

Even so, while the Argentine ground forces struggled to cope, the Argentine pilots, both from the Argentine Navy and the Air Force, showed great skill and courage, earning the respect of their opponents. Despite this, no Sea Harriers were shot down by enemy aircraft. By contrast, at

Goose Green, a battalion of 600 men, 2nd Battalion The Parachute Regiment, overcame an Argentine force three times their number, reversing the perceived wisdom that a successful assault requires the attacking force to outnumber their opponents by a ratio of three to one. This was at the cost of their commanding officer, Colonel 'H' Jones, who was killed in an attack on an Argentine machine-gun post.

On 15 June, British troops entered Port Stanley and the Argentine forces surrendered, a victory for the Royal Navy and for the Fleet Air Arm's Sea Harriers, without which the islands could not have been retaken. The problem was that the seizure could have succeeded had the Argentines been patient. Had they had their aircraft carrier back in service and present off the islands, and had they waited for the planned reductions in British defence capability to be implemented, it would have been virtually impossible for Britain to have retaken the islands.

The outcome also meant that the planned cuts to the Fleet Air Arm were not fully implemented, eventually leaving the Royal Navy with three aircraft carriers, two of which are meant to be available for operations at any one time. The two assault ships were reprieved and two replacements, HMS *Albion* and *Bulwark*, were built. The Royal Navy also gained a helicopter carrier, specifically for commando operations, HMS *Ocean*. Naval gunnery survived as well, and the early Type 22 frigates, which lacked a 4.5-in gun, were later sold to Brazil, while later ships and the new Type 23 Duke-class frigates, were armed with a 4.5-in gun.

One innovation that was brought about by the Falklands campaign was the modification of a small number of Sea King helicopters to act as airborne-early-warning aircraft. These could not fly as high as a fixed-wing AEW aircraft, but in the 'Harrier carrier' Navy, they were much better than nothing.

Chapter 18

A Changing Role

The success of the Falklands Campaign could not disguise the fact that the role of the Fleet Air Arm had changed completely with the retirement of the large, fast, armoured carriers. Indeed, even with the conversion of *Hermes* first to a commando carrier and then to an anti-submarine and 'Harrier carrier'. No longer did the Fleet Air Arm have the capability of taking the attack home to the enemy in the way that it had done during the Second World War, and had continued to be able to do so post-war, especially once equipped with the Buccaneer bomber. In any future war, the Royal Navy's aircraft carriers would be tasked with acting as anti-submarine escorts for a US-led task force, or even, whisper it, a French-led one.

The role of the Fleet Air Arm was confined to the air defence of the fleet and anti-shipping strikes. The original Sea Harrier FSR1s were replaced by the more capable FSR2, and modified to attack shore targets as well, when supporting an expeditionary force of marines or the army ashore. Nevertheless, despite this extension of the role, the Royal Navy no longer had the capability of mounting an attack on vital shore targets *from the air*, but it did have it from *under the sea* as hunter-killer, or fleet, nuclear-powered submarines were modified to launch cruise missiles. Launching cruise missiles from beneath the waves has its advantages, but aircraft could get into position more quickly and even if the Fleet Air Arm did not gain this role, the Royal Air Force could have done it less expensively and reacted more quickly.

Marginalization of the Fleet Air Arm was brought home to the Royal Navy somewhat abruptly when Iraq invaded Kuwait on 2 August 1990. Iraq had long been tempted by its smaller neighbour, and indeed the Royal Navy had prevented a similar action almost thirty years' earlier by deploying HMS *Victorious* and her air group to the Gulf. The Soviet Union had broken up and once again the United Nations was able to call upon forces, known as the 'Coalition', to liberate Kuwait, as it had in Korea. The big difference this time was that the Royal Navy no longer sent an aircraft carrier or carriers to take part. Surface vessels were deployed and they all had their helicopters, but the United States Navy was the only service to send aircraft carriers. This was because the British ships would have had to operate in the confined and relatively shallow waters of the upper Gulf to be within range of Iraqi targets. The Royal Fleet Auxiliary *Argus* transported the troop-carrying Sea King HC4 helicopters of No. 846 NAS to the Gulf in support of the forces ashore.

The shame of this was that there was an acute shortage of secure air bases ashore, and the use of carrier-borne aircraft was an asset in ensuring that a massive volume of air power fell upon the Iraqis. Only the American aircraft carriers could support aircraft with the range to make an impact.

Nevertheless, the demands on the Royal Navy, including the Fleet Air Arm, continued. The break-up of the Republic of Yugoslavia, a non-Warsaw Pact Communist dictatorship, following the death of General Tito, saw the ethnic tensions that had been kept in check for many years boil over into open conflict. The United Nations became involved and on 1 January 1993, a British carrier task group was deployed to the Adriatic to support British land forces in the UN Protection Force in the former Republic of Yugoslavia. The Royal Navy remained in the Adriatic for most of the next decade, with the level of operations varying. On 19 December 1995, after hostilities flared up again and NATO took over control of operations, the British carrier task group was placed under NATO command to provide support for operations against the Bosnian Serbs, and also took part in Operation Deny Flight. The Royal Navy's ships in the area reverted to UK command the following 15 February.

Nevertheless, the Royal Navy and its carriers were not to stay away from the Gulf. After Kuwait was liberated, the Iraqi regime refused to allow United Nations weapons inspectors access to suspected weapons research and manufacturing sites. In Operation Bolton, HMS *Invincible* and RFA *Fort Victoria,* were sent to the Gulf, arriving on 24 January 1998, to fly sorties over the Iraqi 'no-fly' zone until relieved by *Illustrious* on 8 March. Both ships were supported by escort vessels from the Armilla Patrol, which stopped and searched merchantmen bound for Basra, the main Iraqi port. Both Sea Harrier squadrons, 800 and 801 NAS, were involved, as were the helicopters of 814, 829 and 849 NAS. The RAF also based some of its Harrier GR7s aboard the carriers.

A year later, *Invincible* was back with three escorts and two RFAs for Operation Bolton II, arriving on 30 January and remaining until 1 April, when they left for the Adriatic.

On 1 May 2000, *Illustrious* and *Ocean* arrived off Sierra Leone for a UN peacekeeping mission, with Sea King HC4s landing Royal Marine commandos on the beaches in what was known as Operation Palliser.

When the decision was finally taken to invade Iraq in March 2003, known to the British as Operation Telic, the Royal Navy helped mount what was the largest amphibious operation involving British forces for almost fifty years. This required the Fleet Air Arm once again, and HMS

Ark Royal and the helicopter carrier, *Ocean*, were present with the helicopters of 814, 815, 820, 845, 847 and 849 NAS, the last being the Royal Marines own air squadron for close support.

After the battle to liberate Kuwait, another blow fell, with the creation of a Joint Helicopter Command, so that only the small-ship and anti-submarine helicopters were left under direct Fleet Air Arm control. This was followed by the creation of a Joint Force Harrier, with the Fleet Air Arm's Sea Harriers transferred to the new force, commanded by a Royal Navy officer, and moved from their home base at RNAS Yeovilton to RAF Wittering, away from the Royal Navy and its support mechanisms for families. The Sea Harriers were retired and replaced by the new Harrier GR9, an RAF aircraft which was effectively a 'bomb truck' for the support of ground forces, leaving the fleet without any fighter protection until the arrival of the Lockheed Martin F-35 after 2013. The F-35 will be a short take-off and vertical landing aircraft, which will be some reduction in flexibility, but it will be much faster than the Sea Harrier. Not only was the withdrawal of the Sea Harrier premature in the circumstances, but no one seems to have pressed for an equivalent to the GR9, using the Sea Harrier wing and fitted with radar so that fighter protection of the fleet at sea could continue.

The one bright spot on the horizon is the order for two new supercarriers (where have we heard that before?) in excess of 60,000 tons displacement, with the first ship due to be commissioned around 2015. To be named HMS *Queen Elizabeth* and *Prince of Wales*, these ships will be built in sections by several shipbuilders to a French design, overseen by British Aerospace, and the parts of the hull will be towed around the coast to Rosyth for final assembly. The superstructure has been cut down in size so that the ships can pass under the Forth Bridge and the Forth Road Bridge.

Meanwhile, the nominal three aircraft carriers of the Royal Navy, which for many years has meant two in service and one refitting or in reserve, have been reduced to two, as the first ship of the Invincible-class is in a 'very low state of reserve', according to one Admiralty spokesman. One television documentary on Channel 4 recently showed *Illustrious* on a deployment to the Middle East, with just six Sea King helicopters and it was not until she arrived in the Indian Ocean that four Harriers were flown out to join her, so she then had exactly half her planned complement of aircraft.

Yet, we are led to believe that the Royal Navy can recover from its present low ebb to man the two largest warships it has ever had.

Chapter 19

The Future

> *Britannia* (in holiday mood): 'What are the wild waves saying?'
> *Mr Punch*: 'Well, if you ask me, ma'am, they're saying that if you want to go on ruling 'em, you've got to rule the air too.'
>
> *Punch*, 14 June 1922

Just as at one time the Royal Navy was the world's largest, indeed larger than any two navies it was likely to engage, at one time the United Kingdom had the world's largest merchant fleet. Those days are gone, some of which was inevitable. The Washington Naval Treaty ensured that the Royal Navy could, at best, only match the United States Navy, and the Second World War put paid to even that ambition. The emergence of new nations as former colonies became independent also meant that they wanted their own merchant fleets rather than spending scarce foreign exchange on ships belonging to another country. The idea of cross-trading, in which a ship belonging to a third country plied between two other countries, was virtually killed off by international agreements that restricted the third party to no more than 20 per cent of the traffic between two countries.

Yet, despite the importance of air transport and the fact that the South of England is now linked to France by a railway tunnel, most of Britain's imports and much of what is left of our exports still move by sea. As two world wars have shown, without control of the sea lanes, we risk starvation.

It is also interesting that Australia, which got rid of its last aircraft carrier in 1982, is looking for two 27,000-ton helicopter carriers with which to extend the country's reach. If Australia feels the need to do this, without any immediate threat from her neighbours, there seems to be a compelling need for Great Britain to reconsider her needs – after all, Spain and Italy are both continental powers, but they also have aircraft carriers.

The whole point is, of course, whether it is fashionable to care about defence? During the early 1930s, in a Parliamentary by-election a candidate lost because he chose to fight on a rearmament ticket. The current British Prime Minister, Gordon Brown, is on record as saying that he knows nothing about defence, yet that is his primary responsibility. In the United Kingdom, a succession of prime ministers and foreign secretaries have pledged the use of Britain's armed forces on a range of operations from peacekeeping and aid to outright war. Douglas Hurd famously claimed that we 'always punch above our weight'. Well, we do, but for how much longer?

The answer is that politicians love the extra weight that using our armed forces grants the country in international relations, but lack the foresight and even simple common sense to appreciate that the armed forces need to be maintained and planned, that military, and that includes naval, capability does not emerge overnight. Cunningham, that dour and demanding Scottish admiral of the Second World War, once maintained that it 'takes three years to build a ship, three hundred years to build a reputation'. Unfortunately, it now takes far longer than three years to build a ship, but the point about reputation stands.

There is always the problem that decisions taken now and equipment ordered now may become obsolete, or be overtaken by events. That was the problem with the battleship. The major combatants all built battleships before and during the outset of the Second World War, but on the night of 11/12 November 1940, the battleship became obsolete and outdated, something that was confirmed in May and June 1942 at the Battles of the Coral Sea and of Midway.

Yet the aircraft carrier is the most flexible and adaptable of weapons systems. The mix of aircraft dictates the role. It may be that in future the aircraft will be unmanned combat vehicles, or UCVs, but they will still need a mother ship.

What is important to remember is that naval aviation is best left in the hands of mariners, and that the fleet needs to take its own aviation with it. It is also important we do not spend too much time looking at the most sophisticated answer to every military problem. The current in-phrase for the military is 'network enabled'. This presupposes that the ability to communicate between various weapon systems and different allied armed forces is the most important thing of all. It is important but costly and is still not a substitute for boots on the ground and hulls in the water. There are few easy answers.

As someone who believes in naval aviation, the author is not an advocate of the new 'super-carriers'. These are over-complex and their construction programme seems like a logistics nightmare. They are larger than needed and far too expensive, yet carry no more than forty aircraft. We should go back to basics. Merchant vessels today are several generations away from those of the Second World War in size, speed and sophistication. A good fast containership hull would be an economical starting point for a new generation aircraft carrier. The hull of a container ship is open and empty, so the naval architects can fit in the accommodation, fuel tanks, magazines and hangar decks, and on top of it all, the flight deck needed for an aircraft carrier. For the cost of the two ships now building, we could have four or more. After all, apart from planned dry-dock time, ships sometimes don't pass in the night, but instead suffer accidents, and with just two carriers available, the danger is that one will be undergoing a refit and the other damaged.

Appendix I

Naval Air Stations 1914–18

United Kingdom

The rapid growth of the RNAS and its commitment to providing air defence for the United Kingdom, as well as its anti-submarine commitments, meant that a substantial network of naval air stations was quickly established. Some were RFC stations, where the RNAS had what would later be described as 'lodging facilities'. Abroad, the seaplanes and flying boats managed to settle down reasonably quickly alongside the naval bases, but ashore in France and Belgium, in particular, a large number of air stations were used, with units often moving at extremely short notice as the front line varied according to the ebb and flow of the conflict. Many air stations were used, some for very short periods, as in the retreat of late 1914. Some were used either by the RFC or the RNAS, or, of course, by the French and Belgians, as seemed expedient at the time.

While the bases were known as Royal Naval air stations, none seemed to have attracted ships' names at the time, possibly because a high degree of impermanence existed, or perhaps because the RNAS was still officially part of the Army dominated RFC until 1915. The main bases in the UK for aeroplanes were:

Aldeburgh, Suffolk – sub-station or satellite for Great Yarmouth.
Anglesey – doubled up as an airship station.
Ashington, Northumberland – basically an RFC station.
Atwick/Hornsea, Yorks – basically an RFC station.
Bacton, Norfolk – sub-station for Great Yarmouth.
Bangor, North Wales.
Barrow-in-Furness, Lancs – doubled up as an airship station.
Bembridge Harbour, Isle of Wight – sub-station for Calshot.
Bembridge or New Bembridge, Isle of Wight – airfield.
Bowness-on-Windermere, Westmoreland – private seaplane station used temporarily for training.
Brading, Isle of Wight – basically an RFC station.
Burgh Castle, Suffolk – sub-station for Great Yarmouth.
Butley, Suffolk – existed as an experimental station, 1918–19.

Cairncross, Berwickshire – basically an RFC station.
Calshot, Hampshire – seaplane station at the mouth of Southampton Water.
Carnoustie, Forfarshire – provided temporary lodging facilities until RNAS Dundee was ready.
Catfirth, Shetland – flying-boat base.
Cattewater, Devon – seaplane and flying-boat base close to Devonport.
Chickerell, Dorset – special duties station.
Chingford, Essex – training station.
Clacton, Essex – seaplane station.
Covehithe, Suffolk – night sub-station for Great Yarmouth.
Cramlington East, Northumberland – special duties station.
Cranwell North (HMS *Daedalus*), Lincolnshire – training station.
Cranwell South (HMS *Daedalus*), Lincolnshire – training station.
Cromarty, Ross and Cromarty – seaplane station convenient for Invergordon base.
Detling, Kent – night-landing alternate for Eastchurch.
Donibristle, Fife – shore station for shipboard seaplanes when ships visiting Rosyth.
Dover Harbour – seaplane and flying-boat station.
Dover Guston Road – landplane base mainly for fighters.
Dundee Stannergate, Forfar – seaplane and flying-boat base.
Eastbourne, Sussex – training school originally in private hands.
Eastchurch, Isle of Sheppey, Kent – first RN air station and flying school.
East Fortune, East Lothian – originally an airship station but then became a fighter station and also used for carrier aircraft in 1918.
Fairlop, Essex – sub-station for Chingford.
Felixstowe, Suffolk – seaplane and flying-boat station.
Fishguard, Pembrokeshire – seaplane station.
Freiston – sub-station for Cranwell, for bomb-aiming and aerial gunnery training.
Gosforth, Northumberland – manufacturer's aerodrome with lodging facilities for RNAS units.
Gosport, Hampshire – used early in war.
Grain, Kent – initially as a sub-station for Eastchurch, but also used for air defence of the fleet at the Nore and then marine aircraft experimental station.
Great Yarmouth, Norfolk – major seaplane and flying-boat base.
Greenland Top, Lincolnshire – basically an RFC station.
Hawkcraig Point, Fife – experimental station in 1917–1918.
Hendon, Middlesex – civil aerodrome taken over as flying school and aircraft park.
Holt, Norfolk – sub-station for Great Yarmouth for night landings.
Hornsea Mere, Yorks – seaplane sub-station for Killingholme.

Houton Bay, Orkney – seaplane and flying-boat station close to Scapa Flow.
Immingham, Lincolnshire – used by Eastchurch Mobile Squadron, then became kite-balloon base.
Killingholme, Lincolnshire – mainly a seaplane and flying-boat base, but some landplane facilities.
Lee-on-the-Solent, Hampshire – seaplane training station originally intended as sub-station for Calshot, but also became landplane base in due course.
Leuchars, Fife – originally a training station, became Grand Fleet School of Aerial Gunnery and Fighting on 10 November 1918.
Leysdown, Isle of Sheppey – sub-station for Eastchurch.
Luce Bay, Wigtownshire – airship station later used by aircraft.
Machrihanish, Argyll – originally an airship station but later used by landplanes.
Manston, Kent – essentially a sub-station for Westgate.
Martlesham Heath, Suffolk – basically an RFC station but also used as a sub-station for Felixstowe.
Mullion, Cornwall – originally an airship station, but later used by landplanes.
New Haggerston, Northumberland – basically an RFC station.
Newhaven, Sussex – seaplane sub-station for Calshot, despite being some distance away.
Newlyn, Cornwall – seaplane station.
North Coates, Fettes – basically an RFC station.
Owthorne, Yorkshire – basically an RFC station.
Padstow, Cornwall – originally for seaplanes and flying boats, but also used by DH9 units.
Pembroke, Pembrokeshire – airship station soon joined by aircraft.
Peterhead, Aberdeenshire – seaplane station.
Porthholme Meadow, Huntingdonshire – private airfield used as a testing station.
Portland Harbour, Dorset – seaplane sub-station to Calshot, despite distance.
Prawle Point, Devon – seaplane and flying-boat station.
Redcar, Yorkshire – fighter and training station.
Rennington, Northumberland – basically an RFC station.
Ringmer, Sussex – night-landing station for Eastbourne.
Rochford, Essex – fighter station.
Rosyth, Fife – kite-balloon station, also used for ships' aircraft.
Scapa, Orkney – seaplane station but also became aircraft base and repair depot for aircraft from Grand Fleet.
Scarborough, Yorkshire – fighter station.
Seahouses, Northumberland – basically an RFC station.

Seaton Carew/West Hartlepool, Durham – basically an RFC fighter station.
Seaton Carew/Tees, Durham – seaplane station.
Skegness, Lincolnshire – used by Eastchurch Mobile Squadron, briefly.
Smoogroo, Orkney – practice and training station for Grand Fleet.
South Shields, Durham – seaplane station and depot.
Stenness Loch, Orkney – flying-boat station.
Stonehenge, Wiltshire – basically an RFC station.
Strathbeg Loch, Aberdeenshire – seaplane sub-station for Peterhead.
Tallaght, Co. Dublin – opened August 1918 by RAF.
Telscombe Cliffs, Sussex – basically an RFC station.
Torquay Harbour – seaplane and kite-balloon station.
Tregantle, Cornwall – storage depot for naval aircraft.
Tresco, Isle of Scilly – seaplane and flying-boat station.
Trimley, Suffolk – sub-station for Felixstowe.
Turnhouse, West Lothian – basically an RFC station but later used for a fleet aeroplane depot.
Tynemouth, Northumberland – basically an RFC station.
Walmer, Kent – rest station for RNAS units from the Western Front.
Westgate, Mutrix Farm, Kent – landplane base until replaced by Manston.
Westgate, St Mildred's Bay, Kent – seaplane station.
Westray, Orkney – flying-boat station used as sub-station for Houton Bay.
Westward Ho! Devon – air station briefly in summer 1918.
Whitley Bay, Northumberland – fighter station.
Withnoe, Cornwall – storage depot for aircraft.

Naval Air Stations Abroad

France – Bray Dunes, Petite Synthe, Couderkerque.
Belgium – La Panne, Furnes.
Italy – Otranto⁺ (with a sub-station at Santa Maria di Lucia⁺), Taranto⁺.

Note: ⁺ = seaplane stations. Other seaplane stations were at Alexandria, Cherbourg, Gibraltar, Kalafrana (Malta), Mudros, Port Said, Suda Bay, Syra Island.

There were also stations, sub-stations or sheds for airships (* = sub-station or mooring-out site), which included:

Anglesey
Auldbar*, Angus
Ballyliffan*, Donegal
Bridport*, Dorset
Bude*, Cornwall
Capel, Kent
Chathill *, Northumberland
Cranwell, Lincs, with training facilities
East Fortune, East Lothian
Godmersham Park*, Kent
Howden, Yorks
Killeagh*, Co. Cork
Kingsnorth, Kent

Kirkleatham*, Yorks
Laira*, Devon
Larne*, Antrim.
Longside, Angus
Lowthorpe*, Yorks
Luce Bay, Wigtownshire
Malahide*, Co. Dublin
Mullion, Cornwall
Pembroke
Polegate, Sussex
Pulham, Norfolk
Ramsay*, Isle of Man
Slindon*, Sussex
Upton*, Dorset
West Mersham*, Kent

The only overseas airship station was at Mudros. In addition there were overseas kite-balloon stations at Alexandria, Bizerte, Brindisi, Corfu, Gibraltar, Malta.

Appendix II

Naval Air Stations 1939–45

Naval Air Stations in the UK
Note: Identification code letters in parentheses.

Abbotsinch (X), HMS *Sanderling*: Commissioned, 20 September 1943. Previously, FAA had lodger facilities here. Transferred and used for aircraft storage and as maintenance yard.

Angle, HMS *Goldcrest*: Commissioned, 15 May 1943. Moved to Dale, 5 September 1943.

Anthorn (AN), HMS *Nuthatch*: Commissioned, 7 September 1944. Housed No. 1 Aircraft Receipt and Despatch Unit.

Arbroath (A), HMS *Condor*, Arbroath, also known as Aberbrothock: Commissioned, 19 June 1940. Capacity: 200 aircraft. Initially No. 2 Observers' School, also a deck-landing school, and, later, a naval air signals school. Survived post-war, passing to RM, 1971.

Ayr (AR), HMS *Wagtail*: Commissioned, 20 October 1944. Capacity: 110 aircraft. Originally a lodger station. It accommodated disembarked squadrons, FRU, communications squadron, a calibration flight and the Bombardment Training School. Decommissioned, 10 March 1946.

Ballyhalbert (BH), HMS *Corncrake*: Commissioned, 17 July 1945. Capacity: 100 aircraft. Originally lodger facilities from the RAF, but transferred for No. 4 Naval Air Fighter School. Paid off 13 November 1945. Kirkistown commissioned 17 July 1945, as a satellite having previously been lodger facilities on RAF station, and paid off 15 January 1946.

Burscough (O, AH), HMS *Ringtail*: Commissioned, 1 September 1943. At one time a satellite of Inskip, it received disembarking squadrons as well as those working up. Radar training also provided. Operated Woodvale as a satellite. Decommissioned, 15 June 1946.

Campbeltown (P, then AN), HMS *Landrail/Landrail II*: Commissioned, 1 April 1941. Capacity: 85 aircraft. Civil aerodrome, initially a satellite of Donibristle, became *Landrail II* when Machrihanish became the parent station, 15 June 1941. Mainly used for carriers using the Clyde. Decommissioned, June 1945.

Charleton Horethorne (BY), HMS *Heron II*: Commissioned, 1 January, 1943. Satellite for Yeovilton. Decommissioned, 17 April 1945. Exchanged with RAF in return for Zeals.

Crail (C), HMS *Jackdaw*: Commissioned, 1 October 1940. Used for air torpedo training. Decommissioned, April, 1947.

Culham (CM), HMS *Hornbill*: Commissioned, 1 November 1944. No. 2 Aircraft Receipt and Despatch Unit.

Dale (P), HMS *Goldcrest*: Commissioned, 7 September 1943. Airfield for RN Aircraft Direction Centre at Kete, and provided twin-engined aircraft conversion courses. Donibristle (D, then B), HMS *Merlin*: Commissioned, 24 May 1939. Capacity: 220 aircraft. Originally RNAS station in 1917. Housed a communications squadron and an aircraft repair yard, as well as accommodating many visiting units and, towards the end of the war, Flag Officer, Carrier Training. Lodger facilities at Drem, satellites at Campeltown, Evanton and Fearn.

Drem (D), HMS *Nighthawk*: Commissioned, 1 June 1945. Originally lodger facilities, then a satellite of Donibristle from 21 April 1945. Housed Night Fighter School and FRU.

Dundee (A, then AA), HMS *Condor II*: Commissioned, 15 July 1941. Satellite seaplane base for *Condor*. Paid off 15 June 1944.

Dunino (D, then DO), HMS *Jackdaw II*: Commissioned, 15 December 1942. Capacity: 180 aircraft. Satellite of Crail, providing reserve aircraft storage. Decommissioned, 2 April 1946.

East Haven (B, then E), HMS *Peewit*: Commissioned, 1 May 1943. TBR Deck Landing School, providing Part II TBR Training, Deck Landing Control Officer training and aircraft handling training. Decommissioned, August 1946.

Eastleigh (E, then I, EL), HMS *Raven*: Commissioned, 1 July 1939. Shore base for carrier squadrons and housed the Safety Equipment School, School of Air Medicine and Naval Air Radio Installation Unit, as well as fire-fighting training. Lodger facilities at RAF Christchurch. Decommissioned, April 1947.

Eglinton (J), HMS *Gannet*: Commissioned, 15 May 1943. Squadrons working up, or preparing for North Atlantic convoy escort duties.

Evanton (V, then EV), HMS *Fieldfare*: Commissioned, 9 October 1944. Capacity: 500 aircraft. Used by FAA pre-war and lodger facilities in wartime. After commissioning became aircraft maintenance yard. Decommissioned post-war.

Fearn (F), HMS *Owl*: Commissioned, 11 October 1942. Capacity: 96 aircraft. Previously a satellite of Donibristle. Used by TBR squadrons when working up. Decommissioned, 2 July 1946.

Ford (FD), HMS *Peregrine*: Commissioned, 24 May 1939. Immediate reserve storage unit housing Albacores and Swordfish, and accommodating No. 1 Observer School. Returned to RAF, 30 September 1940, but School

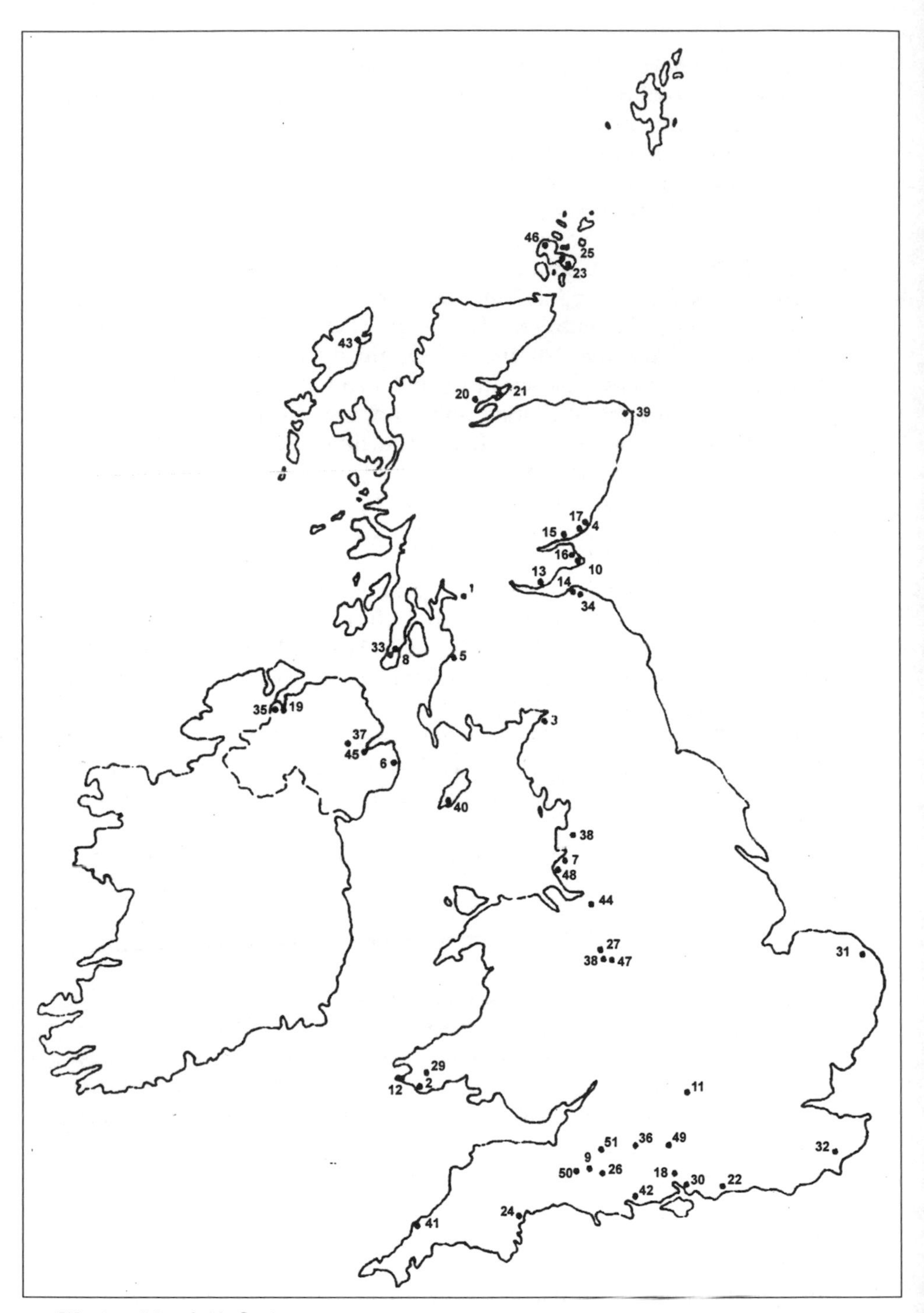

Wartime Naval Air Stations.

of Naval Photography remained as lodgers from *Daedalus*. Returned to FAA and recommissioned, 15 August 1945.

Grimsetter (Z, then GM), HMS *Robin*: Commissioned, 15 August 1943. Capacity: 48 aircraft. Initially a satellite of Hatston. Decommissioned, 31 July 1945.

Haldon (AY), HMS *Heron II*: Commissioned, 18 August 1941. Satellite of Yeovilton. Reduced to care and maintenance basis, May 1943, and name transferred to Charleton Horethorne.

Hatston (H), HMS *Sparrowhawk*: Commissioned, 2 October 1939. Shore base for units embarked with the Home Fleet at Scapa Flow. Decommissioned, 1 August 1945.

Henstridge (G, then N), HMS *Dipper*: Commissioned, 1 April 1943. Capacity: 120 aircraft. No. 2 Naval Air Fighter School. Decommissioned, 11 October 1946.

Hinstock (U), HMS *Godwit*: Commissioned, 14 June 1943. Capacity: 120 aircraft. Originally operated by the Ministry of Aircraft Production, transferred to FAA, 23 July 1942, as a beam approach school under control of Stretton. Home to the Naval Advanced Instrument Flying School. Decomissioned, 28 February 1947.

Inskip (K), HMS *Nightjar*: Commissioned, 15 May 1943. Capacity: 145 aircraft. Housed No. 1 Operational Training Unit and controlled Burscough at one stage. Decommissioned, 2 July 1946.

Lawrenny Ferry (F), HMS *Daedalus II*: Commissioned, 1 February 1942. Seaplane base under the control of *Daedalus*; became care and maintenance only, 24 October 1943.

Lee-on-Solent (L), HMS *Daedalus*: Commissioned, 24 May 1939. Capacity: 100 aircraft. Founded as a seaplane training station, 1917, and expanded to include an aerodrome in 1934. Many squadrons formed while others assembled for passage overseas. Wartime office of the Admiral (Air) and

---

Map 4. Wartime Naval Air Stations with ships' names and code letters (Note: Numbers relate to the map on facing page)

1. Abbotsinch, HMS *Sanderling*; 2. Angle, *Goldcrest*; 3. Anthorn, *Nuthatch*; 4. Arboath, *Condor*; 5. Ayr, *Wagtail*; 6. Ballyhalbert, *Corncrake*; 7. Burscough, *Ringtail*; 8. Campeltown, *Landrail*; 9. Charleton Horethorne, *Heron II*; 10. Crail, *Jackdaw*; 11. Culham, *Hornbill*; 12. Dale, *Goldcrest*; 13. Donibristle, *Merlin*; 14. Drem, *Nighthawk*; 15. Dundee, *Condor II*; 16. Dunino, *Jackdaw II*; 17. East Haven, *Peewit*; 18. Eastleigh, *Raven*; 19. Eglinton, *Gannet*; 20. Evanton, *Fieldfare*; 21. Fearn, *Owl*; 22. Ford, *Peregrine*; 23. Grimsetter, *Robin*; 24. Haldon, *Heron II*; 25. Hatson, *Sparrowhawk*; 26. Henstridge, *Dipper*; 27. Hinstock, *Godwit*; 28. Inskip, *Nightjar*; 29. Lawrenny Ferry, *Daedalus II*; 30. Lee-on-Solent, *Daedalus*; 31. Ludham, *Flycatcher*; 32. Lympe, *Daedalus II*; 33. Machrihanish, *Landrail*; 34. MacMerry, *Nighthawk*; 35. Maydown, *Shrike*; 36. Middle Wallop, *Flycatcher*; 37. Nutts Corner, *Pintail*; 38. Peplow, *Godwit II*; 39. Rattray Head/Crimond, *Merganser*; 40. Ronaldsway, *Urley*; 41. St Merryn, *Vulture*; 42. Sandbanks, *Daedalus II*; 43. Stornoway, *Mentor II*; 44. Stretton, *Blackcap*; 45. Sydenham (Belfast), *Gadwall*; 46. Twatt, *Tern*; 47. Weston Park, *Godwit II*; 48. Woodvale, *Ringtail II*; 49. Worthy Down, *Kestrel*; 50. Yeovilton, *Heron*; 51. Zeals, *Hummingbird*. (*Source: Fleet Air Arm Museum*)

was the main depot for naval air ratings. Portland used occasionally during the war for seaplanes. Satellite airfields and lodging arrangements included Cowdray Park, private airfield for storing withdrawn aircraft; Tangmere until transferred to *Heron;* plus Defford, Ford, Gosport, Heston, Manston and Thorney Island.

Ludham, HMS *Flycatcher*: Commissioned, 4 September 1944. Transferred from RAF as headquarters for the Mobile Naval Airfield organization, until this moved to Middle Wallop in February 1945. Returned to the RAF, 16 February 1945.

Lympe, HMS *Daedalus II*: Commissioned, 1 July 1939, as *Buzzard*, reduced to care and maintenance on 25 September. Reopened as *Daedalus II* later, but handed back to the RAF on 23 May 1940. Accommodated RN Aircraft Training Establishment, providing technical training for air apprentices, air fitters and air mechanics, and W/T training, until this transferred to Newcastle-under-Lyme, May 1940, with the *Daedalus II* name.

Machrihanish (K, then M), HMS *Landrail*: Commissioned, 15 June 1941. Capacity: 85 aircraft. Originally known as Strabane. Transferred from Campbeltown. Mainly used for carriers using the Clyde. Decommissioned, 16 April 1946.

MacMerry, HMS *Nighthawk*: Commissioned, 1 June 1945. Satellite of Drem. Decommissioned, 15 March 1946.

Maydown (N), HMS *Shrike*: Commissioned, 1 January 1944. Capacity: 105 aircraft. Previously satellite of Eglinton. Became HQ for MAC-ship flights and housed Anti U-Boat School, plus refresher and operational training. Decommissioned, 13 September 1945.

Middle Wallop, HMS *Flycatcher*: Commissioned, 16 February 1945. Former RAF airfield taken over as MONAB HQ and Maintenance Test Pilots School. Decommissioned, 10 April 1946.

Nutts Corner, HMS *Pintail*: Commissioned, 11 July 1945. Capacity: 60 aircraft. Used by fighter squadrons. Decommissioned, 31 March 1946.

Peplow, HMS *Godwit II*: Commissioned, 28 February 1945. Satellite of Hinstock.

Rattray Head/Crimond (AT, then I), HMS *Merganser*: Commissioned, 31 October 1944. Capacity: 130 aircraft. Known as Crimond until 1 July 1945. Provided TBR Training Part II. Decommissioned, 30 September 1946.

Ronaldsway (R, AR), HMS *Urley*: Commissioned, 21 June 1944. Capacity: 120 aircraft. Provided TBR training and Naval Operational Training Part III. Decommissioned, 14 January 1946.

St Merryn (M), HMS *Vulture*: Commissioned, 10 August 1940. Capacity: 145 aircraft. Housed School of Naval Air Warfare. Used by many squadrons. Decommissioned post-war. Responsible for *Vulture II*, bombing and gunnery range, with an emergency landing strip.

Sandbanks (S), HMS *Daedalus II*: Commissioned, 15 May 1940. Satellite of *Daedalus* for seaplanes. Decommissioned, 9 October 1943.

Stornoway, HMS *Mentor II*: Commissioned, November 1940. Seaplane base for *Mentor*, RN Stornoway. Decommissioned, June 1941. Transferred to RAF, who granted lodging facilities 1943–4.

Stretton (R, then ST), HMS *Blackcap*: Commissioned, 1 June 1942. Capacity: 180 aircraft. Operational use plus RN Aircraft Maintenance Yard. Post-war, used by RNVR.

Sydenham (Belfast) (Q), HMS *Gadwall*: Commissioned, 21 June 1943. Previously part of HMS *Caroline*. Used for disembarked squadrons, especially those moving from the US and Canada. Housed aircraft maintenance yard. Responsible for the shipment of aircraft overseas with escort carrier berth. Decommissioned, 30 April 1946.

Twatt (T), HMS *Tern*: Commissioned, 1 January 1941. Capacity: 50 aircraft. Originally a satellite of Hatston. Decommissioned, 30 September 1946.

Weston Park, HMS *Godwit II*: Satellite landing strip for Hinstock during 1945.

Woodvale (V), HMS *Ringtail II*: Commissioned, 7 April 1945. Originally lodger facilities at an RAF station, transferred to FAA as satellite of Burscough. Accommodated visiting squadrons. Own FRU. Decommissioned, 28 January 1946.

Worthy Down (W), HMS *Kestrel*: Commissoned, 24 May 1939. Capacity: 150 aircraft. Housed No. 1 Air Gunners School, the School of Aircraft Maintenance and the Engine Handling Unit.

Yeovilton (Y), HMS *Heron*: Commissioned, 1 June 1940. Used earlier. Home to No. 1 Naval Air Fighter School and the Aircraft Direction Centre, and then the Naval Air Fighting Development Unit. Lodger facilities at RAF Duxford, Tangemere and Wittering.

Zeals (Z), HMS *Humming Bird*: Commissioned, 18 May 1945. Ex-RAF, initially a satellite of Yeovilton. Accommodated FRU and provided fighter conversion. Decommissioned, 1 January 1946.

Mobile Naval Air Bases

As the war progressed in the Far East, it became clear that improvised air stations would be needed ashore. It was important for the Royal Navy to be self-reliant because of the political sensitivity in its relations with the United States Navy that would make reliance on USN/USMC bases unacceptable. Mobile naval air bases, or MONABs, were the answer, able to provide the full range of facilities to support squadrons embarked with the fleet.

The headquarters for this new organization was HMS *Flycatcher*, at Ludham, which later moved to Middle Wallop. There were ten MONABs, although the tenth formed too late and never leave the UK, and a

Transportable Aircraft Yard, or TAMY. All received ships' names, started with 'Nab'.

MONAB 1, HMS *Nabbington*: Commissioned at Ludham, 28 October 1944. Disembarked, Sydney, 20 December. Took over RAAF Nowra, 2 January 1945, able to support Corsairs and Avengers. During March and April, problems with the runways at Nowra meant the temporary use of the satellite base of Jervis Bay. Decommissioned, 15 November 1945.

MONAB 2, HMS *Nabberley*: Commissioned at Ludham, 11 November 1944. Took over RAAF Bankstown, becoming operational on 29 January 1945. Able to support every aircraft type in FAA service, including Sea Otters and Expediters. Decommissioned, 31 March 1946.

MONAB 3, HMS *Nabthorpe*: Commissioned at Ludham, 4 December 1944. Reached Sydney, 27 January 1945. Took over RAAF Schofields, 7 February 1945, where it supported Seafires and Fireflies. Decommissioned, 15 November.

MONAB 4, HMS *Nabaron*: Commissioned at Ludham, 1 January 1945. Reached Manus in the Admiralty Islands via Sydney, taking over the USN base at Pityilu on 2 April. Decommissioned, 10 November 1945, in Australia.

MONAB 5, HMS *Nabswick*: Commissioned at Ludham, 1 February 1945. Disembarked Sydney, 29 March. Took over RAAF Jervis Bay, 1 May. Post-war, it moved from Jervis Bay on 15 November and took over Nowra from MONAB 1. Decommissioned, March 1946.

MONAB 6, HMS *Nabstock*: Commissioned at Middle Wallop, 1 April 1945. Reached Sydney, 23 May. Lodged at RAAF Maryborough, 1 June. Took over Schofields from MONAB 3, 15 November. Decommissioned, June 1946.

MONAB 7, HMS *Nabreekie*: Commissioned, Middle Wallop, 1 June 1945. Receipt and despatch unit, it reached the former USN See Bee camp at Meendale, near Brisbane, on 9 August. It shared the airfield at Archerfield with TAMY 1. Decommissioned, 5 November 1945.

MONAB 8, HMS *Nabcatcher*: Commissioned at Middle Wallop, 1 July 1945. Receipt and despatch unit, reaching Kai Tak, via Australia, in September. Decommissioned, August 1946. Kai Tak then came under the control of the shore station, *Tamar*.

MONAB 9, HMS *Nabrock*: Commissioned at Middle Wallop, 1 August 1945. Reached Singapore via Sydney. Decommissioned at Sembawang, 15 December 1945.

MONAB 10, HMS *Nabhurst*: Commissioned at Middle Wallop, 1 September 1945. Decommissioned, 12 October 1945.

TAMY 1, HMS *Nabsford*: Commissioned at Ludham, 1 February 1945. Took over a number of installations near Brisbane, including the civil airfield at Archerfield and an army camp at Focklea. Its role included assembly of aircraft shipped out from the USA and UK, including Corsairs and Seafires. Decommissioned, 31 March 1946.

Overseas Naval Air Stations

Addu Atoll (now known as Gan) (A), HMS *Haitan*: Capacity: 24 aircraft. Secret refuelling base for the Eastern Fleet. Airstrip part of shore base, but operated as a secondary base to China Bay/Trincomalee. Renamed HMS *Moraga*, 1 February 1944.

Aden

Khormaksar, HMS *Sheba*: Shore base with a naval air section at RAF Khormaksar.

Australia

Bankstown (B), HMS *Nabberley*: Loaned from RAAF as base for MONAB 2, 29 January 1945.

Jervis Bay (J), HMS *Nabwick*: RAAF airstrip and satellite to Nowra, taken over 1 May 1945 by MONAB 5.

Nowra (N), HMS *Nabbington, Nabswick*: RAAF station loaned on 2 January 1945 for MONAB 1, until taken over by MONAB 5 post-war.

Canada

Dartmouth/Yarmouth, HMS *Seaborn*: Capacity: 32 aircraft. RCAF Dartmouth provided lodger facilities from September 1940, for disembarked Swordfish and Walruses, operated as part of *Seaborn*. Responsibility was transferred to HMS *Saker* on 1 October 1941, then to HMS *Canada*, which was renamed *Seaborn* on 1 July 1944, by which time it was looking after Swordfish disembarked from MAC-ships bound for Halifax. RCAF Yarmouth, transferred 1 January 1943, for No. 2 Telegraphist Air Gunners School (No. 1 Telegraphist Air Gunners School to the RCN), also controlled by *Canada* until 1 July 1944. The school paid off 30 March, 1945. *Seaborn* paid off 28 January 1946, and Dartmouth returned to the RCAF.

Halifax/Dartmouth/Yarmouth, HMS *Canada*: Overall ship's name for shore stations in Canada, 1942–3.

Ceylon

Colombo Racecourse (L), HMS *Bherunda*: Commissioned, 1 October, 1943. Capacity: 90 aircraft. Accommodation for visiting squadrons, plus FRU and a communications squadron, assembly of aircraft shipped to the Far East and recovery of crashed and damaged aircraft. Local garage acquired to repair engines. Decommissioned, 30 November 1945.

Katukurunda (K), HMS *Ukussa*: Commissioned, 15 October 1942. Capacity: 144 aircraft. Used by visiting squadrons, and included RN Aircraft Repair Yard with aircraft storage. Decommissioned, 27 September 1946.

Maharagama, HMS *Monara*: Commissioned, 1 December 1944. Housed RN Aircraft Training Establishment training Singalese recruits.

Puttalam (P), HMS *Rajaliya*: Commissioned, 1 February 1943. Capacity: 104 aircraft. Previously under control of HMS *Lanka* since May 1942. Facilities for visiting squadrons from the Eastern Fleet and reserve aircraft storage. Decommissioned, 31 October 1945.

Trincomalee/Clappenburg Bay C), HMS *Bambara*: Commissioned, 1 January 1944. Originally RAF China Bay, with lodger facilities, and August 1940 to April 1942, part of shore station, *Lanka*, then part of HMS *Highflyer*. Responsible for Addu Atoll. It later included RN Aircraft Maintenance Yard at Clappenburg Bay. Decommissioned, 31 December 1947.

East Africa

Kilindini and Port Reitz, HMS *Kipanga*: Shore base at Mombasa, Kenya, also responsible for FAA units ashore in East Africa.

Mackinnon Road/Port Reitz (Mombasa)/Voi (R), HMS *Kipanga II*: Capacity: 64 aircraft, Mackinnon Road; two squadrons, Port Reitz. Under control of *Kipanga*, for units using the lodging facilities at the RAF base at Mackinnon Road, used by visiting squadrons and for fighter combat training. Eastern Fleet TBR pool and aircraft erection facilities at Port Reitz, a joint RAF/SAAF station. Voi provided accommodation for disembarked squadrons under the same control. Decommissioned postwar.

Nairobi, HMS *Korongo*: Commissioned, 1 September 1942. Capacity: 160 aircraft. RAF base with naval presence, known as Eastleigh locally, but to avoid confusion referred to as Nairobi by the armed forces. Aircraft repair yard and storage facility. Decommissioned, 15 October 1944.

Tanga, HMS *Kilele*: Commissioned, 1 October 1942. Capacity: 96 aircraft. Accommodated squadrons visiting Tanganyika. Also assembled crated aircraft. Decommissioned, 31 May 1944.

Egypt

Dekheila (D), HMS *Grebe*: Commissioned, 16 September 1940. Capacity: 72 aircraft. Loaned by Egypt, initially as HMS *Nile II*, it remained under the control of the shore base, *Nile*, until 1 April 1941. Used by squadrons from Mediterranean Fleet carriers or in transit to and from the Far East, and for Western Desert operations. Accommodated FRU. Came under control of *Nile* again on 1 April 1943, but retained own ship's name. Decommissioned, 31 January 1946.

Fayid, HMS *Phoenix*: Commissioned, 15 May 1941. Storage for 130 aircraft. Airfield in the Suez Canal Zone, with RN Aircraft Repair Yard. Decommissioned, 28 February 1946.

Gibraltar

North Front (G), HMS *Cormorant II*: Commissioned, 26 September 1940. Capacity: 24 aircraft. Built on racecourse site. Initially landing strip operated by RAF, but RNAS developed and transferred to the FAA, under the control of the local naval base, *Cormorant*. Returned to RAF, 1 August 1941, although lodger facilities remained. Recommissioned, 1 January 1944. FRU. Returned to RAF post-war.

Gold Coast (now Ghana)

Komenda, HMS *Wara*: Commissioned, 1 October 1942. Capacity: 104 aircraft. At Takoradi, uncrated and assembled aircraft to be flown across sub-Saharan Africa as reinforcements. Decommissioned, 7 December 1943.

Iceland

Huitanes/Kaldadarnes, HMS *Baidur*: Shore stations in Iceland, part of local naval base, *Baidur*. Facilities for aircraft disembarked from visiting carriers, mainly on Arctic convoys.

India

Cochin (H), HMS *Kaluga*: Commissioned, 1 February 1945. Lodger facilities on RAF station, but remained under the control of *Garuda* until early 1946. Aircraft erection depot main activity, but limited facilities for disembarked squadrons. Decommissioned: August 1946.

Coimbatore (Q), HMS *Garuda*: Commissioned, 1 October 1942. Capacity: 250 aircraft in storage. RN Aircraft Repair Yard, assembling aircraft shipped from UK and USA. Decommissioned, 1 April 1946.

Sulur (R), HMS *Vairi*: Commissioned, 1 February 1945. Sometimes spelt Sollur. Ex-RAF base. Under the control of *Garuda*. Planned aircraft storage never fully realized, but would have been 300 aircraft. Decommissioned, 1 April 1946.

Tambaram (T), HMS *Valluru*: Commissioned, 1 July 1944. FRU and aircraft maintenance yard, and accommodation for visiting squadrons. Plans for aircraft repair yard abandoned after VJ-Day. Decommissioned, 1 December 1945.

Malta

Ta Kali (M), HMS *Goldfinch*: Commissioned, 1 April 1945. Previously, FAA had lodger facilities at RAF Ta Kali, under control of shore base, *St Angelo*. Housed FRU. Returned to the RAF post-war. Lodger facilities also at RAF Hal Far, transferred to FAA post-war.

Sierra Leone

Hastings (H), HMS *Spurwing*: Commissioned, 22 March 1943. Capacity: 84 aircraft. Civil aerodrome at Freetown, operated by the RAF. Initially under the control of the local headquarters ships, *Edinburgh Castle*. Decommissioned, 31 December 1944.

South Africa

Simonstown/Wingfield/Wynberg (W), HMS *Afrikander*: RN shore base at Simonstown, was responsible for naval units using SAAF Wingfield and Wynberg, although the latter was sometimes known as *Afrikander III*.

Stamford Hill, HMS *Kongoni*: Commissioned, 31 March 1944. Previously SAAF station near Durban with lodger facilties, including an FRU. Decommissioned, 31 January 1946.

Wingfield (W), HMS *Malagas*: Commissioned, 15 March 1942. SAAF base with lodger facilities, originally under *Afrikander* at Simonstown. Air station and aircraft repair yard for Eastern Fleet and ships on passage from the Atlantic to the Eastern Mediterranean via the Cape. Later absorbed air section from Wynberg, and worked up Hellcat squadrons. Decommissioned, 31 May 1946.

United States

Lewiston/Quonset Point/Dartmouth, HMS *Saker II*: Commissioned, 1 October 1942.

Lewiston, Maine, a loaned USN base, relieved pressure on *Saker*, but reabsorbed 1 November 1942. Quonset Point, Rhode Island, became *Saker II* when *Asbury* decommissioned, 31 March 1944.

Quonset Point, Rhode Island, HMS *Asbury*: Commissioned, 1 October 1942. Accommodated FAA squadrons working up after taking delivery of US-built aircraft and escort carriers. Decommissioned, 31 March 1944, to become *Saker II* (see below).

Washington/Halifax/Lewiston/Bunswick, Maine/Squantum/NewYork, HMS *Saker*: Commissioned, 1 October 1941. Accounting and administrative base in Washington for FAA throughout North America. Halifax was the RN base at Halifax, Nova Scotia, under the control of *Saker*, passing to *Canada*, 1 August 1942. Lewiston, Maine, USN base, part of *Saker* from 1943 to 1945. Brunswick, Maine, USN base loaned in August, 1943, part of *Saker* for the next two years, for Corsair squadrons to work up. Pressure on runway and airspace meant that ADDLs, used satellite USN stations at Rockland and Sanford. Decommissioned, 29 February 1948.

West Indies

Bermuda, HMS *Malabar II* and *Malabar III*: Capacity: 12 aircraft. Pre-war seaplane base was used by ships of the America and West Indies Station for their catapult aircraft. Used the ships' names at different times after a landing strip was added. Care and maintenance, 1944.

Palisadoes, HMS *Buzzard*: Commissioned, 1 August 1941. Capacity: 60 aircraft. Name originally used when Lympne transferred from RAF in

1939. Air station in Jamaica operated as part of *Malabar* from 21 December 1940. Accommodated disembarked squadrons and provided reserve aircraft storage. Decommissioned, 15 July 1943, but remained as part of *Moga* until 31 December 1944.

Piarco, HMS *Goshawk*: Comissioned, 6 November 1940. Capacity: 162 aircraft. Housed No. 1 Observer School. Decommissioned, 28 February 1946.

Lodging Facilities at Air Force Bases and Civil Airfields

Operational necessity often meant that Fleet Air Arm squadrons had to make use of other airfields from time to time, mainly RAF bases, and, to a lesser extent, RAAF, SAAF and RCAF bases, and civil aerodromes. Although partly because the FAA was short of air stations at the start of the war, the main reason was that operational requirements were constantly changing. Lodger facilities were not usually accorded ships' names and did not have the prefix RNAS, but did have pre-arranged facilities available to naval air squadrons. The main lodging facilities, with dates used, were:

Aboukir, Egypt: RAF station used throughout the war; during 1941 on the books of *Nile*, the RN shore base at Alexandria.

Aldergrove: RAF, 1939–40, with 774 Squadron attached to No. 3 RAF Bombing and Gunnery School.

Andraka, Diego Suarez, Madagascar: airfield used after invasion, on books of shore station *Ironclad*.

Argentia, Newfoundland: RCAF used for disembarked flights and squadrons from MAC-ships and escort carriers.

Benbecula: RAF.

Bircham Newton: RAF.

Bratton: RAF, used mainly for training facilities for RNAS Hinstock, 1943–4.

Cholavarum, southern India: RAF, with resident RN Air Section.

Culmhead (also known as Church Stanton): RAF, used occasionally.

Detling: 1940–1.

Docking: 1942–4.

Dundonald: used mainly during 1944 by 3rd Naval Fighter Wing.

Duxford: used mainly during 1941–3 as part of the Air Fighting Development Unit, and on the books of *Raven*.

Fraserburgh: used occasionally.

Hal Far, Malta: RAF, used extensively by disembarked squadrons throughout the war and transferred post-war.

Harrowbeer: RAF, 1944.

Heath Row (now Heathrow): Fairey Aviation's airfield, 1944–5.

Heston: also a civilian airfield, used from April 1945 until after the war.

Hyeres La Palyvestre, France: French naval air station near Toulon, used before the fall of France, 1939–40.
Jersey: a civil airport used from 11 March 1940 until it was evacuated on 31 May 1940.
Kalafrana, Malta: RAF, used by disembarked seaplanes.
Lands End (also known as St Just): civil aerodrome used briefly during 1940.
Langham: RAF, 1942–4.
Limavady: RAF, 1944.
Long Kesh: RAF, 1944–5.
Manston: RAF, used occasionally.
Merston: RAF, used occasionally during 1945.
Minneriya, Ceylon: RAF, with resident RN Air Section.
Mullaghmore: RAF, 1944–5.
Norfolk, Virginia: USN used by disembarked squadrons and those working up with US-built aircraft, transferred to Quonset Point, November 1942.
North Coates: 1940–1.
Pembroke Dock: RAF, 1940–1.
Perranporth: RAF, 1944, under control of St Merryn.
Peterhead: RAF, 1942–4.
Port Ellen: RAF, 1943.
Prestwick: RAF, 1940–1.
St Eval: RAF, 1940–4.
St Thomas Mount, Madras, southern India: extensive lodger facilities for up to seven FAA squadrons, plus resident RN Air Section.
Santa Cruz, southern India: extensive lodger facilities for up to four FAA squadrons, plus resident RN Air Section.
Sigriya, Ceylon: RAF, with resident RN Air Section.
Skitten: RAF, 1940–1.
Speke: RAF, 1942–5, with a resident RN Air Section which eventually moved to *Ringtail II* in April 1945.
Squantum: USN, TBR Avenger squadrons working up, 1943–4.
Sullom Voe: RAF, RN Air Section under control of *Sparrowhawk*, resident from mid-1940 to mid-1941 for disembarked seaplanes.
Sumburgh: RAF, 1941–2.
Tain: RAF, 1942–4.
Thorney Island: RAF, used from 1940 onwards.
Turnhouse: RAF, 1942–4.
Vavuniya, Ceylon: RAF, with resident RN Air Section.
West Freugh: RAF, 1940–3.
Westhampnett: RAF, 1945.
West Raynham: RAF, 1945.
Wick: RAF, 1939–40.

Appendix III

Seaplane Tenders and Aircraft Carriers 1914–18

Ark Royal (1914)
LOA: 366 ft. Beam: 50.75 ft. Displacement: 7,020 tons. Triple expansion steam engines delivering 3,000 hp through a single screw. Max speed: 10.6 knots. Complement: 180. Armament: 4 × 12-pdr; 6 × 21-in torpedo tubes. Converted from collier.

Converted Packet Ships
1914. A varied assortment of ships originally built between 1904 and 1911. LOA: 311–375 ft. Beam: 40–46 ft. Displacement: 1,675–2,651 tons. Turbines with three screws. Max speed: 21.5–24.5 knots. Complement: 250. Armament: 5 × 4.7-in; 1 × 3-in AA; 2 × 2-pdr; 6 × 21-in torpedo tubes.

Ben-my-Chree (x), *Empress* (s), *Engadine* (s), *Manxman* (m), *Riviera* (s), *Vindex* (x).
Key: (m) ex-Midland Railway Irish Sea packet; (s) ex-South East & Chatham Railway Channel packet; (x) ex-Isle of Man Steam Packet Company.
Ben-my-Chree sunk by Turkish shore batteries, 1917.

Nairana (1917)
LOA: 352 ft. Beam: 45.5 ft. Displacement: 3,042 tons. Turbines delivering 6,700 hp through two screws. Max speed: 20 knots. Complement: 278. Armament: 2 × 12-pdr; 2 × 12-pdr AA. Seaplane carrier converted from passenger vessel.

Pegasus (1917)
LOA: 332 ft. Beam: 43ft. Displacement: 2,070 tons. Turbines delivering 9,500 hp hrough two screws. Max speed: 21 knots. Complement: 278. Armament: 2 × 12-pdr; 2 × 12-pdr AA. Seaplane carrier converted from passenger vessel.

Campania (1914)
LOA: 622 ft. Beam: 65 ft. Displacement: 18,000 tons. Triple expansion steam engines delivering 28,000 hp through two screws. Max speed: 22 knots.

Complement: 600. Armament: 6 × 4.7-in, 1 × 3-in AA. Seaplane carrier converted from Cunard liner. In 1916, her fore funnel was divided to allow a longer flying-off deck. In 1918, she was sunk in collision with the battlecruiser *Glorious* in the Firth of Forth.

Vindictive
Conversion incomplete at the Armistice and reconverted to a cruiser in 1925.

Aircraft Carriers
Sometimes referred to in the literature of the day as 'Aerodrome Ships'.

Furious (1917)
LOA: 786.5 ft. Beam: 88 ft. Displacement: 22,000 tons. Geared turbines delivering 94,000 hp through four screws. Max speed: 32.5 knots. Complement: 737. Armament: 10 × 5.5-in; 5 × 3-in AA and smaller weapons. 20 aircraft. Armour: Belt 2–3 in, Deck 1–3 in. Originally laid down as a battlecruiser similar to *Glorious* and *Courageous*, but with 2 × 18-in guns; commissioned in 1917 with only the aft 18-in gun while a flying-off deck replaced the forward gun; an aft landing deck was added in 1918.

Argus (1918)
LOA: 565 ft. Beam: 68 ft. Displacement: 15,775 tons. Turbines delivering 22,000 hp through four screws. Max speed: 20.5 knots. Complement: 760. Armament: 6 × 4-in AA and smaller weapons. 20 aircraft. Laid down as a liner for Italy, she was completed as a carrier and the first to be built as a genuine 'flat top' with a through flight deck and no superstructure.

Appendix IV

Aircraft Carriers 1939–45

Fleet Aircraft Carriers

Argus (1918)

Passenger liner for Italy, converted on slipway. Displacement: 14,000 tons standard; 16,500 tons deep load. Armament: 6 × single 4-in; 4 × single 3-pdr; 4 × single MG; 1943. 13 × single 20 mm Oerlikon added. Endurance: 5,200 miles at 12 kts. Complement: 760. Aircraft: originally 20, 15 in 1941. Lifts: 2, but aft lift removed, 1941. Catapults: 1, 1936. Accommodation ship, Chatham, August 1944.

Ark Royal (1938)

Displacement: 22,000 tons standard; 27,720 tons deep load. Armament: 8 × twin 4.5; 4 × octuple 2-pdr pompom; 4 × single 3-pdr; 8 × single MG. Endurance: 11,200 miles at 10 kts. Complement: 1,580. Aircraft: Originally 60, 54 in 1941. Lifts: 3. Catapults: 2. Torpedoed 13 May 1941; sank 14 May 1941. 1 crew member lost.

Courageous-class

Courageous (1928), *Glorious* (1930)

Converted from battlecruisers. Displacement: 22,500 tons standard; 27,560 tons deep load. Armament: 16 × single 4.7-in; 4 × single 3-pdr; 10 × single .303 MG. Endurance: 2,920 miles at 24 kts. Complement: 1,260. Aircraft: 48. Lifts: 2. Catapults: 2, 1936. *Courageous* torpedoed 17 September 1939 by *U-29* in SW Approaches, with loss of 518 lives. *Glorious* sunk by gunfire from German battlecruisers *Scharnhorst* and *Gneisenau*, 8 June 1940, withdrawing from Norway. Lost most of her crew.

Eagle (1924)

Converted from battleship *Almirante Cochrane* being built for Chile. Displacement: 22,600 tons standard; 27,500 tons deep load. Armament: 9 × single 6-in; 5 × single 4-in; 2 × octuple 2-pdr (1937); 12 × single 20 mm Oerlikon (1942); 4 × single 3-pdr; 2 × twin 0.303 MG. Endurance: 3,000 miles at 17 kts. Complement: 988. Aircraft: 22 in 1942. Lifts: 2. No catapults. Ship evaluated concept of starboard island. Hit by four torpedoes from *U-73*, 11 August 1942, while on Malta convoy; sank with loss of 160 lives.

Furious (1918)
Converted in stages from battlecruiser as first aircraft carrier. Displacement: 22,450 tons standard; 27,165 tons deep load. Armament: 6 × twin 4-in; 4 × octuple 2-pdr pompom; 4 × twin 20 mm Oerlikon; 7 × single 20-mm Oerlikon. Endurance: 3,700 miles at 20 kts. Complement: 1,218. Aircraft: 33 in 1939. Lifts: 2. No catapults.

Hermes (1924)
Displacement: 10,850 tons standard; 13,700 tons deep load. Armament: 6 × single 5.5-in; 3 × single 4-in; 2 × quadruple 0.5-in. Endurance: 2,930 miles at 18 kts. Complement: 700. Aircraft: 12 in 1939. Lifts: 2. No catapults. Sunk by Japanese aircraft off Ceylon, 9 April 1942.

Illustrious-class
Formidable (1940), *Illustrious* (1940), *Victorious* (1941)
Displacement: 23,207 tons standard; 28, 619 tons deep load. Armament: 8 × twin 4.5-in; 5 × octuple 2-pdr pompom; 3 × single 40 mm Bofors; 19 × twin 20 mm Oerlikon; 14 × single 20 mm Oerlikon. Endurance: 11,000 miles at 12 kts. Complement: 1,997. Aircraft: 54. Lifts: 2. Catapults: 1. *Victorious* extensively rebuilt between 1950 and 1958 to emerge as one of the worlds most advanced carriers.

Modified Illustrious-class
Indomitable (1941)
Design modified to incorporate a lower hangar. Upper hangar was fitted with rails to increase capacity to three squadrons of Seafires and reduce handling damage to the aircraft, but this had to be abandoned as the system proved cumbersome under intensive combat conditions. Displacement: 24,680 tons standard; 29,730 tons deep load. Armament: 8-in plus 6 × octuple 2-pdr pompom; 2 × quad 40 mm Bofors; 2 × twin 40 mm Bofors; 21 × twin 20 mm Oerlikon; 18 × single 20 mm Oerlikon. Complement: 2,100. Aircraft: 56. Lifts: 2. Catapults: 1.

Implacable-class
Implacable (1944), *Indefatigable* (1944)
Modifications included upper and lower hangars, although forward lift only served upper hangar; four propeller shafts instead of three. Displacement: 23,450 tons standard; 32,110 tons deep load. Armament: 8 × twin 4.5-in; 5 × octuple 2-pdr pompom; 3 × quad 2-pdr pompom; 21 × twin 20 mm Oerlikon; 19 × single 20 mm Oerlikon. Endurance: 12,000 miles at 10 kts. Complement: 2,300. Aircraft: 81. Lifts: 2. Catapults: 1.

Unicorn (1943)
Originally intended as a maintenance and support carrier, but deployed operationally on occasion. Displacement: 16,530 tons standard; 20,300 tons deep load. Armament: 8 × 4-in; 16 × 2-pdr pompom; 13 × single 20 mm

Oerlikon. Endurance: 11,000 miles at 12 kts. Complement: 1,094. Aircraft: 36. Lifts: 2. Catapults: 1.

Light Fleet Carriers
Colossus-class

Colossus (1944), *Glory* (1945), *Ocean (1945)*, *Pioneer* (ferry carrier) (1945), *Venerable* (1945), *Vengeance* (1945).

Built to merchant standards to permit construction in yards not familiar with warship work. One hangar deck. Displacement: 13,190 tons standard; 18,040 tons deep load. LOA: 695 ft; Beam: 112.5 ft. Armament: 6 × quad 2-pdr pompoms; 11 × twin 20 mm Oerlikon; 10 × single 20 mm Oerlikon; 4 × single 3-pdr saluting. Endurance: 8,300 miles at 20 kts. Complement: 1,300. Aircraft: 42. Lifts: 2. Catapults: 1.

Colossus loaned to French Navy as *Arromanches*, 6 August 1946, purchased 1951. *Venerable* sold to RNethNavy, 1 April 1948, becoming the new *Karel Doorman*, 28 May 1948. Sold to Argentina as *25 de Mayo*, 1 September 1969. *Vengeance* loaned RAN, 13 May 1952; Reserve RN 13 August 1955; sold to Brazilian Navy as *Minas Gerais*, 13 December 1956.

Auxiliary or Escort Carriers

These ships were known to the Admiralty, and at first to the United States Navy, as auxiliary aircraft carriers, but the USN later adopted the term 'escort carrier', and this has passed into popular use. In fact, these ships did very much more than simply act as escorts, becoming anti-submarine carriers, aircraft transports and maintenance carriers, as well as providing flight decks for combat aircraft covering forces ashore. The only thing they did not do was operate in fleet actions because of their low speed.

Activity (1942)

Laid down as refrigerated cargo vessel *Telemachus* for Ocean Steamship, but converted on slipway. Displacement: 11,800 tons standard; 14,529 tons deep load. Armament: 1 × twin 4-in; 6 × twin 20 mm Oerlikon; 8 × single 20 mm Oerlikon. Speed 18 kts. Complement: 700. Aircraft: 10. Short hangar 100 ft long, single lift aft, arrester gear but no catapult.

Ameer or Ruler-class

Ameer (1943), *Arbiter* (1943), *Atheling* (1943), *Begum* (1943), *Emperor* (1943), *Empress* (1943), *Khedive* (1943), *Nabob** (1943), *Premier* (1943), *Patroller* (1943), *Puncher** (1944), *Queen* (1943), *Rajah* (1944), *Ranee* (1943), *Reaper* (1944), *Ruler* (1943), *Shah* (1943), *Slinger* (1943), *Smiter* (1944), *Speaker* (1943), *Thane* (1943), *Trumpeter* (1943), *Trouncer* (1944).

(Note: *Crewed by Royal Canadian Navy, but with RN Fleet Air Arm personnel.)

Sometimes referred to as the Ruler-class. Similar in design, but larger, to the Avenger-class and US Bogue-class, these were built as carriers rather than converted, although still using merchantman hulls. Displacement: 11,400 tons standard; 15,400 tons deep load. Armament varied according to role, but generally included: 2 × 5-in; 8 × twin 40 mm Bofors; 20 × 20 mm Oerlikon. Complement: 646. Aircraft: 20. Arrester gear aft and hangar with two lifts, with single accelerator on port side forward capable of handling heavier aircraft. Speed: 18 kts.

Archer (1941)
Laid down as a US merchant vessel, *Mormcamacland*, using a standard C3 hull, converted at Newport News with a wooden-planked flight deck and a small starboard side island for navigation and air control, but no smoke-stack as exhaust fumes discharged horizontally. Suffered considerable technical problems that delayed entry into service. Displacement: 10,220 tons standard; 12,860 tons deep load. Armament: 3 × 4-in; 6 × 20 mm twin Oerlikon; 7 × 20 mm single Oerlikon. Speed: 16.5 kts. Complement: 550. Aircraft: 12–15. Quarter-length hangar with single lift aft, arrester gear aft and a single hydraulic accelerator.

Attacker-class
Attacker (1942), *Battler* (1942), *Chaser* (1943), *Fencer* (1943), *Hunter* (1943), *Pursuer* (1943), *Ravager* (1943), *Searcher* (1943), *Stalker* (1942), *Striker* (1943), *Tracker* (1943)
These ships were identical to the USN's Bogue-class and transferred to the Royal Navy under Lend-Lease. Displacement: 10,200 tons standard; 14,400 tons deep load. Armament: 2 × 4-in; 4 × twin 40 mm Bofors; 4 × twin 20 mm Oerlikon; 4 × 20 mm Oerlikon. Speed: 18.5 kts. Complement: 646. Aircraft: 20. Arrester wires aft. Lifts: 2. Single hydraulic accelerator forward.

Audacity (1941)
Norddeutscher Line cargo vessel *Hannover*, converted after capture. Displacement: 10,200 tons standard; 11,000 tons deep load. Armament: 1 × 4-in; 1 × 6-pdr; 4 × 2-pdr; 4 × single 20 mm Oerlikon. Aircraft: 8 fighters. Arrester gear aft but no hangar, lifts or catapults. Speed: 15 kts. Torpedoed by *U-751* off Portugal, 20 December 1941.

Avenger-class
Avenger (1942), *Biter* (1942), *Dasher* (1942)
Displacement: 12,150 tons standard; 15,700 tons deep load. Armament: 3 × 4 in; 19 × single 20 mm Oerlikon. Complement: 555. Aircraft: 15. Arrester gear aft and hangar with single lift, while flight decks were extended to 440 ft on arrival in UK. Machinery: single diesel driving one shaft. Speed: 16.5 kts. *Avenger* torpedoed by *U-155* off Gibraltar, 15 December 1942, exploded and sunk. Post-war, *Biter* transferred to French Navy as *Dixmude*. *Dasher* exploded as result of an aviation fuel explosion and sunk in Firth of Clyde, 27 March 1943. Also *Charger*, Avenger-class ship retained

by USN for carrier deck landing training for RN pilots trained in the US under the 'Towers Scheme' and not transferred to UK.

Campania (1944)
Riveted construction similar to *Nairana* and *Vindex* but slightly longer and wider. First British escort carrier to have an Action Information Organisation (AIO). Displacement: 12, 450 tons standard; 15,970 tons deep load. Armament: 2 × 4-in; 16 × 2-pdr; 8 × twin 20 mm Oerlikon. Aircraft: 18. Complement: 700. Arrester gear aft but no catapults and just one lift. Speed: 16 kts.

Nairana-class
Nairana (1943), *Vindex* (1943)
Using a refrigerated cargo ship hull design with riveted construction. Displacement: 13,825 tons standard; 16,980 tons deep load. Armament: 2 × 4-in; 16 × 2-pdr. Aircraft: 21. Complement: 700. Arrester gear aft but no catapults and just one lift. Speed: 16 kts. *Vindex* slightly smaller. *Nairana* transferred to the Royal Netherlands Navy on 23 March 1946 as *Karel Doorman*.

Pretoria Castle (1943)
Conversion of the armed merchant cruiser and formerly Union Castle passenger liner of the same name. Officially an escort carrier – by far the largest auxiliary or escort carrier operated by the RN – was used solely for trials and training. Displacement: 19,650 tons standard; 23,450 tons deep load. Armament: 4 × 4 in; 16 × 2-pdr; 20 × single 20 mm Oerlikon. Complement: 580. Aircraft: 21. Arrester gear aft, accelerator and hangar with one lift forward. Speed: 18 kts.

Appendix V

Post-war Aircraft Carriers

Only two of the pre-war carriers, *Furious* and *Argus*, both dating from the First World War, survived the Second World War, and although all of the fast armoured carriers and the maintenance carrier, HMS *Unicorn*, survived the war, of these only *Victorious* remained for any length of time after what was probably the longest and most comprehensive refit and rebuilding in British naval history. All of the US Lend-Lease escort carriers were deleted at the end of the war, with some sunk, such as *Dasher*, most returned to the US where they were scrapped, and a few, too badly damaged or worn out, handed back *in situ*, but never crossed the Atlantic. Two were transferred to the Royal Netherlands Navy and the *Marine Nationale*. Likewise, many of the Colossus-class carriers and the more robust Majestic-class that followed it, ended up with other navies, with ships of these classes serving in Australia, Brazil, Canada, France, India and the Netherlands, possibly a unique achievement for any warship class, but certainly one for an aircraft carrier class. The only ship that did remain with the Royal Navy was the escort carrier *Campania*, which survived for many years as a trials carrier.

For details of the fast armoured carriers, and *Unicorn*, please look at Appendix IV.

It is important to remember that the light fleet carriers were an expedient, being built to merchant-ship standards so that they could use shipyards, such as Harland & Wolff in Belfast, unaccustomed to warship building. This is not to say that they were based on merchant-vessel designs, as were the escort or auxiliary carriers, because they were designed as carriers from the keel upwards and looked the part; certainly none of them was ever even considered for conversion to a merchant vessel. Yet, while far superior in speed and aircraft accommodation to the escort carriers, they also had their shortcomings. This was why as soon as the war ended, the Admiralty turned to building new fleet carriers, the result being a new *Eagle* and a new *Ark Royal*, while to provide new light fleet carriers the Centaur-class was developed, being larger and faster than the Colossus and Majestic-classes. Many would suggest that a modernized version of the Centaur-class would have been superior to the Invincible-class, but that is to overlook the harsh political realities that led to these ships being ordered, and for many years the Fleet Air Arm was thankful to have any flight decks at all. Some have suggested that the most cost-effective design is that of the helicopter carrier, *Ocean*, but she lacks the speed of a true aircraft carrier, however, she deserves far better than to be dismissed by the Ministry of Defence as a 'helicopter landing platform'.

Fleet Carriers
Eagle-class

Essentially a development of the Implacable-class with two hangar decks and four shafts.

Ark Royal (1955), *Eagle* (1951).
Displacement: 36,800 tons standard; 45,720 tons deep load. LOA: 803.75 ft; Beam: 112.5 ft (hull). Armament: 16 × 4.5-in; 32 × 40 mm. Endurance: 5,000 miles at 24 kts. Complement: 2,250. Aircraft: 80. Lifts: 2 (initially 3 *Ark Royal*). Catapults: 2. Both ships much modified during service. *Eagle* received half-angled deck in 1955 and later an angled deck in 1964, as well as later receiving a waist catapult and then three-dimensional radar. *Ark Royal* commissioned with half-angled deck and later an angled deck was added with a waist catapult while the deck-edge lift was removed at the same time. A development of these ships, the Malta-class, with broader beam and a single hangar deck with substantial headroom, and having the same hangar area as the Eagle-class, was cancelled.

Light Fleet carriers
Colossus-class

Colossus (1944), *Glory* (1945), *Ocean* (1945), *Perseus* (1945),
Pioneer (ferry carrier) (1945), *Theseus* (1946), *Triumph* (1946),
Venerable (1945), *Vengeance* (1945), *Warrior* (1948).
Built to merchant standards to permit construction in yards not familiar with warship work. One hangar deck. Displacement: 13,190 tons standard; 18,040 tons deep load. LOA: 695 ft; Beam: 80 ft. Armament: 6 × quad 2-pdr pompoms; 11 × twin 20 mm Oerlikon; 10 × single 20 mm Oerlikon; 4 × single 3-pdr saluting. Endurance: 8,300 miles at 20 kts. Complement: 1,300. Aircraft: 42. Lifts: 2. Catapults: 1.

Colossus loaned to French Navy as *Arromanches*, 6 August 1946, purchased 1951. *Venerable* sold to RNethNavy, 1 April, 1948, becoming the new *Karel Doorman*, 28 May 1948. Sold to Argentina as *25 de Mayo*, 1 September 1969. *Vengeance* loaned RAN 13 May 1952; Reserve RN 13 August 1955; sold to Brazilian Navy as *Minas Gerais*, 13 December 1956. *Warrior* initially loaned to the Royal Canadian Navy, then returned to RN and operated as an aircraft transport during the Korean War. Sold to Argentina as *Independencia* in 1958. *Triumph* served off Korea and was later converted to a repair ship, operating mainly in the Far East during the confrontation with Indonesia, and supported the Beira patrol.

Majestic-class

Hercules (1961), *Leviathan* (not completed), *Magnificent* (1947), *Majestic* (1955), *Powerful* (1957), *Terrible* 1948.

Developed version of the Colossus-class to handle heavier aircraft, but also built to merchant standards to permit construction in yards not familiar with warship work. One hangar deck. Completion was delayed at the end of the Second World War and ships were finally completed as and when sold to mother navies. Displacement: 14,000 tons standard; 17,800 tons deep load. LOA: 695 ft; Beam: 75 ft. Armament: 6 × quad 2-pdr pompoms; 11 × twin 20 mm Oerlikon; 19 × 40 mm Oerlikon; 4 × single 3-pdr saluting. Endurance: 8,300 miles at 20 kts. Complement: 1,300. Aircraft: 37. Lifts: 2. Catapults: 1.

Terrible transferred to Royal Australian Navy in 1949 and commissioned as HMAS *Sydney*. *Magnificent* was loaned to the Royal Canadian Navy in 1947 and was subsequently sold to Canada as HMCS *Magnificent*. *Powerful* sold to Canada in 1952 and completed, much modified, in 1957 as HMCS *Bonaventure*. *Majestic* completed, much modified, for the Royal Australian Navy in 1955 as HMAS *Melbourne*. *Leviathan*, never completed but hulked and then scrapped in 1968. *Hercules*, completed much modified for the Indian Naval Service in 1961 as INS *Vikrant*.

Centaur-class

Albion (1954), *Bulwark* (1954), *Centaur* (1953), *Hermes* (1959).

One hangar deck. Displacement: 18,300 tons standard; 24,500 tons deep load. LOA: 737 ft; Beam: 100 ft. Armament: 32 × 40 mm Oerlikon. Endurance: 6,000 miles at 20 kts. Complement: 1,390. Aircraft: 42. Lifts: 2. Catapults: 2.

Centaur appeared with half-angled deck, but refitted extensively in the late 1950s and emerged with steam catapults. *Albion* and *Bulwark* incorporated a number of improvements and a half-angled deck, which involved a port-side extension, and were refitted as commando carriers, appearing in 1962 and 1960 respectively, capable of accommodating 750 men and sixteen Westland Wessex helicopters. *Hermes* incorporated many improvements, including an angled flight deck and had her flight deck widened to 160 ft at the maximum, including a starboard extension, to accommodate Sea Vixen and Buccaneer aircraft, while also having a larger island. She was modified in 1971–72 to become a commando carrier, losing her three-dimensional radar, but was converted to carry Sea Harriers in 1976–77, with a ski-jump forward, due to delays with the *Invincible*. Placed in reserve in 1984 after action off the Falklands, she was sold to India and commissioned as the INS *Viraat*.

Invincible-class

Ark Royal (1985), *Invincible* (1980), *Illustrious* (1982).

One hangar deck. Displacement: 16,000 tons standard; 19,500 tons deep load. LOA: 677 ft; Beam: 115 ft. Armament: 2 × Sea Dart SAM. Endurance: 5,000 miles at 18 kts. Complement: 900. Aircraft: 20. Lifts: 2.

Invincible modified with ski-jump 1977 before entering service. All ships have since been modified losing the Sea Dart missile system forward in favour of a larger deck area, while gaining Goalkeeper AA and anti-missile multi-barrel gun systems.

Ocean (1998)

One hangar deck. Displacement: 17,500 tons standard; 19,500 tons deep load. LOA: 660 ft; Beam: 92 ft. Armament: Phalanx AA and anti-missile multi-barrel 20 mm. Endurance: 6,300 miles at 16 kts. Complement: 445. Aircraft: 18. Lifts: 2.

Appendix VI

Standard Convoy Air Patrol Code Names

(Note: All suitable for a single aircraft.)

Adder: Patrol ahead of convoy at distance of 8 to 12 miles, with the length of patrol 30 miles, that is, 15 miles on either side of the centre line.

Alligator ... port or starboard: Patrol on side indicated at distance of 10 miles from the convoy along a line parallel to the convoy's course. The length of patrol would be 20 miles, that is 10 miles ahead and astern of the aircraft's position on the convoy's beam.

Cobra 'Y': Patrol around convoy at a distance of Y miles, with Y being the distance from the convoy so that the instruction Cobra 12, would mean patrol at a distance of 12 miles.

Crocodile 'Y': Patrol ahead of convoy from beam to beam at radius 'Y' miles, in effect a half Cobra. This was popular with fast convoys since they had little to fear from a U-boat sneaking up from astern.

Frog 'Y': Patrol astern of convoy at distance of 'Y' miles. Length of patrol would be two 'Y' miles, that is 'Y' miles on either side of the centre line. This was to stop U-boats trailing the convoy, often shortly before dusk. It was also essential prior to any change of course so that the U-boat commander would keep his craft submerged and not realize that the change had taken place until it was too late.

Viper: Patrol around convoy at distance of visibility.

'X' Lizard 'Y': Search sector bearing 'X' to a depth of 'Y' miles.

'X' Mamba: Search along bearing 'X' to a depth of 30 miles and return.

'X' Python 'Y': Given when a submarine had been spotted, so that the aircraft would patrol on bearing 'X' at a distance of 'Y' miles, and would carry out a square search around the indicated position for twenty minutes.

Chronology

1909

7 May: Admiralty signs order for first airship, HMA1, also named *Mayfly*.

1911

25 April: First four naval pilots complete flying training at Eastchurch, Isle of Sheppey.

24 September: Dirigible *Mayfly* wrecked outside her shed at Barrow.

1912

10 January: First aircraft launched from a British warship when Lieutenant Charles Rumney Samson flies a Short S27 from the battleship HMS *Africa* while at anchor.

13 April: Royal Flying Corps formed by Royal Warrant.

2 May: First launch of an aircraft, a Short S38 flown by the then Lieutenant Charles Rumney Samson, from a ship under way, the battleship *Hibernia*, off Portland.

15 July: Naval Wing formed within RFC.

3 September: Leading Seaman O'Connor becomes first rating to qualify as pilot.

1913

First RNAS station commissioned on then Isle of Grain, River Medway.

7 May: *Hermes*, light cruiser, recommissioned after being converted as first ship to fly seaplanes.

1914

1 July: RNAS formed from the Naval Wing, Royal Flying Corps.

28: First successful aerial torpedo drop by Squadron Commander Arthur Longmore (later Air Chief Marshal Sir Arthur, RAF), using Short Folder seaplane flying from Calshot, Southampton Water.

4 August: At 08.30, Admiral Sir John Jellicoe relieves Admiral Sir George Callaghan as Commander-in-Chief of the Grand Fleet at Scapa Flow. At 23.00, British ultimatum expires and the United Kingdom and Germany are at war.

25 August: Royal Marines land at Ostend, but have to be withdrawn on 31 August.

27: First RNAS squadron arrives at Ostend. German cruiser *Konigsberg* sinks HMS *Pegasus* in the harbour at Zanzibar.

5 September: Launch of seaplane carrier *Ark Royal* at Blyth after conversion on slip from collier to seaplane carrier. Renamed *Pegasus* in 1934 and becomes catapult ship in 1941.

3 October: First units of the Royal Naval Division arrive at Antwerp.

8: RNAS Sopwith Tabloid makes the first destruction of a Zeppelin, *LZ.25*, in her shed at Dusseldorf.

9: RNVR AA Corps established to provide air defence, initially of London. Seaplane carrier *Ark Royal* commissioned.

21: Three RNAS Avro 504s attack Zeppelin sheds at Friedrichshafen.

21: First night bombing raid on Ostend by Wing Commander Charles Rumney Samson.

25: Seven seaplanes flown off from the seaplane carriers *Engadine, Riviera* and *Express* to attack the German airship sheds at Cuxhaven in the first bombing raids by ship-borne aircraft.

31: Seaplane carrier *Hermes* sunk by *U-27* in Straits of Dover.

1 November: Three RNAS Avro 504s attack Zeppelin sheds at Friedrichshafen.

9 December: *Ark Royal* laid down as collier, commissioned as seaplane carrier.

25: RNAS seaplanes attack Cuxhaven operating from *Empress, Engadine* and *Riviera*.

1915

15 January: RNAS aircraft attack U-boat alongside the mole at Zeebrugge.

29: RNAS airship shed at Walney Island, off Barrow-in-Furness, shelled by *U-21* operating in the Irish Sea.

18 February: Germany declares British territorial waters to be an unrestricted war zone. U-boat campaign starts.

19: Anglo-French bombardment of the outer forts of the Dardanelles begun.

25: Bombardment of Dardanelles forts resumed.

15 March: German aircraft attack merchantman *Blonde*, the first to be attacked from the air.

18: First ascent of the non-rigid airship SS-1 (Submarine Scout) at Kingsnorth, River Medway.

6 April: False bow waves to be painted on all ships.

25: Royal Navy provides support for landings by British and Australian troops on the Gallipoli peninsula.

17 May: First Sea Lord Admiral of the Fleet Lord Kilverstone ('Jacky' Fisher) walks out of Admiralty, aged seventy-four.

24: Italy joins the war on the side of the Allies against Austria-Hungary.
28: Admiral Sir Henry Jackson succeeds Fisher as First Sea Lord.
31: First ascent by C1 (Coastal Patrol) non-rigid airship.
June: U-boat campaign spreads to Mediterranean using bases in the Adriatic.
7: First RNAS VC to Flight Sub Lieutenant Reginald Warneford for destroying Zeppelin *LZ.37* near Ghent.
7: RNAS aircraft destroy *LZ.38* in her shed at Evere, Belgium.
15: RNAS aircraft and warships destroy German cruiser *Konigsberg* in Rufiji River, German East Africa.
8 August: Sopwith Tabloid (aka Sopwith Schneider) flown off *Campania* by Flight Lieutenant William Welsh (later AM Sir William, RAF).
12: Short 184 seaplane from the seaplane carrier *Ben-my-Chree* makes the first successful aerial torpedo attack against a Turkish cargo ship, previously damaged by a submarine, and sinks her in the Dardanelles.
18: Chief Petty Officer Michael Keogh of *Ark Royal* awarded Albert Medal (later GC) for attempt to rescue fatally injured Captain C.H. Collett RMA, from burning aircraft at Imbros air station.
19 November: Victoria Cross awarded to Squadron Commander Richard Bell-Davis for landing behind enemy lines at Ferrijk Railway Junction in Bulgaria to rescue a fellow pilot who had been shot down.
18 December: Wing Commander Charles Rumney Samson drops first 500-lb bomb on Turkish forces.

1916
16 February: War Office takes over control of anti-aircraft defences from the Admiralty.
25 March: Five seaplanes sent from seaplane carrier *Vindex* in unsuccessful attempt to bomb airship shed at Hoyer on the coast of Schleswig Holstein, but three come down in German territory and their crews are captured.
1 April: East Coast towns attacked by German Zeppelin airships, while *L.15* becomes the first Zeppelin to be brought down by AA fire, landing in the Thames Estuary and surrendering to a British warship.
14: RNAS aircraft based on Mudros bomb Constantinople (now Istanbul).
24: Submarine *E22* conducts 'float-off' trials with two Sopwith Schneider seaplanes to see if these can intercept Zeppelins over the North Sea before they can reach the East Coast.
4 May: Zeppelin *L.7* brought down by light cruisers *Galatea* and *Phaeton* south of the Horns Reef. *E31* rescues seven survivors and destroys *L.7*.
31: Battle of Jutland, with the first use of aerial reconnaissance by a seaplane flown off the seaplane carrier *Engadine*. British force heavily outnumbers and outguns the Germans, but battle is plagued by poor visibility and poor communications between British scouting forces and

the Grand Fleet, while the Admiralty does not pass on information from intercepted signals traffic. In fast-moving battle, Beatty loses the battle-cruisers *Indefatigable*, *Queen Mary* and *Invincible*, and the armoured cruisers *Defence*, *Warrior* and *Black Prince*, plus another five smaller warships, a total tonnage of 155,000 tons, and other warships are damaged, while the Germans lose eleven warships, with a total tonnage of 61,000 tons, before managing to regain the safety of their harbours. The Royal Navy lose 6,090 men against 2,550 for the Germans.

17 June: Zeppelin *L.48* shot down and German naval signal book found in wreckage.

9 August: Submarine *B10* sunk by Austrian aircraft while being repaired at Venice – the first submarine sunk by enemy aircraft.

15: *Furious* launched at Armstrong Whitworth on Tyneside with flight deck replacing forward 18-in gun turret. Later returned to builders to have landing-on deck built aft, replacing aft 18-in gun turret.

24 September: Zeppelin *L.32* shot down and new German naval signal book salvaged from the wreckage.

27 November: First successful flight by RNAS rigid airship, the *R9*.

28: RNAS shoots down Zeppelin *L.21* 8 miles off Lowestoft.

1917

11 January: Seaplane carrier *Ben-my-Chree*, sunk off Kastelorizo by fire from Turkish batteries.

11 February: Lieutenant D.P.T. Stembridge awarded George Cross for the rescue of a pilot from a burning aircraft (the GC had just replaced the Albert Medal at this time).

6 April: United States declares war on Germany.

14 May: RNAS flying boat destroys Zeppelin *L.22* off the Texel.

20: RNAS flying boat sinks *UC-36* in North Sea – the RNAS's first U-boat.

29: First air-sea rescue by RNAS flying boat.

14 June: Curtiss H-12 flying boat destroys Zeppelin *L.43* off Vlieland.

22: First destruction of Zeppelin by aircraft flown off a cruiser as Sopwith Pup shoots down Zeppelin *L.23* off Lodbjerg, Denmark.

22: RNAS observer officers to wear wings instead of eagle on their sleeves.

9 July: RNAS aircraft from Mudros bombs *Sultan Selim* and *Midilli* (aka *Goeben* and *Breslau*) in Constantinople.

24: RNAS flying boat sinks U-boat *UC-1* in North Sea.

28: Two RNAS Curtiss H-12 flying boats sinks U-boat *UB-20* in North Sea.

2 August: Squadron Commander E.H. Dunning makes the first deck-landing on a ship underway, landing aboard *Furious* in a Sopwith Pup. He was drowned in a later attempt when his aircraft went over the side.

22: Sopwith Pup landplane flies off cruiser to destroy Zeppelin *L.23* off the Danish coast, the first time this was achieved.

14 September: George Cross awarded to Ordinary Seamen G.E.P. Abbott, R.J. Knowlton and Gold for rescue of pilot of seaplane crashed on top of a 360 ft mast on Hornsea Island.

23: RNAS Curtiss H-12 Large America flying boat bombed and sinks *UB-32* near the Sunk Lighthouse, English Channel. The first U-boat to be sunk by an aircraft.

28: Curtiss flying boat sinks *UC-6* in North Sea.

1 October: Squadron Commander Rutland makes the first flight from a platform on top of a gun turret in a Sopwith Pup using B turret aboard the battlecruiser *Repulse*.

1918

5 February: Order in Council signed that establishes Royal Air Force, with effect from 1 April.

6 March: Award of George Cross to Flight Lieutenant V.A. Watson for saving life in blazing airship gazetted.

15: *Furious* recommissioned with landing-on deck and the first aircraft lifts.

1 April: Royal Air Force founded, absorbing 55,000 RNAS personnel and 2,500 aircraft.

4: First successful launch of a two-seat reconnaissance aircraft from a ship when a Sopwith 1½-strutter flies off a platform on a forward gun turret of HMAS *Australia*.

8 June: *Eagle* launched at Armstrongs after being converted on the slip from the Chilean battleship *Almirante Cochrane*. First carrier with starboard island and first with round down after end to flight deck to reduce turbulence on approach.

1 July: Aerial attack on the airship sheds at Tondern with seven aircraft flying from the aircraft carrier *Furious* succeeding in destroying *L.54* and *L.60*. This is the first successful attack by landplanes flying from an aircraft carrier.

28 August: RAF (ex-RNAS) aircraft and HMS *Ouse* sink *UC-70* off Whitby.

14 September: First flush-deck carrier, *Argus*, commissioned.

5 November: Seaplane carrier *Campania* sinks after collision with *Royal Oak* and battlecruiser *Glorious* in Firth of Forth.

11: Armistice ends First World War. Most modern German warships and all U-boats ordered to Scapa Flow, but these are scuttled on 21 June 1919.

1919

30 July: Aircraft from seaplane carrier *Vindictive* attacks Kronstadt harbour.

11 September: *Hermes* launched at Armstrong Whitworth on Tyneside: the first ship laid down as an aircraft carrier.

1920

16 June: Seaplane carrier *Ark Royal* joins battleships and destroyers in action against Turks at Istria.

1923

1 May: *Hermes* commissioned as first aircraft carrier designed as such and the first with a starboard island.

1924

1 April: Fleet Air Arm formed within Coastal Area of the Royal Air Force. Only shipboard flights included.

1926

1 July: First night landing aboard an aircraft carrier: Blackburn Dart flown by Flight Lieutenant Boyce lands on *Furious*.

1928

1 March: *Courageous* recommissioned after conversion to aircraft carrier, the first to have transverse arrester wires.

1931

2 April: Rear Admiral R.G.H. Henderson becomes the first Rear Admiral Aircraft Carriers.

1934

17 April: First flight of Fairey Swordfish.

1935

9 September: First landing of rotary-wing aircraft on an aircraft carrier when a Cierva C30A autogyro is flown onto *Furious* by Wing Commander Brie.

1937

30 July: 'Inskip Award' recommends that Fleet Air Arm be transferred from the Royal Air Force to the Royal Navy.

30 July: Cabinet approves Inskip recommendations.

1939

5 April: *Illustrious*, the first of the famous six fast armoured aircraft carriers of the Second World War launched at Vickers, Barrow-in-Furness: the yard's first aircraft carrier.

May: Fleet Air Arm comes fully under Admiralty control, with 1,500 RAF personnel electing to transfer to the Royal Navy's new Air Branch. In preparation, the Admiralty is given authority to triple the size of the FAA.

3 September: Britain and France declare war on Germany after an ultimatum expires.

17: Aircraft carrier *Courageous* torpedoed by *U-29* and sunk.

26: Dornier Do18 flying boat shot down by Blackburn Skua from *Ark Royal*, the first German aircraft to be shot down in the war.

13 December: Battle of the River Plate in which cruisers *Ajax*, *Achilles* and *Exeter* inflict serious damage on the 'pocket' battleship *Admiral Graf Spee*, which seeks refuge in Montevideo, but returns to sea and is scuttled on 17 December.

1940

In this year, as the full pressure of total war became apparent, a massive expansion and relocation of training establishments was undertaken while the length of shore-based courses was cut in half.

9 April: Germany occupies Denmark and begins invasion of Norway.

Mid-April: British and French troops land in Norway, *Furious* covers the landings and afterwards acts as an aircraft transport, *Ark Royal* joins her. *Glorious* recalled from Mediterranean.

10: Luftwaffe attacks Home Fleet south-west of Bergen, sinking a destroyer and causing minor damage to the battleship *Rodney* and the cruisers *Devonshire, Glasgow* and *Southampton.*

10: Skuas of 800 and 803 NAS flying from HMS *Sparrowhawk,* RNAS Hatston, on Orkney attack and sink the German light cruiser *Konigsberg* at Bergen, the first major warship to be sunk by naval aircraft.

11: First coordinated attack by aircraft from more than one squadron as *Furious* sends aircraft from 816 and 818 NAS against Trondheim.

26 May: Operation Dynamo, the evacuation of the British Expeditionary Force from Dunkirk, begins under the command of Vice Admiral Ramsay at Dover.

8 June: Aircraft carrier *Glorious* caught and shelled by *Gneisenau* and *Scharnhorst* during withdrawal from Norway. Carrier and two escorting destroyers *Acasta* and *Ardent* sunk, although *Acasta* scores torpedo hit on *Scharnhorst.*

13: Aircraft from *Ark Royal* attack *Scharnhorst* at Trondheim, but only one bomb hits the ship and this fails to explode.

13: Aircraft of No. 767 Squadron flown by instructors from base in south of France bomb Genoa.

17: French seek armistice, meaning that the Royal Navy is on its own in the Mediterranean.

28: Force H assembled in response to surrender of France, includes *Ark Royal.*

30: Aircraft from 830 NAS based in Malta attack Augusta in Sicily.

2 July: Disembarked Swordfish of 812 NAS attack invasion barge concentration near Rotterdam with RAF Coastal Command.

3: Battle of Mers El-Kebir, attacking Vichy French warships near Oran after French admiral refuses to surrender. French battleship *Bretagne* blows up, while battleship *Provence* and battlecruiser *Dunkerque* crippled.

5: Fairey Swordfish of 813 NAS from *Eagle* sink an Italian destroyer and a freighter at Tobruk.

5: Swordfish of 830 NAS from Malta attack Catania airfield, Sicily.

6: Swordfish of 810 NAS from *Ark Royal* torpedo and damage French battlecruiser *Dunkerque* and sink trawler escaping from Oran.
8: Aircraft from *Hermes* accompanied by two heavy cruisers attack Vichy French fleet at Dakar, damaging the battleship *Richelieu*.
9: Battle of Punta Stilo/Calabria sees British and Italian battleships clash, with *Guilio Cesare* badly damaged by shell from *Warspite*, forcing Italians to withdraw. This was the only action during the war when two full battle fleets engaged. Near misses from Italian bombers damage the carrier's fuel system.
9: U-boat sunk by 830 Squadron aircraft.
10: Aircraft of 813 and 824 NAS from *Eagle* sink Italian destroyer *Leone Pancaldo* in harbour at Augusta.
25: Swordfish of 824 NAS from *Eagle* sink two Italian destroyers and a freighter off Tobruk.
2 August: Operation Crush, twelve Swordfish of 810, 818, 820 NAS from *Ark Royal* attack Elmas airfield, Cagliari and mine harbour.
7: Nine Skuas of 801 NAS flying from RNAS Hatston, Orkney, destroy fuel tanks at Dolvik, Hardangersfjord.
15: Mediterranean Fleet battleships and cruiser *Kent* bombard Italian positions around Bardia and Fort Capuzzo, with *Eagle*'s Swordfish operating from a shore base.
22: Three Swordfish of 842 NAS from *Eagle* sink depot ship *Monte Gargano*, a destroyer and the submarine *Iride* in the Gulf of Bomba.
22/23: Destroyers bombard seaplane base at Bomba, west of Tobruk, joined by three of *Eagle*'s 842 NAS Swordfish operating from a shore base, and sink two Italian submarines, a depot ship and a destroyer with three torpedoes.
31: Disembarked Swordfish of 812 NAS attack oil tanks at Rotterdam.
4 September: Disembarked Swordfish of 812 NAS attacked invasion barges at Terneuzen.
17: Swordfish of 815 and 819 NAS from *Illustrious* sink two Italian destroyers at Benghazi.
23–26: Attack on French fleet at Dakar by Force H, including *Ark Royal*, 810, 814, 818 and 820 NAS.
13 October: Fifteen Swordfish of 815 and 819 NAS off *Illustrious* attack Port Laki on the island of Leros.
16: Operation Dhu, eleven Swordfish and three Skua aircraft of 816 and 801 NAS from *Furious* bomb oil storage tanks and seaplane base at Tromsø.
27: Eight Swordfish of 813 and 824 NAS off *Eagle* bomb airfield at Maltezana, Stampalia.
9 November: Operation Crack, *Ark Royal* sends Fulmar, Skua and Swordfish of 810, 818 and 820 NAS to attack airfield at Elmas, Sardinia.
11/12: Twenty-one aircraft of 813, 815, 819 and 824 NAS fly from *Illustrious* to attack the Italian fleet at Taranto, putting three battleships out of

action, and damaging several other ships and shore installations for the loss of two aircraft. Meanwhile, the Mediterranean Fleet cruisers carry out a diversionary operation in the Straits of Otranto.

17: Fourteen Hawker Hurricanes flown off *Argus* for Malta, but only four reach the island as the others run out of fuel.

26: Fifteen Swordfish of 815 and 819 NAS from *Illustrious* bomb Port Laki on Leros.

14 December: Eight Swordfish of 830 NAS, based on Malta, bomb Tripoli.

17: *Illustrious* sends her aircraft to attack airfields on Rhodes.

20: Ten Swordfish of 830 NAS, based on Malta, bomb Tripoli and mine the harbour.

21: Nine Swordfish of 915 and 819 NAS flown from *Illustrious* sink two Italian ships from convoy off Tunisia.

22: Fifteen Swordfish of 915 and 819 NAS flown from *Illustrious* bombed Tripoli.

1941

10 January: *Illustrious* attacked by Luftwaffe and badly damaged during Operation Excess, the handover of a convoy from Gibraltar to Alexandria off Malta. Ship puts into Malta for emergency repairs.

11: First operational launch from *Pegasus*, a Royal Navy catapult launch ship, but failed to down an enemy aircraft.

16: *Illustrious* provokes an intensified blitz during her stay in Malta for emergency repairs, reaching a peak on this day.

23: *Illustrious* leaves Malta for the United States via the Suez Canal for permanent repairs.

1 February: Aircraft from *Ark Royal* attack the Tirso Dam and power plant in Sardinia.

1: Operation Breach Albacores of 826 and 829 NAS flying from *Formidable* attack Mogadishu in Italian Somaliland.

9: Force H in the western Mediterranean, including the battleship *Malaya* and the battlecruiser *Renown* and aircraft carrier *Ark Royal*, with a cruiser and ten escorts, attacks targets in the Gulf of Genoa, with the battleships bombarding Genoa, and aircraft bombing Leghorn and mining the port of La Spezia.

21: Albacores of 826 and 829 NAS flying from *Formidable* attack Massawa, Eritrea.

1 March: Flying from *Formidable*, 826 NAS's Albacores attack Massawa again.

6: Churchill announces the start of the Battle of the Atlantic.

28: Battle of Cape Matapan with Mediterranean Fleet having battleships *Warspite*, *Valiant* and *Malaya*, aircraft carrier *Formidable* and four cruisers as well as aircraft based ashore in Crete, while the Italians have the battleship *Vittorio Veneto* and eight cruisers. *Vittorio Veneto* badly damaged and stopped at one stage, while three Italian cruisers and two destroyers are sunk. Carrier-borne NAS include 803, 806, 826, 829, as well as 815 flying from Maleme, Crete.

1 April: 824 NAS Swordfish, disembarked from *Eagle*, wrecks Italian destroyer *Leone* off Massawa, Eritrea.

3: Swordfish of 813 and 824 NAS disembarked from *Eagle* attack four Italian destroyers, sinking two, off Port Sudan.

6/7: German troops attack both Yugoslavia and Greece, while the Luftwaffe bombs Piraeus blowing up a British ammunition ship that takes ten other ships with her and damages many more, putting the port out of action.

12: Twenty Hurricanes flown off *Ark Royal* to Malta.

15: RAF Coastal Command comes under Admiralty operational control.

21: Mediterranean Fleet bombards Tripoli supported by aircraft from *Formidable* and Malta, with 803, 806, 826, 829 NAS, inflicting serious damage.

23: Greek Army surrenders and Mediterranean Fleet helps in the evacuation of British forces to Crete.

27: *Patia*, fighter-catapult ship, sunk by Luftwaffe off River Tyne.

18–27 May: Battleship *Bismarck* escorted by the heavy cruiser *Prinz Eugen* makes her maiden sortie, causing the battlecruiser *Hood* and the new battleship *Prince of Wales* to intercept. They are soon followed by the battleship *King George V*, the battlecruiser *Repulse* and the aircraft carrier *Victorious*. The cruisers *Suffolk* and *Norfolk* sight the German ships and proceed to track them on radar. *Hood* and *Prince of Wales* engage the German ships, but after five minutes *Hood* blows up. *Prince of Wales* is badly damaged and breaks off the fight, but *Bismarck* is also damaged with a fuel leak and has to divert to Brest. Late on 24 May, Swordfish from *Victorious* attack *Bismarck*. On 25 May, Force H, with *Renown*, *Ark Royal* and two cruisers, leaves Gibraltar. The following day, Swordfish from *Ark Royal* score two torpedo hits, while that night destroyers make an unsuccessful torpedo attack. The next day, *King George V* and *Rodney* plus two cruisers engage *Bismarck*, and after ninety minutes she is dead in the water and on fire, later sinking.

20: German airborne landings on Crete leaves the Royal Navy to disrupt the follow-up seaborne invasion. Battle continues until 1 June, with *Formidable* damaged 'beyond local repair'. 803, 805, 806 NAS involved.

21: *Ark Royal* flies off RAF Hurricanes to reinforce the air defence of Malta.

22: Luftwaffe attacks Mediterranean Fleet, sinking cruisers *Fiji* and *Gloucester* as well as a destroyer, damaging *Warspite* and cruisers *Carlisle* and *Naiad*.

26: Battleships *Queen Elizabeth* and *Barham* with aircraft carrier *Formidable* and nine destroyers attack Axis airfields in the Dodecanese, but shortage of aircraft limits the effect and the Luftwaffe seriously damages the carrier. This leaves the Royal Navy with the task of evacuating 17,000 British, Commonwealth and Greek troops from Crete.

27: First operational use of catapult aircraft merchantman, CAM-ship, *Michael-E,* but torpedoed and sunk on 30 May.

16 June: Swordfish of 815 NAS from Nicosia, Cyprus, torpedo and sink Vichy destroyer *Chevalier Paul* off Turkish coast.

22 and 30 July: To help the USSR, invaded by Germany in June, aircraft from *Victorious* and *Furious* attack Petsamo and Kirkenes north of the Arctic Circle with little success, losing fifteen aircraft.

September: The United States Navy starts to escort convoys as far as the mid-ocean meeting point, easing the pressure on the Royal Navy.

12: Malta-based Swordfish of 830 NAS join RAF Blenheims in attacking Axis convoy for Tripoli, sinking or damaging several ships.

21: Martlets (Wildcats) of 802 NAS flying from *Audacity* shoot down Focke-Wulf Fw200 Condor while escorting Convoy OG74.

1 November: First operational launch from a CAM-ship, *Empire Foam,* escorting Convoy HX156.

9: Force K from Malta, two cruisers and two destroyers, follows aerial reconnaissance report of an Italian convoy and using radar makes a surprise attack, sinking all seven merchantmen in the convoy and one out of the six escorting destroyers. By this time, the flow of men and materiel between Italy and North Afirca is effectively stopped.

13: *U-81* torpedoes *Ark Royal,* crippling the ship and she sinks the following day.

7 December: Aircraft from the Japanese carriers *Akagi, Kaga, Shokaku, Zuikaku, Hiryu* and *Soryu* send 353 aircraft in two waves to attack the US Pacific Fleet in its forward base at Pearl Harbor in Hawaii, bringing the United States into the war.

14–23: A convoy battle develops off Portugal as convoy HG76 on passage from Gibraltar to the UK is attacked by twelve U-boats. The thirty-two merchantmen have Britain's first escort carrier, *Audacity,* three destroyers and nine smaller warships, but the carrier's aircraft and the escorts together manage to sink five U-boats for the cost of three merchantmen, a destroyer and the carrier herself (sunk on 21 December).

21: Swordfish of 812 NAS disembarked to Gibraltar sink *U-751* offshore.

1942

15 January: No. 815 NAS Swordfish sinks *U-577* north-west of Mersa Matruh.

23: Four Swordfish from 830 NAS, based on Malta, torpedo and sink Italian merchantman bound for Tripoli.

7–15 February: Japanese forces take Singapore with its major naval base.

12: *Gneisenau, Scharnhorst* and *Prinz Eugen* leave Brest for the 'Channel Dash', but are detected by the British too late due to technical and organizational failures. Attacks by MTBs and destroyers are beaten off, while all six Swordfish sent to attack are shot down, for which Lieutenant Commander Eugene Esmonde receives the Fleet Air Arm's first VC posthumously.

15: First Royal Marine Commando formed, now No. 40 RM Commando.

6 March: German attempt to attack convoy PQ12 to the USSR using the battleship *Tirpitz* and three destroyers is foiled by bad weather. Later, an attack by aircraft of 817 and 832 NAS from *Victorious* is beaten off.

April: Heavy attacks by the Luftwaffe throughout the month see three destroyers and three submarines sunk, as well as a number of smaller vessels.

5: Japanese carrier-borne aircraft attack Colombo Harbour in Ceylon (now Sri Lanka), damaging the harbour and merchant shipping. At sea, the cruisers *Cornwall* and *Dorsetshire* are attacked by fifty carrier-borne aircraft and sunk within minutes.

9: The carrier *Hermes*, escorted by an Australian destroyer, is caught by Japanese carrier-borne aircraft and both are sunk off the coast of Ceylon: the first sinking of an aircraft carrier by carrier-borne aircraft. Meanwhile, Japanese aircraft attack Trincomalee, Ceylon, and cruisers raid merchant shipping in the Bay of Bengal.

20: USS *Wasp* flies off forty-eight Spitfires to Malta, of which forty-seven arrive, but twenty destroyed and twelve badly damaged by air attack within minutes of landing.

3–8 May: Battle of the Coral Sea, the first major carrier-to-carrier battle, includes three British cruisers and two destroyers as part of US Task Force 17.

5–8: British forces invade Madagascar in Operation Ironclad, with an initial landing at Diego Suarez, supported by the battleship *Ramillies*, aircraft carriers *Illustrious* and *Indomitable*, cruisers and eleven destroyers, finding weak opposition. On 6 May, Swordfish of 829 NAS flying from *Illustrious* sink Vichy submarine *Heros*.

9: *Eagle* and USS *Wasp* fly off sixty-four Spitfires to Malta, of which sixty-one arrive.

2 June: Swordfish of 815 NAS and Blenheims of 203 Sqn RAF, cripple *U-652* off Solum.

10–15 August: Convoy, Operation Pedestal, sees a fourteen ship convoy from Gibraltar to Malta with a heavy escort including the aircraft carriers *Eagle, Furious, Indomitable* and *Victorious,* and the battleships *Nelson* and *Rodney*, seven cruisers and twenty-seven destroyers. Shortage of fuel keeps the Italian fleet in harbour, but E-boats, U-boats and the Luftwaffe attack continuously. On 11 August, *Eagle* is sunk by *U-73*, while the cruisers *Manchester* and *Cairo* and a destroyer are also lost, along with nine merchantmen. The cruisers *Nigeria* and *Kenya* are badly damaged. The convoy effectively lifts the siege of Malta.

12–18 September: Convoy PQ18 to the Soviet Union is the first Arctic convoy to have an escort carrier, *Avenger*, with another twenty warships, to escort forty-one merchantmen. Ten merchantmen are lost to aerial attack, another three to U-boats, but the Germans lose three U-boats, one of which, *U-589*, is sunk by a Swordfish working with a destroyer, and forty aircraft.

8 November: Operation Torch, the Allied landings in North Africa, supported by the United States Navy and Royal Navy. Overall command of naval forces is with Admiral Sir Andrew Cunningham, and the Royal Navy covers two of the three task forces. Centre Task Force has two escort carriers, three cruisers and thirteen destroyers, while Eastern Task Force has the carrier *Argus*, an escort carrier, three cruisers and sixteen destroyers. The eastern flank of the invasion forces is covered by a reinforced Force H which is deployed in the western Mediterranean with the battleships *Duke of York*, *Nelson* and *Rodney*, the aircraft carriers *Formidable*, *Furious* and *Victorious*, plus three cruisers and seventeen destroyers. Operation supported by 800, 801, 802, 804, 807, 809, 817, 820, 822, 832, 883, 880, 882, 883, 884, 885, 888, 891 and 893 NAS.

15: *Avenger* sunk by *U-155* west of Gibraltar.

21: Albacore of 817 NAS flying from *Victorious* sinks *U-538* in North Atlantic.

1943

27 March: *Dasher*, escort carrier, blows up and sinks in three minutes while south of Little Cumbrae Island, Firth of Clyde, with loss 379 lives.

25 April: Aircraft of No. 811 NAS from *Biter* and destroyer *Pathfinder* sink *U-203* in NW Atlantic while escorting Convoy ONS4.

May: resupply of Axis forces in North Africa has become impossible, forcing them to surrender shortly afterwards.

12: Destroyer *Broadway* and frigate *Lagan* with Swordfish of 811 NAS from *Biter* sink *U-89* in North Atlantic while escorting Convoy HX237.

28: Swordfish from *Archer* sinks *U-752* in Atlantic in first successful attack using rocket projectiles while protecting Convoy HX239.

1 June: First Corsair squadron, 1830 NAS, formed.

11–12: Operation Corkscrew results in the capitulation of the Italian islands of Lampedusa and Pantelleria under British naval and air attack.

10 July: Operation Husky, the Allied landings in Sicily, with Admiral Sir Andrew Cunningham once again in command of the naval forces. The USN provides the Western Naval Task Force, the RN the Eastern. No less than 580 warships and 2,000 landing craft are used, covered by Force H and the Mediterranean Fleet with the battleships *King George V*, *Howe*, *Nelson*, *Rodney*, *Warspite* and *Valiant*, the carriers *Formidable* and *Indomitable*, with 807, 817, 820, 880, 885, 888, 889 and 893 NAS, six cruisers and twenty-four destroyers. Naval firepower breaks up a German armoured division making a counter-attack.

3 September: Allied forces cross the Straits of Messina to land at Calabria.

9: Operation Avalanche, the Allied landings at Salerno, is covered by Force H with the battleships *Nelson* and *Rodney*, and the carriers *Formidable* and *Illustrious*, while Force V under the command of Rear Admiral Sir Philip Vian with *Unicorn* and four escort carriers, *Attacker*, *Battler*, *Hunter* and *Stalker*, covering ground forces ashore with aircraft from 807, 808, 809, 810, 834, 878, 879, 880, 886, 887, 890, 894, 897 and 899 NAS.

9: Following Italian surrender, the Italian fleet sails for Malta and is escorted by the battleships *Howe*, *King George V*, *Valiant* and *Warspite*, which also cover a landing at the major Italian naval base of Taranto. German air attack sees *Warspite* and the cruiser *Uganda* damaged, as well as two American cruisers.

1 October: First Fairey Firefly squadron, 1770 NAS, formed at RNAS Yeovilton.

4: British carrier-borne aircraft attack German convoys around Narvik, sinking 40,000 tons of shipping.

28 November: Royal Navy and United States Coast Guard commence trials with a Sikorsky XR-4 helicopter aboard SS *Dagheston*.

1944

2 January: Sikorsky R-4 helicopters flown by RN personnel off the SS *Daghestan* help protect convoy HX274.

22: Operation Shingle, Allied landing at Anzio, involves four cruisers and a number of destroyers. Cruiser *Spartan* sunk by air attack on 29 January, the cruiser *Penelope* is torpedoed by a U-boat and sunk on 18 February.

10 February: Swordfish from *Fencer* sinks *U-666* in Western Approaches.

4 March: Swordfish from *Chaser* joins *Onslaught* in destruction of *U-472* off North Cape while escorting Convoy RA57.

5: Same Swordfish as above sinks *U-366* off northern Norway.

25: Lieutenant Commander Eric 'Winkle' Brown lands a de Havilland Sea Mosquito aboard HMS *Indefatigable*, the first time a twin-engined aircraft has landed aboard a British aircraft carrier.

3 April: Operation Tungsten, carrier-borne bombers from *Furious* and *Victorious* and three escort carriers, *Emperor*, *Pursuer* and *Searcher*, attack *Tirpitz* and put her out of action for a further three months.

3: Avengers and Wildcats from *Tracker*, and Swordfish from *Activity*, sink *U-288* in Barents Sea while protecting Convoy JW58.

19: Operation Cockpit, aircraft from *Illustrious* and the USS *Saratoga* attack Sabang on Sumatra.

26: Aircraft of 804, 827, 880, 1834 and 1836 NAS from carriers *Furious*, *Victorious*, *Emperor*, *Pursuer* and *Searcher*, attack German convoy off Bodø, Norway in Operation Ridge.

1 May: Swordfish from *Fencer* sinks *U-277* off northern Norway while escorting Convoy RA59.

2: Swordfish from *Fencer* sinks *U-674* and *U-959* off northern Norway while escorting Convoy RA59. The first time one aircraft sank two U-boats in one day.

17: Operation Transom sees Force 66 mount air attack on Japanese base at Surabaya, with carriers *Illustrious* and USS *Saratoga*, with 832, 851, 1830 and 1833 NAS.

6 June: Operation Overlord, the Allied invasion of Normandy, sees naval forces commanded by Admiral Ramsay, and in addition to manning many of the landing craft, the Royal Navy provides a bombardment group with the battleships *Warspite* and *Ramillies*, twelve cruisers and twenty destroyers, with a reserve force including *Nelson* and *Rodney* and three cruisers. Attacks by German destroyers and E-boats see a British destroyer sunk as well as two German ships. Other Allied destroyers sunk by mines, as are a number of landing craft.

30: Operation Pedal, air strike on Port Blair and Andaman Islands by Force 60, by aircraft of 810, 847, 1830,1833, 1837 NAS off *Illustrious*.

17 July: Operation Mascot, Fleet Air Arm attacks *Tirpitz* in Norwegian fjord, but smokescreen protects battleship.

25: Aircraft from *Illustrious* and *Victorious* in the Indian Ocean attack Sabang on Sumatra while their escorts shell the dock areas.

15 August: Operation Dragoon, Allied landings in the South of France, with fleet of nine escort carriers including five British ships, *Attacker*, *Emperor*, *Khedive*, *Searcher* and *Stalker*.

31: Aircraft from *Indomitable* and *Victorious* attack Padang on Sumatra and later the airfield at Sabang, which is also bombarded by surface vessels of the British Eastern Fleet.

31: Operation Goodwood sees aircraft from 801, 820, 826, 827, 887, 894, 1770, 1840, 1841 NAS from *Formidable*, *Furious*, *Indefatigable*, attack German battleship *Tirpitz* in the Altenfjord, Norway. Operation repeated on 29 August, but ship not seriously damaged.

2 September: Swordfish from *Vindex* joins four escorts in sinking *U-394* off Lofoten Islands.

September/October: British naval forces enter the Aegean, with seven escort carriers, seven cruisers, nineteen destroyers and frigates, to attack the German evacuation from Greece and destroy the remaining German naval units in the area.

17 September: Air strike on Sigli, Sumatra, Operation Light, with 815, 817, 822, 1834, 1835, 1839 and 1844 NAS operating from *Indomitable* and *Victorious*.

30: Swordfish of 813 NAS flying from *Campania* sink *U-921* in Arctic waters while escorting Convoy RA60.

17–19 October: Aircraft from *Victorious, Illustrious* and *Indomitable*, Force 63, attack the Nicobar Islands, involving 815, 817, 1834, 1836, 1839, 1844 NAS.

24: Operation Hardy, aircraft from 852 and 846 NAS off *Campania* and *Trumpeter*, lay mines in Lepsorev and Harrhamsfjord while radio stations on Vigra and Hanoy attacked.

26: Operation Athletic, *Implacable*, a cruiser and six destroyers attack shipping between Bodø and Rorvik, involving 828, 841, 887, 894 and 1771 NAS.

27: *Implacable*'s 1771 NAS Fireflies play a part in the sinking of *U-1060* off Norway.

20 November: Operation Handfast, aircraft of 856 and 881 NAS from *Premier* and *Pursuer* lay mines at Haugesund.

7/8 December: Operation Urbane, minelaying at Salhusstrommen, Norway, by aircraft of 856 and 881 NAS flying from *Premier* and *Trumpeter* on 7 Dec and by 881 NAS and 1771 NAS flying from *Trumpeter* and *Implacable* on 8 Dec.

13: Two Swordfish of 813 NAS flown from *Campania* sink *U-365* in Arctic waters.

20: Force 67 mounts Operation Robson against harbour and oil installations at Medan, Sumatra, but unsuccessful. Aircraft from 854, 857, 1830, 1833, 1839 and 1844 NAS flown from *Illustrious* and *Indomitable.*

1945

4 January: Aircraft from *Indomitable, Victorious, Illustrious* and *Indefatigable* attack oil refineries in north-eastern Sumatra.

15: HMS *Thane* torpedoed off the Clyde by *U-482* and damaged beyond repair.

24: Aircraft from *Indomitable, Victorious, Illustrious* and *Indefatigable* attack oil refinery at Palembang on Sumatra.

29: The operation of 24 January is repeated.

21 February: First flight of Fleet Air Arm's last piston-engined fighter type, the Hawker Sea Fury.

25 March: First deck landing of a twin-engined aircraft aboard a British ship – a de Havilland Sea Mosquito aboard *Indefatigable.*

26 March–25 May: The British Pacific Fleet operates as TF57 against the Sakashima Gunto group of islands, Operation Iceberg, cutting Japanese reinforcements to Okinawa.

1 April: British Pacific Fleet reinforces the US Fifth Fleet at the landings on Okinawa, providing the aircraft carriers *Indomitable, Victorious, Illustrious* and *Indefatigable* with 220 aircraft, and the battleships *King George V* and *Howe*, with five cruisers. *Indefatigable* badly damaged by Kamikaze strikes, but operational again on 2 and 6 April.

7: Major Japanese Kamikaze attacks with some 2,000 suicide pilots; amongst the ships hit are *Formidable*, *Victorious* and *Indefatigable*.

11: British Eastern Fleet, with the battleships *Queen Elizabeth* and the French *Richelieu*, bombards Sabang on Sumatra, supported by two escort carriers, two cruisers and five destroyers.

12: Task Force 57 with *Indefatigable* attacks airfield at Shinchiku and harbour at Kiirun, both on Formosa, with aircraft from 820, 887 and 1770 NAS, as part of Operation Iceberg Oolong.

13: Task Force 57 with *Indefatigable* attacks airfields at Shinchiku and Matsuyama, both on Formosa, with aircraft from 820, 887 and 1770 NAS, as part of Operation Iceberg Oolong.

16: Operation Sunfish, Force 63 attacks Emmahaven, Padang, Sumatra, and air-strike element includes aircraft from auxiliary carriers *Emperor* and *Khedive*.

19: First flight of de Havilland Sea Hornet, Fleet Air Arm's first single-seat, twin-engined, fighter.

30: Bombardment and air strike on Nicobar Islands by Force 63, which includes 804 and 851 NAS operating off *Empress* and *Shah*.

4 May: Last air attack on Kilbotn by Home Fleet, with carriers *Queen*, *Searcher*, *Trumpeter*, and 846, 853 and 882 NAS. Two German surface vessels and *U-711* sunk.

4 and 9: Kamikaze attack on *Formidable*. Latter date sees seven aircraft lost on deck and another twelve in the hangar.

5: The British Pacific Fleet, TF57, resumes operations against the Sakashima Gunto group of islands, Operation Iceberg, cutting Japanese reinforcements to Okinawa.

6: Operation Bishop, air attacks on Japanese forces in Burma, with aircraft from 800, 807, 808 and 809 NAS flying from *Emperor*, *Hunter*, *Khedive* and *Stalker*.

9: Liberation of Copenhagen, Operation Cleaver, with *Queen*, *Searcher* and *Trumpeter* present.

15: Air strike and bombardment of Truk in the Carolines, Operation Inmate, including *Implacable* and *Ruler*, 801, 828, 880, 1771 NAS.

15–16: British destroyers sink the heavy cruiser *Haguro* as she steams through the Straits of Malacca in a night torpedo attack, after the ship had been spotted by aircraft from HMS *Emperor*.

18: Armourer working on Corsair in *Formidable*'s hangar accidentally fires guns and starts fire in which thirty aircraft are destroyed.

17 July: First combined attack on Japanese home island of Honshu by RN and USN, with British Task Force 37 including aircraft from *Formidable*.

24 and 28: Fleet Air Arm attacks shipping in Japanese Inland Sea.

9 August: Lieutenant Robert Hampton Gray RCNVR, leading a strike of Corsairs of 1841 NAS from *Formidable*'s 1841 and 1842 Squadrons, comes under heavy AA fire as he attacks a destroyer in the Onagawa Wan. He presses ahead with his attack despite severe damage to his aircraft and is awarded a posthumous VC.

10: Final day of operations by TF37 over Japanese Inland Sea.

29 November: First air/sea rescue by Fleet Air Arm helicopter, a Sikorsky R-5.

3 December: Lieutenant Commander Eric 'Winkle' Brown makes the first landing of a jet aircraft aboard an aircraft carrier, putting a de Havilland Sea Vampire aboard HMS *Ocean*.

1947

7 May: First full helicopter squadron, 705 NAS, formed at RNAS Gosport, HMS *Siskin*.

1950

30 June: First operations in Korean waters with British naval force including *Triumph*.

1951

17 August: First operational FAA jet squadron, 800 NAS, formed at RNAS Ford using Supermarine Attackers.

1952

9 August: Flight of four Sea Furies of 802 NAS from *Ocean* led by Lieutenant (later Commander) Paul 'Hoagy' Carmichael attacked by eight MiG-15s over Korea, with Carmichael shooting one down and two others damaged.

13 December: First operational helicopter squadron, 848 NAS, sails in *Perseus* for Far East, with first operational sorties on 26 January 1953.

1953

2 March: Hawker Sea Hawk enters service for the first time at RNAS Brawdy, joining No. 806 NAS.

20: Fleet Air Arm's first heli-lift of troops into combat during the Malayan emergeny.

1954

20 March: No. 890 NAS reformed at RNAS Yeovilton with the RN's first all-weather jet fighter, the Sea Vixen.

1 October: Official naval battle honours promulgated in Admiralty Fleet Order, includes FAA squadrons as well as ships.

1955

25 February: Fourth *Ark Royal* commissioned, the first British carrier to be completed with an angled deck.

1956

6 November: British forces land in Suez Canal Zone, with Royal Marines of 45 Commando flown in aboard Whirlwind and Sycamore helicopters from *Ocean* and *Theseus*.

1957

18 February: RNVR (Air Branch) disbanded.

1958

15 October: Emergency operations off Jordan and Lebanon involve *Albion*, *Bulwark* and *Eagle*.

28: First flight of Westland Wasp, first specially designed small ships' helicopter.

1960

19 January: *Bulwark* recommissioned as the first commando carrier.

1961

1 July: Iraq threatens to invade Kuwait, but 42 RM Commando landed by Westland Whirlwinds of 845 NAS from *Bulwark*, while 45 RM Commando flown in from Aden by RAF. Air cover provided by aircraft from *Victorious* and *Centaur*.

4: First fully equipped ASW helicopter squadron, 815 NAS, commissioned at RNAS Culdrose with Westland Wessex.

1963

1 February: Admiralty authorizes use of the term 'sonar' as 'Asdic' no longer suitable.

8: Experimental 'touch-and-go' landing by Hawker P1127 VTOL aboard *Ark Royal* off Portland.

1964

28 May: Fleet Air Arm Museum at RNAS Yeovilton opened by HRH Prince Philip, Duke of Edinburgh.

1965

14 October: First Blackburn NA39 Buccaneer unit, 801 NAS, formed at RNAS Lossiemouth.

1966

14 February: Super carrier CVA01 cancelled, leading to resignation in protest by First Sea Lord, Admiral Sir David Luce in April.

1967

13 March: FAA bombs wreck of super tanker *Torrey Canyon*, run aground on the Longstones. Buccaneers from RNAS Brawdy break open the hull, while Sea Vixens from RNAS Yeovilton ignite the fuel.

9 August: First radar-equipped ASW helicopter, Wessex HAS3, joins 814 NAS.

1968

1 September: Flag Officer Aircraft Carriers, FOAC, becomes Flag Officer Aircraft Carriers and Amphibious Ships, FOCAS.

1969

31 March: First operational Phantom squadron, No. 892 NAS, formed at RNAS Yeovilton.

11 May: RN Phantoms of 892 NAS win *Daily Mail* transatlantic air race with west-to-east time of 4 hrs 46 mins 57 seconds, a true airspeed of 1,100 mph (the timing includes using helicopters and bicycles at both ends to travel from the Empire State Building in New York to London's Post Office Tower).

1970

13 May: Sea King of 700 NAS makes record 602.95-mile flight from Land's End to John O'Groats in 4 hrs 19 mins, 21 secs. Fitted with extra fuel tanks.

1974

14 July: *Hermes* with two escorts evacuates British subjects from Kyrenia, Cyprus, during Turkish invasion.

1977

3 May: *Invincible*, the first warship designed to operate V/STOL aircraft, launched by HM The Queen at Barrow-in-Furness.

1978

27 November: Last catapult launch in the Royal Navy when F4K Phantom of 892 NAS flies off *Ark Royal* to RAF St Athan.

15 December: 892 NAS decommissioned at Leuchars, the last conventional fixed-wing squadron in Fleet Air Arm.

1979

14 February: Britain's last conventional carrier, *Ark Royal*, paid off at Plymouth.

18 June: First operational Sea Harrier delivered to RNAS Yeovilton.

1980

11 July: *Invincible*, first 'through-deck cruiser', commissioned.

1982

2 April: Argentine forces invade Falkland Islands. Planning for recovery of the islands under Operation Corporate begins.

5: *Hermes* and *Invincible* sail for Portsmouth to the South Atlantic as Operation Corporate begins.

22: Wessex from destroyer *Antrim* rescues SAS personnel from Fortuna Glacier, South Georgia in bad weather.

25: Helicopters from *Antrim, Brilliant, Endurance* and *Plymouth* cripple Argentiune submarine *Sante Fe* off South Georgia. Helicopter from *Endurance* believed to have been first to sink an enemy vessel using missiles.

26: Helicopters from *Antrim, Brilliant, Endurance* and *Plymouth* land men from 43 RM Commando and SAS to retake Leith on South Georgia.

1 May: First bombing of airfield at Port Stanley by Sea Harriers and first Sea Harrier air-to-air sorties.

9: Argentine trawler *Narwal* bombed by Sea Harriers and then boarded by Royal Marines, who find that it is under naval command and that CO has failed to destroy his orders.

1984

1 January: HMS *Fearless* and RFA *Reliant,* with helicopters from No. 846 NAS evacuate 5,000 civilians from Lebanon over four weeks.

1990

23 March: Post of Flag Officer Naval Aviation established, replacing those of Flag Officer Naval Air Command, and the aviation responsibilities of Flag Officer Flotilla Three and of the Assistant Chief of Staff (Aviation) to Commander-in-Chief, Fleet.

1 August: Iraqi forces invade Kuwait.

1993

1 January: British carrier task group deployed to the Adriatic to support British land forces in the UN Protection Force in the former Republic of Yugoslavia, with the Royal Navy present in the Adriatic for most of the next decade.

1995

27 December: British carrier task group in Adriatic placed under NATO command to provide support for operations against the Bosnian Serbs and also take part in Operation Deny Flight. Reverts to UK command, 15 February 1996.

1997

14 November: *Invincible* deployed to Mediterranean ready to move to the Arabian Gulf to support diplomatic action following Iraq's refusal to allow UN weapons inspectors access to suspected sites. While in Mediterranean, enters Adriatic twice, 8–10 December 1997 and 8–11 January 1998, on Operation Deliberate, for sorties over former Yugoslavia in support of NATO ground forces. Sea Harriers of 800 and Sea Kings of 814 and 849 NAS embarked.

1998

24 January: Start of air sorties from British carriers based in the Gulf against Iraqi targets in support of UN weapons inspectors. Initially

Invincible and RFA *Fort Victoria* deployed on Operation Bolton. Relieved by HMS *Illustrious* on 8 March.

20 February: Britain's first purpose-built helicopter carrier, *Ocean*, named by HM Queen at Barrow-in-Furness.
30 September: *Ocean* commissioned.

1999
30 January: Start of Operation Bolton II, with *Invincible* and three escorts, plus two RFA, back in the Gulf with 800, 814, 849 NAS.
24 March: UK naval forces deployed to Adriatic to support NATO operations against Serbian ethnic cleansing in Kosovo, involving *Invincible* and 800, 814, 849 NAS.
17 November: *Ocean*'s Sea Kings provide humanitarian relief after major earthquake around Duzce, Turkey.

2000
1 April: Air Officer Commanding 3 Group RAF and Flag Officer Maritime Aviation established as joint appointment at RAF High Wycombe. RAF Sea Harriers join RAF Harriers to form Joint Force Harrier.
1 May: *Illustrious* with escorts and RFA deployed to Sierra Leone in support of UN operations with *Ocean* on Operation Palliser to aid government against rebel forces.
24: 42 RM Commando landed by Sea King HC4 on beaches at Sierra Leone in Operation Palliser.

2003
20 March: Britain joins the United States in what becomes known to the British as Operation Telic (the invasion of Iraq), involving the largest amphibious landings by British forces for almost fifty years. Involves HMS *Ark Royal* and *Ocean*, with 814, 815, 820, 845, 847, and 849 NAS.
22: Two Sea Kings of No. 849 NAS flying from *Ark Royal* collide over northern Arabian Gulf, with the loss of all aboard – two pilots and five observers.

Bibliography

Adlam, Henry 'Hank', *On and Off the Flight Deck: Reflections of a Naval Fighter Pilot in World War II*, Pen & Sword, Barnsley, 2007.

Brooke, Geoffrey, *Alarm Starboard: A Remarkable True Story of the War at Sea*, Patrick Stephens, Cambridge, 1983.

Hanson, Norman, *Carrier Pilot*, Patrick Stephens, Cambridge, 1979

Hobbs, Commander David, *Aircraft Carriers of the Royal & Commonwealth Navies*, Greenhill Books, 1996.

Johnson, Brian, *Fly Navy*, David & Charles, Newton Abbot and London, 1981.

Kilbracken, Lord, *Bring Back My Stringbag: A Stringbag Pilot at War*, Pan Books, London, 1980.

Masters, A.O. 'Cappy', *Memoirs of a Reluctant Batsman*, Janus, London, 1995.

Poolman, Kenneth, *Escort Carrier: HMS* Vindex *at War*, Secker & Warburg, London, 1983.

Roskill, Captain, S.W., *The Navy at War, 1939–45*, HMSO, London, 1960.

Sainsbury, Captain A.B., RN, and Phillips, Lieutenant Commander F.L., RN, *The Royal Navy Day by Day*, Sutton, Stroud, 2005.

Sturtevant, Ray and Balance, Theo, *The Squadrons of the Fleet Air Arm*, Air Britain, Tonbridge, 1994.

Thetford, Owen, *British Naval Aircraft since 1912*, Putnam, London, 1958–82.

Winton, John, *Air Power at Sea, 1939–45*, Sidgwick & Jackson, London, 1976.

——, *Carrier Glorious*, Leo Cooper, London, 1986.

——, *The Forgotten Fleet*, Michael Joseph, London, 1960.

Woodman, Richard, *Arctic Convoys*, John Murray, London, 1974.

Woods, Gerard A., *Wings at Sea: A Fleet Air Arm Observer's War, 1940–45*, Conway Maritime, London, 1985.

Wragg, David, *The Fleet Air Arm Handbook*, Sutton, Stroud, 2001.

——, *Carrier Combat*, Sutton, Stroud, 1997

——, *Wings Over The Sea: A History of Naval Aviation*, David & Charles, Newton Abbot and London, 1979.

Index